The Sherlock Effect

How Forensic Doctors and Investigators Disastrously Reason Like the Great Detective

I0885226

The Sherlock Effect

How Forensic Doctors and Investigators Disastrously Reason Like the Great Detective

Thomas W. Young

CRC Press
Taylor & Francis Group
Boca Raton London New York

CRC Press is an imprint of the
Taylor & Francis Group, an **informa** business

CRC Press
Taylor & Francis Group
6000 Broken Sound Parkway NW, Suite 300
Boca Raton, FL 33487-2742

First issued in paperback 2022

ISBN 13: 978-1-03-240190-4 (pbk)
ISBN 13: 978-0-8153-6194-7 (hbk)

DOI: 10.1201/9781351113830

Library of Congress Cataloging-in-Publication Data

Names: Young, Thomas W. (Forensic doctor), author.
Title: The Sherlock effect : how forensic doctors and investigators disastrously reason like the great detective / Thomas W. Young, MD.
Description: Boca Raton, FL : CRC Press, Taylor & Francis Group, [2018] | Includes bibliographical references and index.
Identifiers: LCCN 2017058263| ISBN 9780815361947 (hardback : alk. paper) | ISBN 9781351113830 (ebook : alk. paper)
Subjects: LCSH: Forensic pathology--Popular works. | Holmes, Sherlock--Fiction--History and criticism. | Detective and mystery stories, English--History and criticism. | Private investigators--England--Fiction. | Literature and science.
Classification: LCC RA1063.4 .Y68 2018 | DDC 614/.1--dc23
LC record available at https://lccn.loc.gov/2017058263

Visit the Taylor & Francis Web site at
http://www.taylorandfrancis.com

and the CRC Press Web site at
http://www.crcpress.com

Contents

Author ix
Introduction xi

1 Reasoning Backwards 1
Notes 8

2 Sherlock and His Successors 9
Notes 17

3 Categorical Intuitive Deduction 19
Note 25

4 How Detective Fiction Turned into Medical Science 27
Notes 35

5 Good Cop, Bad Cop 37
Notes 42

6 You Don't Know What You Don't Know 43
Notes 51

7 Can't Shake This Feeling 53
Notes 60

8 The Emperor Wears No Clothes 61
Notes 70

9 Broken Bones in Babies 71
Notes 80

10 The Unified Hypothesis **81**

Notes 90

11 Failing the Infamous **93**

Daily Mail, June 11, 2012: The Dingo DID Do It: Lindy Chamberlain in Tears at Verdict after 32 Years 93

Radar Online, June 8, 2016: Natalie Wood Coroner Dodges Lawyer's Attempts to Bring Robert Wagner to Justice 95

ProPublica, July 5, 2011: Casey Anthony Trial Shows the Limits of Forensic Science in Proving How a Child Died 96

Bustle.com, September 16, 2016: Who Is Werner Spitz? The Forensic Pathologist Has a JonBenet Ramsey Theory 97

The New York Times, July 13, 2013: Zimmerman Is Acquitted in Trayvon Martin Killing 99

Billboard, May 29, 2007: Coroner Provides Graphic Details at Spector Murder Trial 100

Notes 105

12 The Deadly Bed **107**

Notes 117

13 Failing the Numerous Not-So-Infamous **119**

The Charlotte Observer, September 21, 2015: State Budget Boosts Pay, Training for Medical Examiners 119

The Charlotte Observer, October 2, 2015: As N.C. Struggles, Nation's Top Medical Examiners Meet in Charlotte 124

Notes 130

14 The Double Dip **131**

The News Journal (Wilmington, DE), October 2, 2015: Ex-Chief Medical Examiner Gets Probation 133

The Atlanta Journal-Constitution, October 3, 2015: Outside Work Challenges Medical Examiner's Credibility, Judgment 135

Notes 141

15 Modern-Day Sherlocks 143

Daily Mail, October 10, 2015: Doctor Whose Blunder Left Couple Accused of Abusing Their Baby Made the Same Mistake Six Years Ago 143

The Gazette, September 24, 2015: Medical Examiner Testifies to Wounds That Killed Kerry O'Clair Jefferson 145

Great Falls Tribune, September 21, 2015: Jaraczeski Defense Shifts Blame 146

Akron Beacon Journal, November 13, 2015: Evidence Shows Pregnant Woman was Strangled From Behind in 1985, Examiner Testifies in Scott Purk Trial 147

The Wilson Times, November 6, 2017: State Rests Gregory Parks Murder Case on Pathologists' Testimony 150

Cognitive and Human Factors in Expert Decision Making: Six Fallacies and the Eight Sources of Bias 152

Notes 159

16 The Battered Football Player Syndrome 161

The Davis Enterprise, October 19, 2016: Neuropathologist Says Davis Toddler Suffered Abuse-Related Trauma 168

Fitsnews, September 13, 2016: Expert: Hillary Clinton Poisoned by Donald Trump, Vladimir Putin 169

Notes 176

17 Tree People and Forest People 179

Notes 199

18 The Perils of Pediatric Forensic Pathology 201

The Star, October 1, 2008: Payout Urged in Smith Probe 202

Toronto Star, October 7, 2008: Baby Death Review "Daunting" 203

Missoulian, July 11, 2015: Forensic Pathologist Will No Longer Do Work for Montana County Coroners 205

Notes 212

19 Kayakers, Spider Bites, Jack the Ripper, and Speaking for the Dead 213

The New York Times, September 10, 2015: Autopsy Cites "Intentionally Removed" Plug in Ruling Kayaker's Death a Homicide 213

Daily Mail.com, September 16, 2015: EXCLUSIVE: Was Killer Professor Driven Mad by a Spider Bite? Delta State Academic Who Murdered Girlfriend and Colleague Was in Despair Over His Swollen Face 216

WNEM.com, September 16, 2015: Coroner Disputes Delta State Professor "Spider Bite" Theory 217

CBS News, October 25, 2015: The Undying Fascination Over Jack the Ripper 218

Dateline NBC, August 20, 2007: Dead Men Talking: Inside a Medical Examiner's Office and *Eden Prairie News*, November 2, 2017: Speakers for the Dead 220

Notes 224

20 CSI, Adam Ruins Forensic Science, Forensic Tree Teams, Divinity School, and a Bridge in Melbourne 225

Variety, September 17, 2015: "CSI" Farewell Panel Talks How DNA, Hair Fibers & Plushies Changed TV & Society 225

truTVEps, October 21, 2015: "Adam Ruins Forensic Science" 227

Hannibal Courier-Post, September 24, 2015: "Forensic" Team to Look at South Main Tree Death 229

WBUR, November 1, 2017: Opioid Epidemic Inspires New Hampshire Medical Examiner to Enter Ministry 230

The Guardian, October 30, 2015: Murder of Girl Thrown From Bridge by Father "Could Not Have Been Predicted" 231

Notes 238

21 Confessions of a Former Chief Medical Examiner 239

The Marshall News Messenger, October 7, 2016: Kelly Found Guilty, Gets Life With No Parole in Marshall Baby Death 239

Note 245

Index 247

Author

Dr. Thomas W. Young, a forensic pathologist and full-time forensic doctor for nearly 30 years, has testified in court over 460 times both as a prosecution and defense expert. He is a fellow of the American Academy of Forensic Sciences and the National Association of Medical Examiners—two organizations that represent the mainstream of forensic science and pathology. He has written extensively and been published in peer-reviewed journals. He served as a chief medical examiner successfully for nearly 12 years and is a former director of a training program in forensic pathology. As a forensic practitioner, what makes him uniquely qualified to write this book are not only his credentials, but also his research on real-world trials and case studies, his examination of current practices, and his close study of deductive and inductive logic. Thanks to his years as a chief medical examiner and as a current independent forensic-pathology consultant, Dr. Young has a deep understanding of the problem about which he writes.

Introduction

In the early 1980s, Dr. James Malcolm "Taffy" Cameron was the go-to guy in forensic medicine. Director of the Department of Forensic Medicine at the London Hospital Medical College and a past president and then general secretary of the British Academy of Forensic Sciences, he was a living, breathing, twentieth-century Sherlock Holmes. At least that's what Northern Territory law-enforcement investigators believed when they enlisted his help in investigating the sensational Australian dingo case. Prior to Dr. Cameron's arrival, their case had come to a standstill.

A coroner inquest on February 20, 1981, the first televised inquest in Australia, agreed with the claims of the Chamberlain family, that a dingo had killed the infant Azaria Chamberlain after that animal took her from the family tent during a vacation at Uluru, the famous sandstone monolith formerly called Ayer's Rock. The coroner agreed to this in spite of mounting scientific evidence from local forensic scientists supporting a theory generally accepted by law enforcement—and increasingly by a fascinated public—that the Chamberlains, a family of religious fanatics, had murdered their child as a sacrifice in the wilderness.

While in Europe for a forensic science conference, an Australian forensic dentist paid a visit to Dr. Cameron in London, carrying with him the skull of a dingo, pieces of Azaria Chamberlain's bloodstained clothing found a few kilometers from the tent, and portions of clothing from zoo experiments using dingoes. Both the detectives and Australian forensic scientists had great hopes that Dr. Cameron, then the sixth-rated forensic expert in the world, would help make their case.

The doctor did not disappoint. He later testified at a second coroner inquest in the Northern Territory. Using ultraviolet light and his considerable expertise and observational skills, Dr. Cameron discerned prints consistent with the right hand of a young adult female. He further determined that the child met her death by having her neck cut by a sharp instrument—a cut that certainly opened the vital blood vessels and possibly encircled the neck. This finding explained the spray of infant blood found in the floorboard of the Chamberlain's car—a finding recognized by another forensic scientist.

The determination of homicide at the second inquest led to the indictment and conviction of Lindy Chamberlain for the murder of her infant daughter.

The court sentenced her to prison for life on October 29, 1982. Several appeals that went all the way to the High Court in Australia were unsuccessful.

Then, in 1986, while investigating the death of a mountain climber who fell at Uluru, police discovered Azaria's missing matinee jacket in an area full of dingo lairs. This additional evidence immediately falsified the elaborate theory put forth by forensic scientists and Dr. Cameron; the matinee jacket was recovered from a location that would not have been accessible to the Chamberlains. Later, other scientists discovered the spray in the floorboard of the family car was not blood at all but a cross-reaction with the manufacturer's sound-deadening compound.

New evidence prompted a series of appeals. Lindy was released from prison, but the case continued back and forth in the courts in Australia over many years. In 1995, a third coroner inquest resulted in an open finding where the cause and manner of death were declared to be unknown. Finally in 2012, a fourth inquest concluded that the death was due to a dingo carrying the baby from the family tent. Some thirty years after Lindy Chamberlain was convicted, the coroner offered a tearful apology to the Chamberlain family for the loss of their child and for all of the suffering they endured from the justice system.

On June 17, 2003, Professor Cameron passed away in his home in England. His obituary pointed out his contribution as a leading proponent for drug testing in professional sports, particularly swimming.[1] He was also touted as a leading scientist who played critical roles in the Shroud of Turin investigation, the investigations of deaths of many abused and neglected children, and the 1980s Australian dingo case. The author of that article did not, however, point out Dr. Cameron's role in sending an innocent woman to prison, nor did the obit writer stop to wonder why, if that world-renowned forensic doctor was really so good at what he did, did he fail so spectacularly in the Chamberlain case?

***

My name is Thomas W. Young, MD. I am a board-certified forensic pathologist, a member—even a fellow—of a variety of forensic science and pathology organizations, and a former chief medical examiner—a chief doctor who functions like a coroner, who finds out why a person died. I am a forensic doctor.

There are many things I love about what I do. I love good science and I have great confidence in it. I also love death investigation, something that coroners and medical examiners are trained to do. Those loves have never changed for me.

But there is one thing I do not love and actually hate: I hate the way many forensic doctors and scientists daily destroy the lives of innocent people.

You may not be aware of this. In fact, most forensic doctors and scientists are not aware of the harm they have been causing. For many years, I was not aware of the harm I was causing. No one told me what I am about to tell you in this book. I had to discover it for myself.

I want you to be aware of what goes on. One day, God forbid, you or someone you care about may become a victim of a forensic professional. Maybe if you know what goes on, you and many others might be able to stop it.

What I will tell you in the pages that follow is not hard to understand. The basic underlying problem with forensic doctors is so simple that even a 12-year-old could understand it.

You do not believe me? Well, check it out.

It all starts with Sherlock Holmes.

Note

1. Lord C. Professor James Malcolm "Taffy" Cameron: Appreciation for a quiet hero. *Swimming World*, June 18, 2003. https://www.swimmingworldmagazine.com/news/professor-james-malcolm-taffy-cameron-appreciation-for-a-quiet-hero/. Accessed on October 12, 2016.

1 Reasoning Backwards

Even if he wasn't the first fictional detective ever portrayed, Sherlock Holmes is without a doubt the most enduring and influential fictional detective of all time.

In 2012, Guinness World Records announced that Holmes has the world record as the most portrayed literary human character in film and television. He has been on the screen 254 times (Dracula beat Holmes with 272 films, but Dracula is a non-human character). Since 1887, more than 75 actors have depicted Sherlock Holmes. The Guinness organization recognizes Sherlock Holmes as a "literary institution": someone who is just as "compelling" today as he was 125 years before today.[1]

Holmes' fame extends throughout the entire world. He is very popular in China. The people there viewed the first episode of the third season of the British Broadcasting Corporation's production of *Sherlock* over seven million times—somewhat comparable to the ten million times it was viewed in the United Kingdom on prime time. When British Prime Minister David Cameron visited China, Chinese subscribers on a social media site peppered him with questions about the television program.[2]

Sherlock Holmes is as popular as ever everywhere you may go.

Some even look at him wistfully in this modern age, wishing that modern forms of forensic evidence like DNA had not made irrelevant the kind of Sherlock-Holmes-style deduction described in short stories and novels. According to one reporter from the United Kingdom, it is the "size of the DNA database" and not Holmes-like reasoning that puts criminals behind bars these days.[3] This reporter does not understand the power that Sherlock Holmes and his analytical methods have on modern-day forensic doctors and scientists.

Sherlock Holmes is the invention of author Sir Arthur Conan Doyle (1859–1930).

Many authors of detective fiction often use Conan Doyle's general ideas. These authors depict brilliant detectives—people who are smarter than rank-and-file police officers—who solve mysteries through intuition and deduction. The fictional heroes are peculiar people with both serious personal problems and endearing quirks, who wander about looking for "clues." At the conclusion of each tale, the brilliance of each detective catches everyone off guard when he or she weaves the clues into an amazing account. The "bad guy" typically acknowledges the truthfulness of that account by confessing at the end of the story.

Sherlock Holmes had as his sidekick a medical doctor, the famous Dr. Watson. At the conclusion of one Sherlock Holmes novel, *A Study in Scarlet*, Holmes explains how he is able to solve his cases (Holmes talks and Watson responds):

> In solving a problem of this sort, the grand thing is to be able to reason backwards. That is a very useful accomplishment, and a very easy one, but people do not practise it much. In the every-day affairs of life it is more useful to reason forwards, and so the other comes to be neglected. There are fifty who can reason synthetically for one who can reason analytically.
>
> "I confess," said I, "that I do not quite follow you."
>
> I hardly expected that you would. Let me see if I can make it clearer. Most people, if you describe a train of events to them, will tell you what the result would be. They can put those events together in their minds, and argue from them that something will come to pass. There are few people, however, who, if you told them a result, would be able to evolve from their own inner consciousness what the steps were which led up to that result. This power is what I mean when I talk of reasoning backwards, or analytically.
>
> "I understand," said I.[4]

Holmes describes what a person does when he reasons forward: by learning the train of events and knowing (or predicting) what the result of those events would be. He describes this as something that most people do.

Rare and brilliant individuals like Sherlock Holmes, however, solve cases by reasoning backward: by learning the result and, through intuition, describing the multiple steps in the past that led to the result. When a person learns the events of the past first and then describes the result, the reasoning moves forward. When a person learns the result first and then says what led to the result, the reasoning moves backward.

It seems plausible to the casual reader that if there is someone brilliant enough like Sherlock Holmes, that person could solve crimes with the same method of reasoning backwards. The reader is tricked into thinking that backward reasoning is brilliant, but it is not. Backward reasoning does not work. Those described by Sherlock Holmes as "most people" do not do it because it does not work.

If I had often used the Sherlock Holmes' method when I was employed as a medical examiner, I would not have been able to keep my job for as long as I did. Citizens and civic leaders do not appreciate death investigators and police officers who use methods that do not work. The failure of backward reasoning in a case becomes painfully apparent as more is learned about the case.

There is a simple explanation why backward reasoning does not work. For any result, any set of clues, there may be numerous possible "trains of events" that could explain the result. Sherlock Holmes and Conan Doyle may imagine only one "train of events" and may persuade the reader that there is only one possible "train of events," so the reader never considers that there are other possibilities or even imagines them.

Consider an example of backward reasoning that took place earlier in *A Study in Scarlet*. Early in the story, Dr. Watson is introduced to Sherlock Holmes. Holmes looks at Watson and draws the following conclusions about him:

> Here is a gentleman of a medical type, but with the air of a military man. Clearly an army doctor, then. He has just come from the tropics, for his face is dark, and that is not the natural tint of his skin, for his wrists are fair. He has undergone hardship and sickness, as his haggard face says clearly. His left arm has been injured. He holds it in a stiff and unnatural manner. Where in the tropics could an English army doctor have seen much hardship and got his arm wounded? Clearly in Afghanistan.

Of course, Dr. Watson is amazed by how accurately Holmes determined Watson's past from simple but subtle observations. Readers of Sherlock Holmes' novels are also amazed at the brilliance of the super sleuth, but neither Watson nor the reader realize that there are numerous other possible explanations for these observations.

Is the military the only place where one can develop what seems to be "the air of a military man?" Why does Watson have to be an army doctor? Why not a navy doctor?

Are the tropics the only place where one can develop a tan? Is Afghanistan the only country in the "tropics?" Who says that hardship and sickness from military service is the only explanation for a haggard face? Aren't there other places and other ways besides a military conflict where one can wound his left arm?

To the reader, the Afghanistan war is made to seem like the best explanation for all of the findings, but how would we know that it truly is the best explanation?

There is an answer to that question. What if we as detectives were to ask Dr. Watson the following: "Dr. Watson, tell us about yourself. What have you been doing all of these years? Where have you gone? What have you gone through?"

Perhaps Dr. Watson himself could independently and spontaneously provide an explanation for the military bearing, the tan, the haggard face, and the injured arm through his answers. If he freely told his story and if that story happened to explain all of the observations made by Sherlock Holmes, wouldn't that then be the best explanation?

Of course, to do that would be reasoning forward—learning the "train of events" and seeing if those events could explain the result. Asking Dr. Watson would be straightforward, but Sherlock Holmes wants to work in a less straightforward, less certain way. Why is that considered brilliant?

Here is another way to understand this concept, all using the fact that

$$2 + 2 = 4$$

Consider the numbers to the left of the equal sign to be a "train of events"—where one event is added to another event in a series of events. I use only two "events" in this illustration—two added to two—to keep things simple. Now consider the number to the right of the equal sign to be the result of what happened on the left side of the equal sign. Using forward reasoning, we would learn what came before (two being added to two) and see if the result (four) makes sense with what came before. In other words, using Dr. Watson's freely and spontaneously offered story, we would see if his "train of events" explains the clues in Dr. Watson's body. What he said could explain the result...

$$2 + 2 = 4$$

...or it might not explain the result:

$$2 + 3 \neq 4$$

The facts from Dr. Watson might "add up" or they might not "add up."

With this forward approach, the detective learns all available facts. These facts are gathered both from eyewitnesses and observable results of the past events. The detective will then see if everything "adds up." If everything does not add up, there is a red flag; more investigation is called for and more non-leading questions need to be asked.

On the other hand, the backward reasoning approach attempts to tell the past events from the result. Witness accounts are ignored with backward reasoning. Instead, an arrogant and brilliant detective tells the witnesses what they should have supposedly seen. The detective is the one who "fills in the blanks":

$$\_\_ + \_\_ = 4$$

The arrogant and brilliant detective may fill in the blanks with 2 and 2, figuring that to be the best explanation, but in truth, combinations of numbers too numerous to count could be placed into the blanks: 1 and 3, 4 and 0, negative 1 and positive 5, 1.999 and 2.001, etc.

Two and two cannot be considered the best possibility among millions of possibilities. Selecting the best explanation that way would be like correctly guessing the right numbers in a combination lock or the correct order of letters and numbers in a computer password!

Reasoning backward from a result to a complex train of events that is beyond what a person could imagine is not brilliant. It is just the opposite. It is simply guessing with no hope of learning the correct answer.

Perhaps you are a person who does not like mathematics. Maybe you would prefer to think about white beans.

Charles Sanders Peirce (1839–1914) was a logician, mathematician, philosopher, and scientist who lived at much the same time as Arthur Conan Doyle. He offered an illustration of a bag that contained only white beans.[5] If you reached into that bag and grabbed several of those beans, you could reasonably and certainly conclude that when you opened your hand, you would see white beans. He called this a *deduction.* A deduction is a conclusion that is guaranteed to be true as long as the other items are true: the bag contains only white beans and you grabbed the beans from that bag. On the other hand, a *hypothesis* is seeing someone holding white beans in his hand and concluding that he got the beans from the bag of white beans. A hypothesis is a guess requiring further proof. The beans may have come from that bag, but they may have also come from somewhere else: from another bag in another room or from the grocer down the street or from who knows where.

You may have noticed that with the deduction above, the train of events leading to the result is known and witnessed. On the other hand, a hypothesis involves trying to guess or surmise the past events that led to the result without knowing or considering what was witnessed. If the hypothesis is a guess requiring further proof, what would be that proof? Asking the person with the beans in his hand what he did, of course. If he said he got the beans from the special bag with only white beans, you could then conclude that what he said *could have happened.* His account is *consistent* with the result. That would be a deduction.

But if his hand contained only black beans and he said that he grabbed them from the special bag with only white beans, then what he said *could not have happened.* His account is *not consistent* with the result. That would also be a deduction.

Back in 2009, I wrote a statement that I believe sums up what I have written above. I call it the *Inferential Test*:

> One can be reasonably certain if witness accounts of the past are consistent or not consistent with physical evidence in the present, but one cannot reliably surmise past events from physical evidence unless there is only one plausible explanation for that evidence.

I know that sounds wordy and it seems hard to understand at first. What would be a simpler way to say it? How about this: You can listen to an eyewitness with an open mind and see if what he says fits the clues, but you cannot make up a story from the clues and expect it to be true.

"Clues" are what police officers search for at crime scenes or items doctors look for when they examine patients or dead bodies. It is a word I borrowed from detective fiction to illustrate. When a medical examiner looks for clues in dead bodies, it is important for this forensic doctor not to invent a scenario to explain those clues. The doctor should listen to eyewitness accounts of what happened in the past and compare those accounts to the clues he found. Doctors who build scenarios before carefully listening with an open mind to eyewitnesses cause innocent people to be sent to prison.

I know what I have written so far is simple and it seems obvious. It seems obvious that weaving a story around clues while failing to listen to eyewitnesses, the people who were actually there to see what happened, would be asking for trouble.

But what would happen if someone who was seemingly brilliant and had impressive credentials—someone like Sherlock Holmes—were to get up on a witness stand in a courtroom and engage in Sherlock Holmes-like behavior, weaving stories from clues? What if everybody on the jury believed that impressive expert? What if people were sent to prison because of that kind of testimony? Who could stop him? What if nobody was willing to stop him? What if he were allowed to go on, year after year, doing this? What if people actually confessed to doing what he stated in his invented theory? Does this actually happen?

Sadly enough, this actually happens. Many forensic doctors behave this way all the time, everyday; and attorneys, jurors, judges, and the public buy into it. It is a great tragedy with no end in sight.

***

Modern-day Marshall, Texas, is different in time and place from Victorian-era England, but forward reasoning is still forward reasoning, no matter the time or place. If we would have allowed Deterryon Kelly to tell us independently and spontaneously what happened on the night and morning of May 5 and 6, 2014, what follows is what we would have learned. We know this because according to proper police procedure, members of the Marshall Police Department allowed Deterryon to tell that story and properly recorded it in writing and on video.

Deterryon Tyrell Kelly, a 275-pound African-American male who was 26-years-old in May of 2014, grew up in the East Texas town of Jefferson, a small burg of 2,055 souls 21 miles west of the Louisiana state line. A high-school graduate, Kelly worked for Weatherford, an oil and gas service company based in Houston, Texas. The company stationed him at that time in North Dakota, working for three weeks and then taking a break for two. In early May of 2014, he neared the end of his two-week break and was due back at work later that week.

Deterryon was visiting his girlfriend, Jameshia Cooks, and her 21-month-old son, Ja'Keen Sanders, in Marshall, a slightly larger town of 24,500 souls 17 miles south of Jefferson. Jameshia was 7-months pregnant with Deterryon's child. As Deterryon came to the end of his leave, the couple wanted to spend some time together—just the two of them and Ja'Keen—away from other family members who lived in Marshall. They stayed together at a motel on Highway 59, located north of Interstate 20.

The man, his girlfriend, and her child checked into the Best Western motel shortly before 7 p.m. Jameshia watched the television and gave Ja'Keen a bath while Deterryon went to McDonald's and Burger King for food. Later in the evening and after dark, while Jameshia took a bath, Deterryon took the little boy to the vending machine. Jameshia was preparing herself for a sexual encounter with Deterryon, so she dressed in lingerie after her bath.

Deterryon and Ja'Keen walked by the swimming pool on their way to the room with the vending machine. Ja'Keen hadn't eaten much, so Deterryon went to buy him some food. After entering the room and seating the child on either the washing machine or dryer in the room, Deterryon placed his coins in the candy machine, but no candy bar came out. He hit the machine firmly several times and rocked the machine, hoping these maneuvers would work to dislodge the candy. A woman who worked for the motel came to check on what was going on after hearing loud noises caused by Deterryon's efforts. He explained what he did and then asked her if there was any fruit because the child would normally eat fruit. She went off to retrieve a banana.

By that time, it was late in the evening, and the child was getting tired. While the woman went off to get a banana, the man took the child outside. Ja'Keen was whining, so Deterryon tried to entertain him by throwing him high up into the air and catching him. The child was accustomed to Deterryon playing with him in this apparent rough and acrobatic fashion. Deterryon described Ja'Keen as a "tough little guy" who was accustomed to this kind of playfulness. In spite of these maneuvers, Ja'Keen afterward became whiny and acted sleepy because it was already late at night, sometime around 11 p.m.

After the woman delivered the banana, the man and the boy went into the lobby of the motel. Deterryon placed the sleepy child on two chairs to lie down while he checked the computer in the lobby and called Jameshia on his cell phone to find out if she had finished her preparations. After speaking briefly to the manager who asked about problems with the vending machine, the man and the child walked back to the motel room. They sat outside the room while the man tried unsuccessfully to feed the sleepy child a banana.

Finally, the two entered the room. Jameshia asked Deterryon to cover Ja'Keen with a blanket because the child was recovering from a cold. They tried to keep the child covered, but the little boy repeatedly kicked off the blankets. Both adults waited for the child to fall asleep and even sat outside the room for a while to keep from distracting the child from sleeping. During the time when the boy would not fall asleep, his mother would hold the child in her arms to settle him down.

Eventually Ja'Keen fell asleep, and the couple had sex. Deterryon believed he personally fell asleep sometime between 2:30 and 3 a.m. Pregnant Jameshia needed to visit the bathroom several times during the night.

While it was dark in the room shortly after 6 a.m., the girlfriend suddenly awakened Deterryon. "Where's Ja'Keen?" she asked when she did not see the child on the surface of his bed. When the man got up, he felt Ja'Keen with his foot. The child was wedged between the nightstand next to Ja'Keen's bed and the mattress. Quickly, Deterryon bumped the nightstand a little to the side and grabbed Ja'Keen by the waist. Both the man and the child's mother noted the child to be cold, to have "dead weight." Deterryon heard some gurgling from the child, but Ja'Keen did not respond. Deterryon was trained in adult cardiopulmonary resuscitation (CPR), but he placed the child first on the bed to perform chest compressions. A short while later, he remembered he was not supposed to perform chest compressions on a soft surface like a mattress, so he placed the child on the floor for the compressions. He explained to the police shortly after they arrived that he may have performed the compressions too hard. Shortly after Jameshia called 911, they heard and saw rescue units with sirens blaring outside the door. CPR and other life-saving efforts continued as the child was rushed to the hospital.

During his interview with the police later that day after the child had been pronounced dead, Deterryon expressed his hope that an autopsy would tell him what happened. Nearly a month after that autopsy had been performed and completed, the police arrested Deterryon Tyrell Kelly. A grand jury charged him with capital murder.

Notes

1. Guinness World Records News. Sherlock Holmes awarded title for most portrayed literary human character in film & TV. May 14, 2012. http://www.guinnessworldrecords.com/news/2012/5/sherlock-holmes-awarded-title-for-most-portrayed-literary-human-character-in-film-tv-41743/. Accessed on November 11, 2017.
2. Taylor A. The Unreal Popularity of "Sherlock" In China. Business Insider, Jan 3, 2014. http://www.businessinsider.com/the-unreal-popularity-of-sherlock-in-china-2014-1. Accessed on November 11, 2017.
3. McDonagh M. We still believe in Sherlock Holmes, even in the age of DNA. The Telegraph, May 21, 2009. http://www.telegraph.co.uk/comment/personal-view/5363777/We-still-believe-in-Sherlock-Holmes-even-in-the-age-of-DNA.html. Accessed on November 11, 2017.
4. Doyle AC. *A Study in Scarlet*. United Kingdom: Ward Lock & Co, 1888.
5. Peirce CS. Illustrations of the logic of science. Sixth paper—Deduction, induction, and hypothesis. *Popular Science Monthly* 1878;13:470–482.

Sherlock and His Successors

2

The model for the great detective Sherlock Holmes was not a detective at all; he was a forensic doctor. Dr. Joseph Bell (1837–1911) was a surgeon and a teacher of physicians and surgeons at the University of Edinburgh in Scotland. During his celebrated lectures, Dr. Bell would amaze his students with his keen observational and diagnostic skills. He would invite patients to his lectures, place them in front of his students, and make very dramatic pronouncements about the patients. One of those students recorded his memories of a portion of one of those lectures:

> Well do I remember the gasping astonishment of an outpatient to whom he suddenly remarked, "I know you are a beadle and ring the bells on Sundays at a church in Northumberland somewhere near the Tweed." "I'm all that," said the man, "but how do you know? I never told you." "Ah," said Bell, when the outpatient had left bewildered, "of course, gentlemen, you all know about that as well as I did. What! You didn't make that out! Did you not notice the Northumbrian burr in his speech, too soft for the south of Northumberland? One only finds it near the Tweed. And then his hands. Did you not notice the callosities on them caused by the ropes? Also, this is Saturday, and when I asked him if he could not come back on Monday, he said he must be getting home to-night. Then I knew he had to ring the bells tomorrow. Quite easy, gentleman, if you will only observe and put two and two together."[1]

This is remarkably similar to the observations of Dr. Watson made by Sherlock Holmes in *A Study in Scarlet*. The keen observations and conclusions of Dr. Bell sound brilliant, but they are undercut by something that few of Bell's admirers would have realized.

The bell ringer was a patient in a clinic where Dr. Bell provided medical care. When a doctor sees a patient for the first time, the doctor takes a *history*. This is a patient's first-hand account of what is ailing him and what has ailed him in the past. A history includes many personal details besides the patient's chief complaint: among them the patient's social circumstances, information about his family, and even what he does for a living. It is not hard to spot in Dr. Bell's "observations" the kind of information often included in a patient history.

After taking a history, a doctor performs a *physical examination*, a detailed observation of the patient's body, often using, among other things, a stethoscope, a device for listening to sounds coming from inside a patient's body. Often, the history guides the doctor's observations, allowing the physical examination to help him figure out what is wrong with the patient. The doctor writes down all of these items in a medical record, and medical records are filed and maintained in the clinic. Any person working in the clinic, including Dr. Bell, would have ready access to the information in a medical record.

The students, of course, would never imagine that their revered teacher, a person who could observe detailed historical information from finger calluses and subtle regional accents, would ever pull such a trick on them. Few would imagine they might have been part of a rigged game.

The consequences of this might have been less far-reaching had Dr. Bell confined his amazing "skills" to the lecture hall. He did not. Bell's "skills" came to the attention of the Edinburgh Police Department; they asked him to help them solve some of their crimes. Scotland Yard eventually consulted the doctor in 1888 during their hunt for notorious serial killer, Jack the Ripper. Dr. Bell studied handwriting samples and even came up with the name of a suspect for the Ripper.

Thus was born a policeman with a stethoscope; medicine meets crime-solving. Elementary!

Another admiring student sitting in the lecture hall listening to Dr. Bell was Arthur Conan Doyle. Doyle—or Conan Doyle as he is often called—was a physician who made his name not from practicing medicine but from writing crime novels. If it wasn't for the fame of Sherlock Holmes, it is not likely that we would pay any attention to Dr. Bell. Conan Doyle credits his mentor in a letter he wrote to Dr. Bell in 1892: "It is most certainly to you that I owe Sherlock Holmes."[2] Conan Doyle's autobiography also clearly credits Dr. Bell not only for his profound influence but also for his "eagle face," his "curious ways," and his "eerie trick of spotting details."[3] Anyone familiar with Conan Doyle's writings would see these as apt descriptions of Sherlock Holmes.

A news article commemorating the 100th anniversary of Bell's death wistfully muses about Dr. Joseph Bell. The reporter considers that if Joseph Bell were alive, he would no doubt be smiling, considering "that he had a part in it all."[4]

There is no doubt about the smiling. All the world has been duped by the seeming deductive powers of Dr. Bell, but Dr. Bell did not offer deductions—conclusions that can be certain. He offered hypotheses—conclusions that cannot be certain—and made them look like deductions. He did this like a magician pulling a rabbit out of a hat, a clever party trick. But the upshot of Bell's tricks, amplified and immortalized in Baker Street's most famous imaginary resident, are no laughing matter.

There is no question that Conan Doyle was a great writer of fiction. Indeed, he was so good that he made the methods of Sherlock Holmes plausible not only to a general readership but also to a wide variety of forensic doctors, academicians, and scientists. People seem to have forgotten that Sherlock Holmes is make-believe. It is both sad and terrifying to note that professionals from the Victorian Era to the present day apply fictional methods to true-life happenings.

Let's back up a second: How do I know that Dr. Bell peeked at the medical records of the Northumbrian church bell ringer before giving his lecture and demonstration? The answer is: I don't. For me to know that for certain, I would need to have watched him do it. There were no witnesses who saw him look at the medical records, but the mere presence of the medical records in the clinic visited by the bell ringer would call into question Dr. Bell's claim that he could "put two and two together" simply by looking at the patient and—without knowing anything else about him—say where he was from and what he did for a living. Dr. Bell's classroom demonstration cannot turn a hypothesis—a guess with multiple possibilities—into a deduction—a conclusion which he can claim certain knowledge—no matter what he might say.

> Then I *knew* he had to ring the bells tomorrow. Quite easy, gentleman, if you will only observe and put two and two together.

Consider this: What if a student who took an examination was found to have the answer key to the examination in his backpack? We would not know for certain whether or not he looked at the key before taking the test or how the answer key got into his backpack, but it would still call into question whether or not he cheated, whether or not the examination results reflect his knowledge. In Dr. Bell's case, Dr. Bell had the medical record in his "backpack."

It would have been fine if Sherlock Holmes remained a character in the pages of a novel and his crime-solving techniques the creation of a superb literary imagination; unfortunately, several doctors positioned themselves as real-life Sherlocks. One of these was Sir Bernard Spilsbury (1877–1947), a pathologist who did autopsies—examinations of dead bodies for the purpose of finding evidence of disease or injury.

Pathology is the study of disease. Most pathologists practice their study in hospitals and are familiar with the course of natural disease, but the police were looking for doctors who could help them solve crimes from violent injury—unnatural deaths. By the early 1900s, Scotland Yard employed doctors to examine the bodies of murder victims, looking for clues that would help them solve crimes. The British were not the first to use forensic doctors for criminal cases. Forensic medicine had, in fact, been in existence for several centuries by that time, and by the late nineteenth century, doctors were already performing autopsies in several medicolegal institutes on the European continent, notably in France and Germany. Academic departments of forensic medicine in universities scattered throughout the continent provided medical consultants for the courts—"public physicians"—from the time of Napoleon in the early part of the nineteenth century and onward. Scotland Yard, however, was late to discover the usefulness of forensic medicine. A few doctors from St. Mary's Hospital in Paddington, specialists in surgery and internal medicine, developed interests in trauma pathology and toxicology, the study of the detection of poisons. While continuing with their clinical practices, these doctors also found employment as "Home Office Pathologists" or "Home Office Analysts." Rather than being subjected to the humiliating disciplinary pecking order so prevalent in academic institutions in Europe and elsewhere, these doctors were granted a far freer free rein. St. Mary's Hospital and Scotland Yard became breeding grounds for overconfident, larger-than-life personas similar to Sherlock Holmes.

Following a succession of these doctors (A. P. Luff, William Willcox, Augustus Joseph Pepper), Bernard Spilsbury, a 33-year-old pathologist employed by St. Mary's Hospital, accepted work as a Home Office pathologist in 1910. His career spanned 40 years, and he supposedly performed about 20,000 autopsies. I use the word "supposedly" because it is inconceivable how any pathologist could have performed 500 autopsies per year and still have had time to eat and sleep, let alone perform many other duties including court testimony. Spilsbury testified for the prosecution in some 200 trials and was eventually knighted for his service to King and Country.

Like Sherlock Holmes, Spilsbury was also quirky and seemingly brilliant. In addition to being handsome and impeccably dressed, he was flamboyant and dogmatic in the courtroom and always rigidly certain about his opinions. To this day, attorneys prefer experts who, like Spilsbury, can put on a good show before a jury and who are persuasive enough to move jurors to convict. One person sentenced to death as a result of Spilsbury's testimony, convicted murderer Norman Thorne, made a chilling statement in writing shortly before his execution in 1925, claiming himself as a "martyr to Spilsburyism."[5] Ironically, Thorne's case was one where Conan Doyle himself questioned whether or not it was clearly proved. By then, however, Spilsbury's celebrity and certitude brooked little contradiction.

Among Spilsbury's most famous cases were the "Brides in the Bath" murders. Using aliases, serial polygamist George Joseph Smith married three women who each were found dead in a bathtub. Smith was a con man, a reform school graduate with a criminal record who developed talents for charming women and stealing from them. Several of the women survived after Smith stole their savings, but mysteriously, three of these women were found following separate marriages to be submerged in tubs filled with water. Mr. Smith was the one who "discovered" each of his dead wives. The father of one of the victims noted similarities among his daughter's death and those of two other victims reported in the newspapers, so he alerted the authorities.

The police exhumed the three bodies, and Dr. Spilsbury performed the autopsies. There were no clues found at autopsy to show how the women died, and there were no witness accounts of what happened to the women before they died; however, this did not stop the Magnificent Spilsbury, as he was known, from weaving a past-event account. Dr. Spilsbury concluded that while the women reclined in bathtubs filled with water, Smith grabbed them by the ankles and pulled upwards, submerging them under water so quickly that each lost consciousness instantly.[6]

As further confirmation of this theory, a police investigator hired women divers who had physiques similar to the victims. He pulled the legs of one of the divers and quickly submerged her, and he was alarmed when she no longer moved. After removing her from the tub, it took over 30 minutes to revive her. Apparently, the rush of water into her airway triggered a reflex that caused her to lose consciousness.

The term "theory" is often used in the courtroom to describe past events that were not witnessed by anybody. In spite of an impressive experiment that showed that a woman could lose consciousness if her head were quickly submerged, Spilsbury's theory and other complex past event theories like it are not likely to be true. This is easy to demonstrate.

There are six elements to Spilsbury's theory, and we can number them from 1 to 6:

1. The husband would first need to be in the same room as his wife while she is taking a bath.
2. Then he would need to put his hands around her ankles.
3. Then he would need to grip her ankles firmly.
4. Then he would need to pull her legs upward "sharply out of the bath."
5. Her head would have to go underwater quickly.
6. She would then have to lose consciousness.

Note that in order for number two to have occurred, number one would have had to occur first. Then note that for number three to have occurred, numbers one and two would have had to occur first. For number four to have occurred, numbers one, two, and three would have had to occur first. For number five to have occurred, the first four would have had to have occurred first in order. Finally, in order for her to lose consciousness and drown, the first five would have had to occur in order for this to be a murder. Furthermore, for all three murders, these steps would have had to occur in the same order, without any failure or deviation. Is this probable?

We can demonstrate the improbability with the tossing of a coin. How probable is it for a coin toss to lead to "heads?" Any twelve-year-old can tell you: "50-50." Probability is calculated by taking the desired result (heads) and dividing it by the number of possible results (heads and tails). One divided by two is 0.5, or 50%.

What about getting heads twice in a row: having heads first occur and then heads occur again after the first time? That would be 0.5 divided by two or 0.25: 25%.

What about getting heads to occur after getting heads to occur the first and second times? That would be 0.25 divided by two or 0.125: 12.5%.

Now let's make this like the Spilsbury theory above: What about getting heads to occur the sixth time after occurring the first five times? That would be one divided by two, divided by two, divided by two, divided by two, divided by two, divided by two or 0.015625: about 1.6%.

If each event in the Spilsbury theory were to be given even odds of happening or not happening, then the probability of Spilsbury's theory being true is about 1.6%. This would also mean that the probability of Spilsbury's theory being not true is about 98.4%.

And that is only with one bride; with all eighteen events in succession from three brides, the probability is so ridiculously close to zero that it is hardly worth mentioning or calculating.

But it is even worse than that. I only mentioned six past events. In truth, past events occurring over time can be divided into fractions of a second, causing separate events to be numerous in a way that is not even imaginable. With any variation in the train of events over fractions of a second, the result could be highly variable. Furthermore, the train of events could be expanded to include activities before and after the six events that need to be accounted for. Earlier I mentioned combination locks and computer passwords as an illustration. In truth, coming up with a complex order of past events in the way Spilsbury did is even less likely than guessing the right combination or the right computer password.

It is entirely understandable for one to be suspicious of George Joseph Smith. His police record indicated past criminal behavior. He seemed to have motive and opportunity for killing the women. It also seemed that the deaths under the same circumstances were not likely to be coincidentally natural, accidental, or suicidal.

But testimony in a courtroom offered by a forensic doctor has to go beyond suspicion. The courts require medical experts to be certain of their opinions. Suspicion is not certainty; it is simply a hunch. A hypothesis. Furthermore, invented complex scenarios such as the one offered by Spilsbury in this case and in many of his other cases are already demonstrably improbable.

Since Spilsbury's death from suicide in 1947 and even before, a few others have also found problems with Spilsbury's court testimonies. In a lecture about expert evidence, a former United Kingdom attorney general admitted that the doctor's "inflexibility" may have "led to miscarriages of justice."[7]

Did George Joseph Smith kill his wives? Not according to him. Even to the very end, Smith proclaimed he was innocent, never explaining how and why the women died. If he had killed them, he took that information to the gallows at Maidstone Prison.

We will never know what happened. Why? Because there are no witness accounts for us to consider and no physical evidence for us to compare to the witness accounts. The only witness who might have been able to tell us what happened is dead.

If an impressive doctor like Spilsbury can support our suspicions, we feel much better and even certain about convicting and executing a criminal, regardless of flaws in the doctor's reasoning. We might be inclined to believe a doctor who supports our suspicions rather than listen to a witness who denies them. Even if Smith were alive, who would be willing to listen to him and consider carefully what he had to say after all that damning medical testimony?

***

While conducting his scene investigation, a crime scene investigator of the Marshall Police Department became wary of Deterryon Kelly's account of what happened. "Before leaving," he wrote in his narrative, "I was looking at the bed where Sanders was said to have been sleeping and the nightstand. It didn't look feasible for Sanders to have been trapped in between the bed and nightstand." He further described, "I then used an l-ruler to show the distance between the two. It measured approximately 80 millimeters or just over 3 inches." It seemed to him that the nightstand and the bed were too close together to allow Ja'Keen to be wedged between the two items.

The lead detective on the case viewed surveillance videos from the hotel. He saw "some sort of activity happening" inside the vending machine room "in which Kelly can be seen grabbing and hitting Sanders." After performing a walk-through of the first-floor motel room, where visible blood or fluid stains were not observed, another crime scene investigator and the lead detective inspected the vending machine room. The officers observed that on the Coke machine and a food vending machine, "there was a layer of dust on the top, therefore Sanders was not placed on the top of either machine, as was mentioned previously." Officer Hodges made no mention of either the washing machine or dryer next to the vending machines against the same wall. Deterryon Kelly said he placed the child on the washer or the dryer as he was manipulating the vending machine.

The justice of the peace of Harrison County—the Texas equivalent to a coroner -pronounced the death in the Emergency Department of Good Shepherd Hospital in Marshall, and she ordered an autopsy on the child to be performed at Forensic Medical in Tyler, Texas, a small, rectangular, one-story facility located a little over 50 miles to the west of the hospital. According to one of the crime scene investigators, "I arrived and spoke briefly with the Pathologist Dr. Lyons that would be performing the autopsy."

Board-certified forensic pathologist Robert E. Lyon, DO, performed a meticulous autopsy, even making additional incisions outside the usual head, chest, and abdominal incisions to examine the body further for injuries below the skin. Dr. Lyon carefully examined the exterior of the body. The clothing the little boy wore was not bloodstained, and his disposable diaper was clean and dry. The child weighed 23 pounds. He was well-developed and well-nourished, appearing the stated age of 21 months.

Dr. Lyon noted no injuries of any kind in the skin of the head or face, nor were there any injuries in the nose, ears, or mouth. The child had no injuries in the neck. The skin of the chest and abdomen, however, revealed numerous injuries. A cluster of small oval purple bruises lay centrally in the skin of the chest over the sternum—a shield-like bone in the central front of the chest lying over the heart—covering an oval area a little over two inches in diameter. Also, the lower front of the chest below the sternum and the upper central abdominal skin had another oval area of purple bruising slightly larger than the cluster of bruises over the sternum—an area little more than three inches in diameter. He also noted skin bruises in both arms. Although he found bruises in the skin—bruises are areas beneath the skin where blood has leaked out of blood vessels because of trauma—there wear no scrapes or tears of the skin and there were no underlying fractures of any bone.

When Dr. Lyon made incisions into the body to examine for injuries that were more than skin deep, he made more serious findings. About 25 mL of blood (less than 1 fluid ounce) leaked from the abdominal cavity from his opening abdominal incision. He found 150 mL of fluid blood (about 5 fluid ounces) in the abdominal cavity. The backside of the left lobe of the liver had a linear tear, and an estimated 50 mL of hemorrhage (a little over one and a half fluid ounces) lay in soft tissues attached to the nearby large intestine. Further incisions into other areas of the body revealed hemorrhages in the soft tissues of the upper abdominal wall, the back, and the deep scalp tissues of the head. One of the deep scalp hemorrhages was on the top of the head and another in the lower part of the backside of the head. He found hemorrhages in the subcutaneous fatty tissues of the arms and in the connective tissues surrounding the muscles. Dr. Lyon saw smaller deep areas of hemorrhage in the legs.

The doctor saw nothing abnormal about the brain or any diseases in any of the organs.

On May 6, 2014—the same day as the autopsy—Dr. Lyon released a "provisional pathologic diagnosis" and "cause of death" of "blunt impact to scalp, torso, and limbs." The cause of death is a description of the events that led to the death. Dr. Lyon believed that a beating had occurred. Someone brutally kicked or punched the young boy multiple times, and these injuries led to death; that much seemed obvious to him.

He would determine the "manner of death"—homicide, suicide, natural, or accident—at a later time after the completion of the testing of the child's body fluids for drugs and after examining the tissues of the child under the microscope. These examinations eventually disclosed nothing new, so Dr. Lyon released his final determination on June 12: the cause of death was "blunt impact injuries" and the manner of death "homicide."

Notes

1. MacGillivray CW. Some memories of Old Harveians. *Edinburgh Medical Journal* new series 1912;VIII:121.
2. History.com Staff. Was Sherlock Holmes based on a real person? History.com; July 29, 2014. http://www.history.com/news/ask-history/was-sherlock-holmes-based-on-a-real-person. Accessed on November 11, 2017.
3. Doyle AC. *Memories & Adventures.* London: Hodder & Stoughton, 1924.
4. Fiction imitates real life in a case of true inspiration. *Irish Examiner*, November 4, 2011. http://www.irishexaminer.com/viewpoints/analysis/fiction-imitates-real-life-in-a-case-of-true-inspiration-172752.html. Accessed on November 6, 2017.
5. Burney I, Pemberton N. Bruised witness: Bernard Spilsbury and the performance of early twentieth-century English forensic pathology. *Medical History* 2011;55(1):41–60. https://www.ncbi.nlm.nih.gov/pmc/articles/PMC3037214/. Accessed on November 8, 2017.
6. Solved: How the brides in the bath died at the hands of their ruthless womanising husband. *Daily Mail* April 22, 2010. http://www.dailymail.co.uk/femail/article-1267913/Solved-How-brides-bath-died-hands-ruthless-womaniser.html. Accessed on November 11, 2017.
7. Goldsmith PH. Expert Evidence—The Problem Or The Solution. Reprinted in Networked Knowledge: http://netk.net.au/Experts/Expert1.asp. Accessed on November 3, 2017.

3 Categorical Intuitive Deduction

I know at this point it seems that I am picking on the United Kingdom.

For those of you out there who love everything British (and I would include myself among Anglophiles), I do not mean to suggest that all forensic folly originated there. Throughout the world, all systems of justice have suffered from human failure. No one can claim to be immune from jumping to conclusions or prejudice. But when a very bad idea is made to sound like a very good idea, such notions often start from somewhere—much like the source of a serious disease comes from the leaking sewer pipe that contaminates the town water supply.

By the 1950s, the contamination had spread well beyond Great Britain. It spread to the United States. Mistakes from Sherlock Holmes-style backward reasoning had a serious effect on the fledgling medical practice of forensic pathology—the application of the science of pathology to the public arena.

Forensic pathologist Alan R. Moritz (1899–1986) was one of the pioneers of that nascent specialty. Although he was not well known to the general public, many of his ideas shaped the development of death investigation in the United States. Dr. Moritz began his career as a hospital pathologist and rose in academic rank at Western Reserve University in Cleveland. While there, he developed an interest in legal medicine through his frequent interaction with the local coroner; his office was located near the county morgue. Dr. Moritz eventually founded Harvard University's Department of Legal Medicine and taught many other pioneering forensic pathologists who would later lead major medical examiner offices in the United States.

One article well known among forensic pathologists is an article entitled, "Classical mistakes in forensic pathology."[1] The article is a reprint of an address Dr. Moritz gave before a meeting of pathologists in 1956.

The article lists various mistakes that a forensic pathologist who performs medicolegal autopsies on behalf of the public can make, such as the "mistake of not being aware of the objective of the medicolegal autopsy," the "mistake of performing an incomplete autopsy," the "mistake of permitting the body to be embalmed before performing a medicolegal autopsy," the "mistake of regarding a mutilated or decomposed body unsuitable for autopsy," etc.

Dr. Moritz describes one mistake as "one of the most dangerous mistakes in forensic pathology": the "mistake of substituting intuition for scientifically defensible interpretation."

Here is what he said (the italicized print is mine):

> This brings me to one of the most dangerous mistakes in forensic pathology, and one that is particularly prevalent among experienced forensic pathologists who, for one reason or another, acquire a propensity for what might be called "categorical intuitive deduction." This *Sherlock Holmes type of expert* may see certain bruises in the skin of the neck and conclude without doubt that they were produced by the thumb and forefinger of the right hand of the stranger. He may see an excoriation of the anus and maintain unequivocally and without benefit of other elements of scientific proof that the assailant was a sodomist. He ignores the essential component for proof of the correctness of any such scientific deduction, namely, the nonoccurrence of such lesions or changes in control cases. Such a pathologist usually has the happy faculty of failing to remember the many similar bruises of necks that were known to have been produced by mechanisms other than pressure by the thumb and fingers. He fails to remember that many anal and rectal excoriations that were caused by injuries other than sodomy.

This dangerous expert is one who invents a train of events from clues found at the autopsy—just like Bell, Conan Doyle, and Spilsbury. The expert fails to realize that for any set of clues there are often other trains of events that can explain the clues. Bruises in the neck have other causes besides a right-handed strangler. Scrapes of the anus could be caused by hard bowel movements and not just by a criminal who inserts an object. This expert does not consider carefully the accounts of people who were present at the time of the injury because the expert is too busy inventing his own detective fiction.

Dr. Moritz describes the Holmes-like doctor's failure as a "happy faculty": a "service" that doctor is happy to provide to any who will listen to him. He is happy to be a policeman with a stethoscope. Why deal with the mundane existence of seeing patients in a clinic when he can put away bad guys and receive praise for it?

Dr. Moritz goes on:

> Such a pathologist is a delight to newspaper reporters owing to the fact that he "makes good copy." He may be highly esteemed by the police and the prosecuting attorney because he is an emphatic and impressive witness. His prestige, together with his exclusive access to the original evidence, places him in an exceedingly powerful position in the courtroom. Rarely can the defense attorneys find anyone with comparable experience to evaluate the postmortem findings. On the other hand, if they do, it seems obvious to the jury 1) that the outside expert was hired to say something that would help the accused, and 2) that the outside expert, unlike the state's witness, was handicapped by the fact that he did not see the evidence with his own eyes.

"Emphatic and impressive." Like Sherlock Holmes. Like Joseph Bell. Like Bernard—*Sir* Bernard—Spilsbury. When such a renowned and powerful doctor steps up to the witness stand, who dares to contradict him? Even though such a doctor spouts nonsense and fiction, nobody will accept that it is nonsense and fiction, particularly the judge and the jury.

Dr. Moritz then concludes:

> It is difficult to estimate how much harm is done by these people. I know of a man who was hanged largely on the weight of such uncritical evidence. The ordinary hospital pathologist is not accustomed to being so continuously unchallenged as to permit him to acquire a full-blown God complex of the kind that I am discussing. The hospital pathologist must be able to defend his interpretations against clinicians who also have a certain amount of information about the facts in issue. It is only the full-time forensic pathologist who is likely to become accustomed to having his opinions go virtually unchallenged. The stakes are too high to play hunches in forensic pathology.

When Dr. Moritz delivered his speech in 1956, he could not have anticipated how bad this problem would eventually become. He mentioned that he knew of one man "who was hanged largely on the weight of such uncritical evidence," but since then, countless numbers of people have had their lives destroyed by such doctors. Nor did he realize that this problem would spread well beyond forensic pathology and involve physicians of all clinical disciplines.

Medical care in the clinic or hospital setting has an element that is not typically seen in forensic medicine. That element is *self-correction*. When doctors make mistakes in patient care, those mistakes become apparent with time. When medical care does not work, patients do not improve. They get worse. They die. They (or their survivors) even sue. Great efforts are made to avoid bad results, and such efforts are demonstrated through quality-assurance practices, medical-licensing practices, and a whole host of committees formed by patient care providers and non-providers.

Forensic medicine for the most part has no self-correction. Wrongful executions are rarely discovered because there is typically no way to detect them without additional evidence coming to light. Few people sue medical experts for a wrongful conviction because the medical experts are believed to be above everybody else. After all, if other medical experts disagree with the erroneous opinions brought forth during a trial, who can say which expert is right or if any of them are right or wrong? By checking witness accounts, you say? Unfortunately—as of now—witnesses who were present to see what happened have far less credibility than doctors who invent events.

It is no wonder that testifying doctors might develop a "God complex." Unchallenged doctors come to believe they are smarter than they really are.

The lack of challenge brings out the worst in human behavior—the emphatic certainty, the dogmatism, the sneering, and even the flamboyance. That same mild-mannered hospital pathologist who must defer to his fellow physicians in a clinical setting can turn into Genghis Khan on the witness stand in front of judges and jurors who all too rarely question his knowledge and expertise.

What, you might wonder, about the rigorous cross-examination in court that doctors go through?

Contrary to what we see on television, most defense attorneys who cross-examine experienced prosecution medical experts are easily fooled and intimidated by them—just as the judges and juries are.

The experienced prosecution medical expert often has little to fear from a cross-examination. On the other hand, the medical expert hired by the defense attorney who dares question the prosecution expert is often discredited as a "hired gun" who simply adjusts his opinions to help the defense. He is an untrustworthy money-grubber from out of town who was never present in the autopsy room. These kinds of unflattering characterizations are why defense medical experts are few and far between: doctors do not want to be treated badly. It's also true that defense attorneys rarely challenge the local prosecution expert too vigorously because they will rely on that local doctor for information for their future cases; they have an ongoing relationship to maintain. On the other hand, prosecutors will vigorously—even viciously—challenge the out-of-town expert who serves them no useful purpose.

Few people perceive the injustice and the inequity in all of this. Few appreciate the plight of someone who is wrongly accused based largely on the opinions of some medical expert. Rarely does anyone question a doctor's ability to create a narrative of events that were never seen by anybody.

Dr. Moritz, early in his statement mentions the words *categorical intuitive deduction*:

> This brings me to one of the most dangerous mistakes in forensic pathology, and one that is particularly prevalent among experienced forensic pathologists who, for one reason or another, acquire a propensity for what might be called "categorical intuitive deduction."

What does "categorical intuitive deduction" mean?

A simple search of the internet shows each word—"categorical," "intuitive," and "deduction"—cited multiple times, but I could never find the three words used together in the fashion described by Dr. Moritz. The only thing we are left to do (since Dr. Moritz is no longer around to explain himself) is to figure out what he meant.

We have already described a *deduction* in Chapter 1. A deduction is a conclusion that is guaranteed to be true as long as the other items leading to and supporting that conclusion—the premises—are true. In Chapter 1, we illustrated a deduction using simple arithmetic and a bag of beans as examples. Deductions are not hunches or even educated guesses; they are conclusions where an expression of certainty is valid.

"Reasoning forward" described by Sherlock Holmes in *A Study in Scarlet* and also referred to in the first part of the Inferential Test, both mentioned in Chapter 1, is deductive. Consider the following:

1. If a train of events is consistent with the clues left by those events, then the accounts of those events can be true.
2. If a train of events is not consistent with the clues left by those events, then the accounts of those events cannot be entirely true.

The conclusions described in those statements are deductive and reliable for an expression of certainty as long as the observations of the clues are accurate and the science describing the cause-effect relationship between the events and the clues is accurate. The hope of the court is that an expert can offer an opinion of that kind of reliability to a "reasonable degree of medical certainty." "Deduction" and "certainty" certainly go together.

"Intuitive" on the other hand indicates a use of the imagination to form a *hypothesis*—another term we have described. In the setting of trying to determine what happened, that would mean imagining the past events in the form of a hunch and then declaring them with certainty to be true. So far, this sounds like Sherlock Holmes and his "reasoning backwards."

But what about "categorical"?

Often these days, forensic doctors do not give a detailed account like Dr. Spilsbury did with the brides in the bath. They instead summarize an otherwise detailed account into a general *category.* A category is a class of people, things, or events that have shared characteristics. With past events, categorizing would involve doctors putting those events into simple and easy-to-understand classes with shared characteristics.

Instead of saying, "The man picked up the infant and slammed his head against the wall with all of his might," the doctor states a category: abusive head injury.

Instead of saying, "The man was upset at the infant's fussiness so he picked up the infant and, with his two hands encircling the infant's chest, shook the infant forward and backward with all his might," the doctor states a category: shaken baby syndrome.

Instead of saying, "The man is vicious and cruel so he hit his child multiple times on more than one occasion," the doctor states a category: battered child syndrome.

Since medical doctors make these determinations, they borrow a term from their clinical practices to use as a form of shorthand. They call these categories *diagnoses.* Using "diagnoses" allows doctors to get away with inventing past events without making it look like they have invented past events. It makes their opinions sound more clinical and scientific.

The findings of forensic doctors have the ring of truth to those who rely on their expertise—juries, attorneys, and judges. The findings sound official, technical, and precise. But as we shall see in the coming chapters, too often diagnoses of past events—"categorical intuitive deductions"—are junk science made to sound like good science.

***

Attorney Richard Hurlburt of Longview, Texas, has an excellent reputation as a trial attorney. Even judges admire his work. "If you ever want to see how a criminal case should be tried," one local judge commented to a law student, "watch Richard Hurlburt."

Attorney Hurlburt, a native son of the Lone Star State, graduated with a Juris Doctor degree from Texas Southern University in 1990 following four years as a law enforcement officer. He remained in Houston for another four and a half years as an assistant district attorney for Harris County, prosecuting criminal cases in the big city. When his father died, Richard Hurlburt relocated to Longview, a much smaller city in East Texas west of Marshall, to take care of his mother. Although serving on occasion as a prosecutor in that part of the state, Mr. Hurlburt focused on criminal defense, practicing that specialty since 1998.

Mr. Hurlburt and several other criminal defense attorneys in the area were on a list of those who would accept indigent cases—cases in which the defendant could not afford the steep costs of mounting a defense, cases in which the court would have to pay the bills. Deterryon Kelly's case was one of those.

Deterryon's attorney knew right away that Deterryon had a problem. Video footage from several surveillance cameras at the Best Western motel showed the defendant tossing around and twirling the young boy as a baton twirler tosses and twirls a baton, also throwing the child five feet in the air several times. The attorney also saw at one point the defendant quickly moving his arm to hit the child in the head after the two walked out of the motel room. A surveillance camera peering through a window into the vending machine room depicted silhouettes of the man picking up the child and rapidly punching toward the child. Hurlburt also saw several instances where the child was not able to stand up, even behaving like he was unconscious. The video cameras seemed to deny Deterryon Kelly's story of not harming the child.

As an experienced trial attorney, Richard Hurlburt knew that cases like this could only be won by thorough preparation, by learning something the police and prosecutor were not aware of. He enlisted the help of Michael Reinhart, a retired Longview police officer who serves as a private investigator, and Kandilyn "Kandi" Ash, a registered nurse who was also a fairly new attorney. All would devote many hours of further investigation and research into this case—a capital murder case with the threat of life imprisonment without parole.

Ms Ash combed through Ja'Keen's medical records—not only those from his final visit to the Emergency Department but also from over thirty visits to the doctor for various concerns. Jameshia was clearly a mother who was deeply invested in and focused on the well-being of her son and who noted every cough and sniffle and sought help for every concern. Would she be someone who would allow a monster to care for her child? Would she fail to notice that her child was lethally injured or fail to do something about it?

Then there was that autopsy report. How were they to understand all of those injuries?

Attorneys at present throughout the United States realize the necessity of obtaining help from medical experts—forensic doctors—who could help them understand complicated principles of anatomy, physiology, pathology, and medical care and who would be willing to offer a second opinion about the autopsy and the scientific evidence. Unfortunately, qualified forensic doctors who are willing to work with defense attorneys are very few and not readily found. Forensic pathologists in particular are already in short supply nationwide and do not have the time to devote to cases like Deterryon's case. Forensic pathologists employed in government positions also do not want to jeopardize the relationships they have with local prosecutors and government officials, who frown on their medical examiners offering help to criminal defense attorneys. When I was a medical examiner, I would consider working as a consultant on a few civil lawsuits during my off hours, but I would refuse requests from criminal defense attorneys. Few government doctors want to expose themselves to those kinds of career-jeopardizing risks.

Attorney Hurlburt communicated with other Texas criminal defense attorneys through the TCDLA (Texas Criminal Defense Lawyers Association) LISTSERV, an electronic mailing list for email communications among the members. He requested the names of qualified forensic pathology experts and received back from the members a list of a few people he could call.

One of the doctors on that short list was a forensic pathologist from Kansas City named Thomas W. Young.

Note

1. Moritz AR. Classical mistakes in forensic pathology. Ward Burdick Award address. *American Journal of Clinical Pathology* 1956;26(12):1383–1397.

4 How Detective Fiction Turned into Medical Science

Meet Virginia Jaspers, an infant nurse and serial killer from the 1940s and 1950s.

Virginia Jaspers was special but not in a good way. Sure, she was the daughter of a senator and she came from a prominent family, but she was considered an ugly "giantess" who was six-feet tall and weighed 220 pounds. According to a colorful article from 1957 written by John M. Ross[1]:

> Nature had dealt her a cruel blow in almost every respect—tremendous hands and feet, a lumpy face, a stumpy neck, weak eyes that squinted cat-like through thick glasses and an awkward gait on elephantine legs. …Until she was 14, the Jaspers girl had been average in size and habits. She liked sports and had many companions. Then, at an age when girls start noticing boys and boys only pretend they don't see them, Virginia underwent a tragic change. She began to grow immense. Her skin became scaly and erupted. Her arms and legs seemed to swell. The boys gave her nicknames "The Horse," "The Ox," and "The Four-Eyed Monster." Her girl friends withdrew from her. But no one recalls Virginia Jaspers ever complaining or answering back.

In spite of being dealt a cruel blow by nature and compared unfavorably to an attractive younger sister, Virginia had a great attitude.

Virginia loved babies. Although she had no boyfriends or social life, she spent her time taking care of the infants and children of the Connecticut community where she grew up.

In 1943, following an 18-month course in childcare, Virginia's love for infants turned into a career as a live-in nurse. "I always loved children. I've always wanted children of my own," was her explanation for why she selected this occupation. Parents liked her work and willingly trusted her with their infants, although one parent noted that she was somewhat "heavy-handed" when she would burp babies. Over the next 12 years, Virginia took care of numerous babies.

Virginia Jaspers' career as an infant nurse came to an abrupt end in the early hours of August 23, 1956, at the death of Abbe Kapsinow. Author John Ross gave dramatic details of that tragic event:

> At 3:15 a.m. in the New Haven home of Mr. and Mrs. Allen Kapsinow their 11-day-old daughter Abbe awoke and cried. Nurse Jaspers, on sleep-in duty,

> responded. Changing the baby's diaper, she sensed the child was burning with fever. A thermometer confirmed her suspicions and she immediately aroused the parents. The baby's pediatrician was summoned. He rushed her to the hospital.
>
> Two hours later little Abbe died at the Grace-New Haven Hospital, victim of a cerebral hemorrhage. Nurse Jaspers, who had kept an anxious vigil at the hospital, tried to comfort and assist the distraught parents before packing her bags and checking out of the case.

At that point, there was no description of any violent act: only a description of a child who was desperately ill. Then came the doctors:

> Enter two alert doctors at the New Haven hospital. One, a young and inquisitive resident in pediatrics, had performed two spinal taps prior to the infant's death to determine the cause of the hemorrhaging. His findings were illuminating. Blood was detected in the normally clear spinal fluid—an indication of mishap or, possibly, violence. A post-mortem supported the theory. The membrane covering the brain and spinal cord had been ruptured either by a blow on the head, a fall, or *manhandling.*

Please note my italicized print above for manhandling. This would eventually morph into shaking.

Then, another pediatrician took notice:

> By a remarkable coincidence, the report of the Kapsinow baby's death came to the attention of a New Haven pediatrician (author's note: the doctors have requested that their names be withheld) who had been assigned to supervise the hospital's pediatrics section that month, and the suspicion of mishap to a baby in the big nurse's charge struck a familiar and frightening chord.
>
> This doctor quickly recalled his 1948 case of 13-day-old Cynthia Hubbard, who also had died of a cerebral hemorrhage. "Death from natural causes" had closed the case, but there was a suspicion that the baby might have been dropped or thrown. Miss Jaspers had been the infant's nurse. In 1951 he had learned of another sudden death on a Jaspers case. Jennifer Malkan, two months old, had died of asphyxiation while her mother, soprano soloist Joan Brainerd, was away and Nurse Jaspers had been in attendance. And only the year before, the doctor remembered, he had been summoned to aid Bruce Schaeffer, three weeks old, whose leg had been mysteriously broken while under the Jaspers woman's care.

Each of these cases differed greatly from one another. Two of the cases had cerebral hemorrhage, but the prior case did not have elements to invite suspicion of violence after an investigation. A brain hemorrhage in a very young infant can occur for reasons other than violence. The third case involved some form of infant choking or "asphyxiation," but there is no mention of hemorrhage in the head. The fourth case involved a leg fracture and nothing wrong with the head.

However, what the cases had in common was that all of these children were under the care of Virginia Jaspers, the funny-looking woman who loved children and took care of numerous infants over the past 12 years.

Still, the suspicious pediatrician considered the evidence of foul play at the hands of Virginia Jaspers to be strong:

> The strong evidence in the Kapsinow case now permitted him to proceed. The wheels turned swiftly.
>
> In the two days that followed the death of Abbe Kapsinow, New Haven detectives, contacting the agency through which the nurse operated, checked out the cases Miss Jaspers had handled over a 12-year period…

What were the results?

> The results were staggering. Suspicion of cruelty and mistreatment was everywhere.

Perhaps there was suspicion everywhere, but at this point there was no account from any eyewitness of any "cruelty" or "mistreatment." The details behind each disease and injury were vague, and there was no mention of anyone actually seeing Virginia injure children. After all those years of child care, nobody suspected or witnessed anything from Virginia Jaspers—except for pediatricians who at the end of Virginia's time as an infant nurse only suspected.

Then the case took a strange turn. Armed with all of this "information" provided by doctors, the police asked to interrogate the suspect. The story continued:

> On August 27 Virginia Jaspers was summoned to the New Haven police headquarters for questioning. En route to New Haven, her puzzled father asked her, "Is there anything you want to tell me, Virginia?"

She shrugged her large shoulders in bewilderment.

> "I don't know why they'd want to talk to me," she replied.

She appeared bewildered by why she would need to appear at the police station, but she soon found out why:

> At headquarters, Chief of Police Francis V. McManus and his men confronted her with a compilation of the unusually large number of casualties among the infants who had been entrusted to her care. How did she account for this?

Virginia Jaspers was taken aback. Apparently, the four cases in which no violence was ever witnessed but were suspicious to doctors became the "unusually large number of casualties."

> It was strange, the nurse admitted, but she couldn't explain it. Steadfastly she denied ever hurting any baby. These were anxious moments for the police, who had to entertain the remote possibility that this hulk of a woman simply was clumsy.

It was not going well for the police, but that suddenly changed:

> Suddenly Nurse Jaspers broke down and sobbed.
>
> "I lied to you, Dad, I lied to you," she cried. "I knew why they wanted me all the time…"
>
> Thereupon she began a three-and-a-half-hour recitation of the incredible brutality she had inflicted upon the helpless infants she had professed to love. At one point the police interrupted the confession to send out for a 24-inch baby doll with which the nurse might demonstrate her acts of cruelty.
>
> Wrapping her powerful hands around the doll's upper arms and back, her thumbs pressing into its chest, the nurse calmly showed how she had violently shaken Abbe Kapsinow several hours before her death. The infant had been crying rather long. The nurse became angry. She picked Abbe up, gave her several savage shakes and then threw her back into the crib—a drop of about a foot. The baby struggled for her breath, sobbed a little and then went to sleep. When Abbe awoke later in the night, she was near death from a brain injury.

Virginia Jaspers then attributed all the other deaths and injuries to shaking:

> Cynthia Hubbard had received the same punishment for crying too much, the nurse revealed. And she, too, died but a few hours after the shaking, suffering a damaged brain. Jennifer Malkan had been guilty of being too slow in getting up her last "bubble" after her evening bottle.
>
> "I had been holding her up to my shoulder, burping her," the nurse told police. "She was fussing something awful. Finally I took her down, held her in front of me and shook her a few times. Her head bobbed back and forth and her eyes went funny…"
>
> The nurse demonstrated each step with the doll. Realistically, the doll's eyes rolled in its head. The hardened police officers cringed. Senator Jaspers turned away.
>
> The Jaspers woman paused for a moment in her recitation, and a detective studied her carefully as she unconsciously patted the doll gently.
>
> "Why did you do these terrible things?" he asked.
>
> She wiped her eyes.
>
> "I don't know why I did them," she replied. "It was all uncontrollable. Sometimes children get on my nerves."

> Then why didn't you look for other work?
>
> "I've always loved children," the nurse answered, matter-of-factly. "I've always wanted children of my own."
>
> After admitting responsibility for the three deaths, the nurse cleared up the mystery of Marvin Schaeffer's broken leg. She confessed to shaking him, and then slamming him back into his carriage. She explained that both Mrs. Schaeffer and the family doctor had suspected foul play, but had not challenged her vow of innocence.
>
> "I'll bet you never had a case like this before," she said, as she looked at the stunned officers around the table. A flood of tears came again, and then she added, "And everyone thinks I'm so patient with children..."

Wow! Ladies and gentlemen, what we have here is the great American detective novel! We have the brilliant doctors who think like Sherlock Holmes, Joseph Bell, and Bernard Spilsbury—weaving an account of violence and foul play from clues found during hospital care and autopsy—an account that included "manhandling." When the suspect is confronted with the damning information, she confesses to their foul play scenario just like the bad guy at the end of the novel. Widely different cases were all caused by shaking! Mild mannered but ugly Dr. Jekyll turned into wild Mr Hyde, even though no one ever witnessed a transformation like that during the last 12 years or at any time during her life.

But what is even more amazing is how this lurid detective story turned into medical science.

Forensic doctor and radiologist, John Caffey, presented Virginia Jaspers' case as the main case report for his article on brain damage from "whiplash-shaking of infants," published in a medical journal in 1972.[2] In his report of the case, his writing is even more colorful than that of John Ross, characterizing the "proved pathogenic whiplash-shakings" and "burpings" as "gruesome." Through shaking, Virginia killed three infants and maimed 12 others during a period of eight years. The assaults, according to the main case report in his article, all occurred in the homes of upper middle class, well-educated and well-to-do parents who could afford the expert medical care by highly-trained providers like Virginia. Dr. Caffey described Virginia as "extravagantly kind" to the infants in her care. Her clients even invited her back to care for other children, but she admitted giving some of the infants "a good shaking" as a way of trying to get a "bubble" up, of trying to get the children to burp. According to Dr. Caffey's report, several others in the community disclosed additional infants injured by the nurse once her deeds had come to light.

Prior to Caffey's article, one other doctor suspected and wrote about shaking as a cause of infant brain damage, but none of his reported cases had any documented confessions—only a "very strong reason indeed to suppose" a shaking mechanism.[3] Virginia Jaspers changed suspicion into proof by providing what was lacking. What might have been considered as a suspicion before—a "hypothesis" according to Charles Sanders Peirce—turned into cases of "proved pathogenic whiplash shakings," thanks to the confession of Virginia Jaspers. Over time, this confession formed the basis for the diagnosis of shaken baby syndrome, a diagnosis still held in high esteem by forensic doctors, particularly specialized forensic doctors for children: child-abuse pediatricians. Even today in spite of many problems with the diagnosis, which we will cover later, the shaking of infants continues to be a major public health concern. Parents of infants to this day are warned through public health agencies and hospitals not to shake their children for any reason. These concerns are further supported by highly esteemed general and specialty medical organizations that have made official pronouncements of the dangers of shaking babies. At the time, Virginia Jaspers had little idea of the result her confession would bring.

But the confession must be true, right? Why would she willingly confess to harming children if it was not true? Why would she willingly destroy her life and her reputation with a false confession?

***

A few months before the arrest of Virginia Jaspers in Connecticut, "yours truly"—Thomas William Young—was born on the other side of the country and raised in El Cajon, California, a suburb east of San Diego.

I was the third son of William and Mary Young. My father was a dentist. When I was a child my father told me, "Tom, there are two ways to make a living, two good careers: medicine or dentistry. Which career will you choose?"

I never felt confined by those two options. It never occurred to me to do anything other than medicine. I admired my father. He was great in my eyes: a fine, loving father to my two older brothers, one younger sister, and me and a loving husband to my mother. I happily accepted any advice or choice he gave me.

That choice was the same advice my grandfather gave to my father and my uncle. Although my grandfather was a businessman, my father became a dentist and my uncle became an obstetrician-gynecologist. In my family, my oldest brother became a physician, brother #2 became a dentist, I became a physician, and my younger sister became a dentist.

Still, Bill Young's third son was a different breed of cat.

My early years in elementary school were not successful. I would sit in the classroom and daydream, paying little attention to my teachers and the work they would assign. My mother and father identified me as someone who was slow. Perhaps one day, they would have to buy me a gas station and have my siblings come in to take care of the books.

When I entered the fifth grade, it occurred to me that if I wanted to be a doctor one day, I would have to pay attention in school and work hard. From that time, I excelled in my studies, maintaining straight A's all the way through college.

During those early years in elementary school, I would avidly read mystery fiction, particularly *The Hardy Boys*. I learned about Frank and Joe Hardy who followed the example of their private-investigator father, Fenton Hardy, by solving mysteries and capturing bad guys. These teenage boys, one brunette and the other blonde, did this while maintaining top grades in high school and becoming heroes on their high school football team. They would often solve puzzling mysteries even in countries far from their hometown of Bayport. I didn't simply read the numerous books in the Hardy Boys series; I devoured them, even reading as many as four books in one day when I stayed home sick from school.

I was nothing like Frank and Joe Hardy. I was shy, studious and serious—more like a wallflower than a football hero.

I was not religious. My worldview matched that of another backwardly reasoning scientist from nineteenth-century England named Charles Darwin. While on a voyage as a naturalist, Professor Darwin observed plants and animals in South America. From what he saw, he backwardly reasoned—hypothesized or theorized—that life on earth arose spontaneously from primitive chemicals and evolved into vastly complex organisms over vast periods of time. It is amazing to think how many times Professor Darwin would have had to flip a coin and have it come up heads every time for that story to be true; nevertheless, to me as a teenager, his story made more sense than the fantastic and strange ancient witness accounts offered in the Bible. After all, Darwin was a scientist, and I believed in science.

Still, believing in Darwinian evolution made for a sad and lonely existence for a teenager like me. What I wanted to do in life did not seem to amount for much. If life was about "survival of the fittest," what if I happened to be among the fittest who survived? If I became a successful physician one day, making a lot of money and having a lot of things that people want in life, what would I have to show for having lived when my time was up? What was the point or purpose of my life?

These gloomy thoughts crossed my mind frequently when, at 16 years old, I trudged through the streets of the South American town of Pereira in Colombia. I was a member of Amigos de las Américas, an organization that gave teenagers an opportunity to help people in Central and South America in a health-related way. I went door-to-door, delivering oral polio vaccine to children five years of age and under. Living in a foreign culture among people speaking a foreign language simply accentuated the loneliness in a lonely boy.

That trip to South America had many benefits. The Spanish I took in high school greatly improved—even to the point that I was thinking in Spanish by the time my trip was over.

I also saw an autopsy. While staying in a hospital during my time in Colombia, I would pass by the morgue on my way to the cafeteria, and I would look beyond the open door into the morgue. One day, I saw a pathologist doing an autopsy. He had already eviscerated the organs of the chest and abdomen and was continuing to dissect. I was immediately fascinated. The doctor did not mind my questions as I asked him about what he was doing. After the trip, I asked my uncle, an obstetrician-gynecologist, about pathologists and what they do. I decided at that young age that I would one day become a pathologist.

During my high school years, my father decided he wanted to specialize within dentistry. He applied and was accepted to a master's degree program in endodontics at the dental school at Loma Linda University, a Seventh-day Adventist school of higher learning in Loma Linda, California, just a few hours drive north of El Cajon. He lived in a motor home during the week for the next two years while the rest of the family remained in El Cajon, and he visited us on the weekends.

My oldest brother entered a liberal arts university in Southern California. Even though our family was not religious, we were not nearly as wild socially as the college environment my brother found himself in during the early 1970s. By the time his first year ended, my mother persuaded my father to enroll him in the undergraduate school at Loma Linda located in nearby Riverside, California.

I had never heard of Seventh-day Adventists, figuring them to be a collection of strange religious fanatics. When my brother enrolled at the La Sierra campus of Loma Linda University, he did all he could to fit into a new environment and religious culture, hoping eventually to apply to the School of Medicine in a few years. In the spring quarter of his sophomore year, my brother was baptized and joined the Seventh-day Adventist Church.

Around the time, I recall my mother waking me up early one Saturday morning. "We are going to church," she said, "so get up and get dressed." I remember thinking, "How strange! Why are we going to church on Saturday?"

Shortly later, I learned. The reference to the seventh-day in the church's name refers to the Sabbath, a memorial in time to the creative act of God in forming the earth during the first six days. "Adventist" refers to the hope and belief that Jesus Christ will one day return to earth to take those who love Him home to be with Him in heaven.

During the summer months prior to my senior year in high school, I became acquainted with young people from the Adventist church in nearby La Mesa, learning things from the Bible I never knew existed. I made many new friends as I learned many new things, but more than that, I learned there exists a God who doesn't just like me or even love me. I learned that the person who made me is crazy about me, so much so that He came to earth personally to die on a cross for me, to make it possible for me to have my sins forgiven and to have a relationship with Him.

Over time, an enduring friendship has replaced the lonely feelings that had been my life's undercurrent. The point and purpose for my life became clearly apparent: I was to love Jesus supremely, to be His devoted friend, and to serve Him and others. Every day since that time when I was 17 years old, every morning after I wake up, I give my heart and my life to God, asking Him to guide me where He wants me to go so that I may do what He wants me to do, regardless of the outcome. I do this with the hope that one day, whether I am alive or dead when He returns, I will be part of that group of people who Jesus will take with Him to heaven.

The Seventh-day Adventist Church accepted the rest of my family through baptism in the fall of my senior year in high school, and I transferred to a Seventh-day Adventist high school. I attended La Sierra the following autumn with my two older brothers as a pre-medicine and piano-performance student. Throughout my years growing up, my mother insisted that I practice the piano for 30 minutes every morning and evening, and she wanted to make sure I continued to play the piano. My skills in the piano came in handy because the school had many worship services that needed a pianist.

The piano also came in handy after I became acquainted with a female student named Yara Cerna, a young lady with a beautiful soprano voice who would sing solos and direct the singing for many of the worship services at school. What started as an arrangement of singer and piano accompanist turned into a deep friendship, and that deep friendship turned into love. After receiving an early acceptance into the School of Medicine at Loma Linda after my junior year in college and after accepting a full-ride scholarship and stipend from the United States Air Force for my medical education, I married my only girlfriend and my first love. Together, we raised three children and watched them become adults. At the time of the Deterryon Kelly trial, my daughter was a physician in Salt Lake City, Utah. My two sons worked and taught at Adventist boarding schools—one in Minnesota and the other in Jefferson, a small burg of 2,055 souls north of Marshall, Texas.

Notes

1. Ross JM. The truth about the baby-killing nurse. *The American Weekly* March 3, 1957.
2. Caffey J. On the theory and practice of shaking infants. Its potential residual effects of permanent brain damage and mental retardation. *American Journal of Diseases of Children* August 1972;124(2):161–169.
3. Guthkelch AN. Infantile subdural haematoma and its relationship to whiplash injuries. *British Medical Journal* 1971;2:430–431.

Good Cop, Bad Cop 5

In 1974, America was shocked to see video footage of wealthy newspaper heiress Patricia "Patty" Hearst robbing a bank.

Shortly before, a radical organization known as the Symbionese Liberation Army kidnapped Patty Hearst from her Berkeley, California, apartment. Urban guerrillas held her hostage.

Many in the United States at the time carefully followed media accounts of the abduction and disappearance of Patty Hearst. Most wondered if she was even alive.

Later, images of Patty with the militants robbing a bank shocked the television-viewing and newspaper-reading audience. She wore a black beret and held an automatic firearm during the robbery. Patty Hearst had transformed into newly militant "Tania."

How did this happen?

Psychiatrists offered the label of Stockholm syndrome, a "condition" brought about by "brain washing," in which captives eventually sympathize and even join their captors.

Too often, doctors in general and forensic doctors in particular like to summarize past events and human behavior into oversimplified diagnostic categories. They like to use words like *syndrome*. A syndrome is a term used in patient care to describe a set of signs and symptoms that are all caused by the same underlying medical condition. *Signs* are items a doctor sees when examining a patient, and *symptoms* are complaints a patient may have that are clues to a disease. Forensic doctors take the term syndrome and flip it upside down: instead of a single condition causing multiple signs and symptoms, they use syndrome to describe a train of multiple past events causing a single result—like death or injury. Whenever forensic doctors use the term syndrome, please beware! It is reasoning backwards, with the train of complex past events put into a simple category. Reasoning forward in any case demonstrates how inaccurate such simple categories are.

In the case of Patty Hearst or any person held captive, threatened, isolated, starved, and beaten, the main objective is to stay alive. If she maintains herself on the best possible terms with her captor, then her chances for survival go up. It is not necessary to invent a syndrome to see that in the case of Patty Hearst.

What about Virginia Jaspers? What happened to her?

What happened to Virginia Jaspers is what happens to countless people who are accused of crimes that they could not have committed. Think of what happened to her as a game that none of us would ever want to play if we could help it. We can call the game, "Good Cop, Bad Cop."

In the game, the Good Cop is the forensic doctor, the brilliant sleuth-like person who looks at the clues and explains the train of events that preceded the clues, leading to an accusation. The Bad Cop is the interrogating police officer who gets a confession out of the accused person.

We have already discussed the Good Cop part and have pointed out how what he does is highly unlikely to lead to the right answer. What about the Bad Cop? Does he put two and two together to get four?

Well…no. He actually doesn't put two and two together to come up with anything useful.

With apologies to those who do not like mathematics, let us consider once again that

$$2 + 2 = 4$$

Here we say that two is added to two. What if we were to say instead that two is *not* added to two? What would be the result?

The result would be…no one knows!

If two is *not* added to two, the result might *not* be four:

$$3 + 2 = 5$$

But the result might be four:

$$3 + 1 = 4$$

If the sum might be four or might not be four, then the sum could be anything. If the sum could be anything, then we don't know the sum or even what was added to what. We don't know anything.

Declaring that something is *not* added to something is *presuming negatively*. Without proof, let us say that we presume someone is giving us false information. "Mr Jones says that two was added to two, but we do not believe him! Two was not added to two!" If this is what we start with, will we ever learn the truth?

The answer is simple: No. If we begin with believing that someone is not telling the truth, we will never learn what happened. Starting with a negative—*not* telling the truth—is *not* a good place to start.

In the case of Virginia Jaspers, she may have been a person without a criminal record, who loved children, who was never witnessed to do anything violent, who was a trusted caretaker of many infants for many years, but she was still not to be believed. Why? Because brilliant and highly esteemed doctors—the Good Cop—declared her to be a murderer. Calling someone a murderer before there is proof is presuming negatively, but this is what the Good Cop did. Since the Good Cop had spoken and the Bad Cop believed the Good Cop before any eyewitness, all that was left to do was to get a confession from the eyewitness.

Thanks to Sherlock Holmes and detective fiction, the confession at the end of the case is the goal worthy of reaching. Thanks to Sherlock Holmes, the confession is the gold standard for truth, the undeniable proof that trumps all other proofs.

Stop for a moment to think about this: if a presumed criminal like Virginia Jaspers was a liar when she said she didn't harm any child, what made her a truth-teller when she finally admitted to doing cruel acts to children? Why wasn't she believed before but believed later? Isn't it because the police did not get the answer they wanted before but then got what they wanted later?

There is a name for Virginia Jaspers' situation: it is a "no-win" situation, in which you are "damned if you do and damned if you don't." Regardless of what a suspect says, if she does not confess, she is hounded until she does confess. Once she confesses, everything stops. The case is closed.

How logical and scientific is that?

There are some accused people who are strong willed, who in spite of a lengthy interrogation will insist to the end that they never did anything wrong. In spite of a variety of psychological tricks often used by police officers during an interrogation, these accused people hold out to the end. Deterryon Kelly was someone like this. He didn't understand what had happened to Ja'Keen, but he insisted that he never did anything wrong, in spite of cop-applied pressure to confess.

Not all are like this. It is not uncommon for an accused person to insist on her innocence and then suddenly cave, confessing to horrible acts. Just like Virginia Jaspers. When it happens, the results can be stunning. The Bad Cop thinks, "Finally, she admits to what we have known all along!"

Often with such a switch, there is a calculation made by the accused person. A decision is made and carried out. There is a change in the demeanor of the accused person, a change in the tone of voice, a change in the "body language."

The reasons for the calculation may vary from case to case. It would not be possible for me to give the large list of all the reasons why people might decide to confess, but I can give you a small list.

For example, if a person does not see any hope because of the "no-win" situation, he might lie and confess to something that might sound accidental or not sound as bad as what he is accused of doing. When he does this, he is trapped. He "paints himself into a corner" because what he is confessing does not make any sense. This may lead him to admit to something worse.

Also, a person may make a calculation on behalf of another family member: if he confesses, it may prevent a loved one who could be another suspect from having to go to jail.

Also, a person may believe the Good Cop. The accused person may think he did something to harm the child that he was not aware of. The person then "thinks out loud," saying in front of the police what he considers he might or might not have done. Our minds can play tricks on us when we are put under pressure.

Often, decisions are made quickly in the heat of an interrogation. Once there is a decision, there is no turning back.

So why did Virginia Jaspers confess the way she did?

First of all, it is important to recognize that what she confessed does not make any sense in the real world. No amount of shaking by any human being is going to cause a brain hemorrhage. This will be made evident in chapters to come.

There was clearly something else going on, and what that something might have been can be seen by reasoning forward—by considering what we already know about Virginia Jaspers' life, then by considering the result.

In spite of her pleasant disposition, it would seem that Virginia would have known very well her worth to a society that places great emphasis on the outside of a person and not the inside. Years of taunting by others about her appearance could not have helped but take a toll on her self-image and self-esteem. In spite of coming from a prominent family, it would seem that she believed she would always remain on the fringes of society, not being able to experience what many women enjoy: a husband and family.

But there was one thing she did with her life and did joyfully: she loved and took care of children. She fed them, changed their diapers, played with them, bought gifts for them, and kept pictures of them. She loved them and could have thought that she received love back from her small infant charges. As long as the people from her Connecticut community kept having babies, she would make herself available to take care of them.

It looked like she lived her life for the children. Without them, what could she do?

Then came the police interrogation. Not only did she look like a monster, important and influential people like the police and Sherlock Holmes told her that she was a monster. She was the cruel killer of the children she loved. With a poor self-image, how could she not at some level believe what they were saying?

She could have also seen the end of her career as a pediatric nurse. Regardless of the outcome of any trial, she would never be allowed near children again. That much was certain, and I believe she realized it during a "no-win" interrogation. She may have realized her life was over. She had nothing. Might as well finish it.

"It was all uncontrollable," Virginia moaned. "I don't know why I did it. I ought to be put in the electric chair."[1]

***

While browsing through a bookstore near Loma Linda back in 1983, I found a recently published book written by Thomas Noguchi, the former chief medical examiner/coroner for nearby Los Angeles County.[2] He was the "Coroner of the Stars": his book detailed the autopsies and death investigations of several Hollywood celebrities and public figures. One of the stories in the book involved a police shootout in Los Angeles in 1974 with the Symbionese Liberation Army, the radical group responsible for kidnapping Patty Hearst. Although Ms Hearst was not present with them, several other members of that organization lost their lives in the shootout and the subsequent house fire. Dr. Noguchi and others in his office performed the autopsies. In one chapter, Dr. Noguchi walked through the death scene and, while considering the clues from the scene and the autopsies, described in vivid detail how the deaths of each member took place—much like Sherlock Holmes might do if he were a chief medical examiner.

Needless to say, I was hooked. I had never heard of any doctor or pathologist doing anything like this. I wanted to know more.

After graduating from medical school, the Air Force allowed me to remain in Loma Linda for an internship and residency in pathology. Shortly after reading the book, I spoke to my program director and obtained permission for a two-month elective in forensic pathology. After performing about 70 autopsies under the supervision of the forensic pathologist who performed autopsies for the coroner of San Bernardino County, it became clear that this was the career path meant for me—a path I would pursue once I completed my Air Force obligation.

During my training in Loma Linda, I learned about Lindy Chamberlain, the wife of a Seventh-day Adventist minister from Australia, and the dingo. Rather than accept that a dingo could have taken the baby out of the tent, the authorities in that country and many of the people living there alleged that the minister and his wife were part of a cult of religious fanatics who went to Ayer's Rock to sacrifice their infant daughter in the wilderness. Forensic scientists and an English forensic pathologist offered evidence in support of that wild conspiracy theory. Apparently, many Australians at that time were not familiar with Seventh-day Adventist people. It would never enter the imagination of any Seventh-day Adventist to perform a strange act so clearly condemned in the Bible.[3] "How could scientists come up with evidence supporting something like this?" I remembered thinking.

Following my stint in the Air Force, I trained for one year in Atlanta, Georgia, at the Office of the Fulton County Medical Examiner. Unlike what I first thought, I learned that speculating about what happened from autopsy or other physical evidence, much like what Dr. Noguchi did, was not supposed to be done. My teachers called this "scenario building," a behavior I was to avoid.

I also learned how important it is to consider evidence beyond the autopsy, particularly evidence at the scene of death, before drawing conclusions. A training program to the south of mine in Miami required that their fellows visit every death scene for every autopsy they performed. It seemed like a form of forensic pathology boot camp, where the trainee would drive across town to a death scene in a bad part of town late at night and then perform the autopsy the following morning. Most forensic pathologists in a busy office would not be able to sustain that kind of activity for very long, but the lesson to be learned was incredibly important. According to Dr. Joseph Davis, the program director in Miami at that time, "the scene's the thing"—the place where the forensic pathologist learns what will put him on the right path. I did not train in Miami, but I visited about 70 death scenes during my year of training in Atlanta. Most of those death scenes were disgusting and creepy, but I never avoided them nor minimized their importance. I learned that important information lay beyond the walls of an autopsy suite, and I needed to get that information somehow.

The most valuable lessons I learn as a professional are from my mistakes. I recall one time joining a discussion with detectives while watching my teacher, Dr. Saleh Zaki, perform an autopsy on a homicide victim. While the detectives and I floated several theories of what might have happened, Dr. Zaki put down his scalpel, grabbed my elbow, and took me out of the autopsy room.

"Tom, you need to shut up!" I recall him saying. "Police officers may do what they do, but you are not to do what they do. You are the doctor, and they consider every word from your mouth to be like it came from God or the Pope. One day, one of these detectives may present your half-baked theory in court, claiming you told him that theory. What will you do then? Please, Tom…keep your mouth shut!"

I felt horribly embarrassed, recalling one of the "Classical Mistakes in Forensic Pathology" described by Dr. Moritz: the "mistake of talking too soon, too much, or to the wrong people."

Notes

1. The Boys Jeered Her. *Newsweek* September 10, 1956;48(11):90.
2. Noguchi TT. *Coroner; America's Most Controversial Medical Examiner explores the Unanswered Questions Surrouding the Deaths of Marilyn Monroe, Robert F. Kennedy, Sharon Tate, Janis Joplin, William Holden, Natalie Wood, John Belushi and Many Other of His Important Cases.* Simon and Schuster, New York, NY, 1983.
3. Deuteronomy 18:10 and 12:31. The Holy Bible.

You Don't Know What You Don't Know

6

In the 1960s, Sherlock Holmes entered the modern era in the United States. He did it through the important work of child protection.

Child maltreatment or abuse has been around for thousands of years. Prior to the 1960s, doctors would see young patients with suspicious looking wounds and problems, but, for one reason or another, they would never report these suspicious cases to law enforcement authorities. That all changed after the 1962 publication of a medical article entitled "The battered-child syndrome."[1]

After this article, child abuse was no longer simply a law-enforcement matter involving a crime investigation. Crime became "medicalized"—something that now could be diagnosed and treated in a clinical setting. Clinical doctors now became forensic doctors who applied their expertise to matters of crime and punishment.

Please do not misunderstand me. There is no question that the most vulnerable and disadvantaged in society should be protected. This most definitely includes children. Thankfully most parents love their children and do everything in their power to take care of them, but there are tragic exceptions. In such cases, children of cruel and vicious parents have no other refuge but a society who is aware of the problem and does what it can to protect them.

There is no question that anyone who comes in contact with possibly victimized children—anyone such as a school teacher, a daycare worker, or a doctor—has a responsibility to report suspicious cases to the authorities. There is no question that professionals—particularly professionals who can reason logically and scientifically—should participate in the investigation of cases involving suspected child cruelty.

There is also no question that the intention behind "The battered-child-syndrome" article is worthy of praise.

Unfortunately, good intentions are not good enough. Through the introduction of forensic medicine into the investigation of child abuse, countless numbers of people have had their lives damaged and destroyed. Most in society have no idea how bad the situation has become over the last 50 years.

The challenge now is how to explain the problem of "medicalizing" child abuse to people in a way that can be easily understood. One way to do this is to say, "You don't know what you don't know."

"You don't know what you don't know?" What does this mean, and what does this have to do with a medical diagnosis of child abuse?

No one knows where "you don't know what you don't know" came from. It has a kind of dumb-smart ring to it, similar to the sayings of the late Yogi Berra. Berra was a major-league baseball player, coach, and manager famous for strange quotations like, "It ain't over till it's over."

The idea of "you don't know what you don't know" can be demonstrated in a pie chart. Imagine a pie chart representing everything that can be known in the universe. One thin slice of it could show, "what I know that I know." An example of that could be: "I know that I can drive a car."

A slightly larger slice could show, "what I know that I don't know." Examples of that could be: "I don't know how to speak Japanese, I don't know how to make clothing, and I don't know how to tango."

The rest of the pie could show, "what I don't know that I don't know." An example of that could be… um…

I can't give an example. If I could, then that example would be something that I know I don't know.

Most of us understand this. This is because, over time, we encounter many things that we previously did not know. The process of living brings new information to light—assuming, of course, that we are able to learn new information.

Sherlock Holmes' pie looks different from our pie. With Sherlock Holmes' pie, most of it is made up of "what he knows that he knows." A smaller part of the pie is made up of "what he knows that he doesn't know." "What he doesn't know that he doesn't know" doesn't exist:

> My name is Sherlock Holmes. It is my business to know what other people don't know.[2]
>
> No, no: I never guess. It is a shocking habit—destructive to the logical faculty.[3]

If "what he doesn't know that he doesn't know" doesn't exist, then everything is a simple deductive calculation. This would then allow him to say to Dr. Watson

> "You will not apply my precept," he said, shaking his head. "How often have I said to you that when you have eliminated the impossible, whatever remains, however improbable, must be the truth?"[4]

In order for him to say this, "what he doesn't know that he doesn't know" can't exist.

To demonstrate, let's say while we are putting two and two together…

$$2 + 2 = 4$$

...there is an important past event item that was left out, an item that a witness doesn't mention, an item like, "I shook the baby as hard as I could."

$$2 + \_ = 4$$

We could certainly "eliminate" or "rule out" the "impossible" through a series of *diagnostic tests.* Using the number example above, we could test with various numbers and try each in the blank.

For example, what about zero? Well...zero doesn't work. We have now ruled out zero.

What about one? Well...one doesn't work. We have now ruled out one.

What about three? Well...three doesn't work. We have now ruled out three.

After going through our *differential diagnosis,* a medical term that means other choices we can think of to rule out, we are left with "whatever remains," which is two. That approach could work, at least for Sherlock Holmes.

What about the rest of us? What if there was one more thing out there that could change everything, the thing that we don't know that we don't know, the thing that we have not even imagined? It can be represented by one more blank added to the left side of the equal sign:

$$2 + \_ + \_ = 4$$

If there was such a thing, then "whatever remains" becomes uncertain. We would then not know what would go in the blanks.

This is something that former medical examiners like me are often aware of: there may be some piece of information—some new witness account, some recently learned science, some overlooked clue—that could change everything we thought about the case. What if we were to learn that piece of information? What if we were to learn that "one" goes in the added blank? That new information could change the remaining empty blank from two to one:

$$2 + \_ + 1 = 4$$

For example, "He had to have shaken the baby as hard as he could with his own two hands" could change to "The baby stopped breathing for a while, then started again." (If that sounds confusing right now, don't worry about it: I will discuss this later.)

Of course, with Sherlock Holmes, there is never anything new like that to learn. How can he learn anything new like that when he already knows what he knows or doesn't know?

"The battered-child-syndrome" article from 1962 describes "physical abuse" as a "clinical condition" requiring a "full medical evaluation." Doctors should consider the syndrome if there are certain signs, including

- Evidence of fracture of any bone
- Subdural hematoma (a collection of blood lying in a "space" between the membrane surrounding the brain—the *dura*—and the surface of the brain)
- Failure to thrive (when an infant is not gaining weight or growing as he should)
- Soft-tissue swellings or skin bruising (a bruise is bleeding beneath the skin caused by trauma)
- Any child who dies suddenly
- Where the degree and type of injury is at variance with the history given regarding the occurrence of the trauma.

Dr. Kempe and his colleagues acknowledged that there were items they did not know. There was already a recognition that the signs above could have other causes and, of course, that there are "psychiatric factors" that might be present but not fully understood.

The article called for other conditions that could mimic the battered-child syndrome to be ruled out by a "full evaluation." In clinical medicine, a "full evaluation" means a diagnostic workup, often including X-rays and laboratory tests. Once the other conditions have been ruled out and the diagnosis made certain, the treatment would involve removing the child from the presence and custody of the offending person so that the child would be safe.

It sounds simple, doesn't it? The doctor takes a history, does a physical examination, and notes the signs and symptoms. Then the doctor orders tests to rule out other conditions that may mimic the syndrome. The doctor confirms the diagnosis once the other items in the differential diagnosis are ruled out. Then the authorities take the child away.

What is remarkable is that all of this can be done within the confines of a hospital or clinic. A doctor does not even need to leave the building to do this work. She does not have to remove her white coat or leave the bedside or examination room. All the testing can be done inside the hospital.

On the other hand, "real-life" crime investigation performed by law-enforcement officers means visiting the scene of the injury or death and collecting evidence from the scene. It means talking not only to one or two people who show up to the hospital but also canvassing entire neighborhoods, looking for people who may have seen or heard something important to the case. It means lengthy and painstaking interviews of numerous people. It means looking at and thinking about things that never enter the conscious thoughts of the vast majority of doctors who don't know what they don't know.

With a medical degree comes a sense of entitlement, a sense of thinking that one is a whole lot more intelligent than he or she really is. Society confers authority on persons who have the title "doctor" in front of their names. That authority allows a doctor to become a policeman without police-academy training.

The article also covers important techniques for the evaluation of potential offenders. The doctor should tell the parents that the injuries in the child would not have occurred had the child been adequately protected. The doctor should invite parents to tell the entire story so that he might be able to prevent further similar situations in the future. Sometimes, admissions may help the parents feel that they are atoning for the wrongs they have committed, but the parents may still insist that they are not guilty of any wrongdoing. Still, doctors are encouraged to sound sympathetic, acknowledging that there may be times when parents and caregivers may understandably lose their tempers and that there may be circumstances that could explain their actions—even if those actions were a little too forceful.

The article continues on like this, sounding similar to the "Reid Technique"—an interview and interrogation strategy used by law-enforcement officers since the 1940s and 1950s.[5] What was at one time a "doctor-patient" relationship—where a doctor seeks to help a patient—has now turned into an adversarial relationship—in which a doctor seeks to interrogate parents and caregivers. The healer has now become a policeman with a stethoscope. The healer has become Sherlock Holmes, a cartoon professional who doesn't know what he doesn't know.

So often, the scenes of injury or death where forensic doctors diagnose child abuse have no elements of foul play. When the police return to these scenes to collect evidence, there is hardly any evidence to collect. Usually, when there has been an assault or murder of any person, the scene in the vast majority of cases reflects the violence of the event, but child-abuse scenes typically do not reflect violence. Instead, they often reflect the activity of ambulance personnel who respond to help a child who needs to be resuscitated.

Also, when police investigators typically question multiple witnesses, those witnesses may have plenty to say about the character and habitual behaviors of the accused, but they often do not offer any account of any witnessed traumatic event capable of causing the injuries asserted by doctors. Multiple witnesses in most of the cases in which doctors diagnose child abuse do not see the abusive behavior. Often, in cases of criminal violence, there is ample witness evidence for the violence but not in cases of diagnosed child abuse.

When medical professionals write articles about child abuse, there is typically little understanding or acknowledgement of those scenes of injury or death with little or no evidence. There is typically little understanding or acknowledgement of why witnesses in most cases do not see the behaviors asserted by doctors. It is as if such situations have not entered the conscious thoughts of doctors. The police note these items, or the lack of them, in their reports, but forensic doctors often do not read police reports. They are too busy taking care of their patients in their clinics and hospitals, blissfully unaware of what they don't know that they don't know.

***

I have always loved being a medical examiner. It has always been a thrill for me to apply medical knowledge to issues occurring outside of the hospital. Determining what happened and who—if anyone—was responsible for what happened had been and continues to be my passion.

However, after spending seven years in Atlanta as an associate medical examiner for Fulton County and as a pathologist for the Division of Forensic Sciences, Georgia Bureau of Investigation, in nearby Decatur following my fellowship training in forensic pathology, that love was growing cold. I realized that I had not done my family any favors by choosing to be a medical examiner. Performing an additional year of training in forensic pathology had guaranteed a smaller income. It guaranteed that I would remain among the lowest paid of physicians.

After seven years in Georgia, my salary was $85,000 per year, and there was no raise in sight. In early 1995, my oldest son was 13 years old, and the twins were 11. Tuition at the local Adventist school continued to rise as they progressed in their education. I had hoped to be able to pay for the college educations of all my children, just as my father had paid for the educations of my siblings and me. I did not have a huge debt from my medical education, thanks to the Air Force, but I was finding it more and more challenging to support my family and to put away money for the future.

To make ends meet, I performed additional work during my off-hours as a *locum tenens* pathologist in small hospitals near Atlanta, filling in when the pathologists who practiced full-time needed to take some time off. The income from that work enabled me to make ends meet, but all of that changed when for various reasons those extra-work opportunities disappeared. At that point, I realized I needed to do something. I needed to look for a higher paying job outside of forensic pathology in the local area or move away and take a higher paying job in hospital or forensic pathology or both.

Dr. Zaki understood my plight. He had encouraged me to pursue the *locum tenens* work because convincing county officials to raise salaries had been impossible. When I told him my situation, he understood and encouraged me to do what I needed to do for my family.

No available work opportunities existed locally, so the search began for opportunities nationally. One opportunity came from Kansas City. The Department of Pathology at Truman Medical Center, the county hospital for Jackson County and the main teaching hospital for the University of Missouri at Kansas City School of Medicine, was searching for two board-certified forensic pathologists—one to serve as the Jackson County Medical Examiner and the other to assist. I responded to the inquiry, so I was forwarded airline tickets for a trip to Kansas City two weeks later.

On the day prior to the trip, the department canceled the trip without explaining why. Several more weeks passed before I heard from them again, once again offering to fly me to Kansas City.

I arrived in Kansas City for the interview, and the trip was going well. The pathology department at Truman put me up in a very nice hotel next to the Country Club Plaza, a well-known shopping district in Kansas City. The following day I met with the department chairman and was given a tour of their department and the morgue area in the basement. The pathology department shared the autopsy space with the medical examiner. The chairman showed me the two autopsy rooms they used, but the door to the room with the medical examiner's autopsy table was locked. I asked why he didn't have access to the room. He said that the acting medical examiner would not allow anyone else to enter.

The offices for the medical examiner and the clerical staff were near the autopsy rooms, but the door to these offices was also locked. I was not allowed to enter to take a look, and there was no one in there at the time of my tour. A medical-examiner investigator sat at a desk in the broad space between the autopsy room and the offices. With a grim look on her face, she said nothing to me or even acknowledged my presence.

What was going on?

Later that day, I met with deputy attorneys of the prosecuting attorney's office and with a representative from the Jackson County Executive's office. The representative from the Jackson County Executive explained the situation to me.

Two years before, the Jackson County medical examiner of that time left for a hospital job in Hutchinson, Kansas. He was paid $89,000 per year for his services and had decided to make more money elsewhere. Once he left, the county thought it would be an easy matter to replace him, but no pathologist inquired about the job. What then happened was a crisis. Bodies accumulated in the morgue refrigerator. The medical examiner investigators at that time were able to process bodies that did not need autopsies and release them, but no doctor was available to perform autopsies. There were also no death certificates being signed. News of this crisis made it into the *Kansas City Star*.[6]

At the request of the county executive, the pathology department at Truman Medical Center provided two pathologists to perform the autopsies.

They worked all night, completing their work by the next morning. Both pathologists (doctors I will call pathologist #1 and pathologist #2) were not board-certified forensic pathologists, but they agreed to perform the autopsies until the county hired a permanent medical examiner.

Several days later, pathologist #1 signed a contract with the county, agreeing to serve as a temporary medical examiner. The contractual amount was based on an annual salary of $105,000. The county realized they would need also to hire a full-time assistant, a doctor whose salary would be $90,000.

One year had passed and the county still had not hired a permanent medical examiner. By September of 1994, the county was displeased with pathologist #1, so they did not renew his contract. Shortly after being notified of that non-renewal, pathologist #1 dropped the "corruption" bomb. He alleged that members of law enforcement worked improperly to influence his work on at least 20 death cases, compelling him to close those cases without calling them homicides. Police and county officials bullied him, and he claimed that files from suspected homicides were missing from the office. Pathologist #1 declined to cite any specific instances.[7] The Missouri Highway Patrol, the Missouri attorney aeneral and the Missouri Board of Healing Arts joined the county prosecutor in an investigation of the office, finding that the doctor not only had previously been fired from another medical-examiner office for incompetence but that he also made similar allegations of corruption upon being fired.

The county then passed temporary leadership of the office to pathologist #2; he entered into another contract with the county. By the time of my interview in the spring of 1995, pathologist #2 was estranged from the Truman Pathology Department.

The pathology chairman at Truman decided he wanted his department to have the contract for the medical-examiner function and that he wanted to hire the permanent medical examiner. When the county balked at the idea, the pathology department chairman rescinded his offer to interview me, only to later have me come to Kansas City without finalizing any arrangement with the county.

The representative from the county executive's office told me that they wanted to hire me directly as an employee of Jackson County. I told him I had no problem with that arrangement, but I had four conditions. One of those conditions was an annual salary of $160,000, a major jump from what I had been paid in Atlanta.

They also had a condition: they wanted me to accept pathologist #2 as an assistant, telling me that if he did not work out, I had the option of letting him go. I agreed to the arrangement and was appointed by the county executive as the Jackson County Medical Examiner. I began work in Kansas City in July of 1995.

Notes

1. Kempe C, Silverman FN, Steele BF, Droegemueller W, Silver HK. The battered-child syndrome. *Journal of the American Medical Association* 1962;181(1):17–24.
2. Doyle AC. The adventure of the blue carbuncle. The Adventures of Sherlock Holmes. *Strand Magazine* January 1892.
3. Doyle AC. The sign of the four. Chapter 1—The science of deduction. *Lippincott's Monthly Magazine* February 1890.
4. Doyle AC. The sign of the four. Chapter 6—Sherlock Holmes gives a demonstration. *Lippincott's Monthly Magazine* February 1890.
5. Inbau FE, Reid JE, Buckley JP, Jayne BC. *Criminal Interrogation and Confessions.* Gaithersburg, MD: Aspen Publishers, 2001.
6. Jeffers G. Job vacancy delays eight funerals. *Kansas City Star* November 10, 1993.
7. Jeffers G. Inquiry on office is sought. *Kansas City Star* September 17, 1994.

7 Can't Shake This Feeling

From the moment Virginia Jaspers admitted to "a good shaking,"[1] it became an idea that will never go away.

The idea of shaking hooked radiologist John Caffey when he heard about Virginia Jaspers and her confession. Shaking seemed to explain so much to him. He saw it as a great way to explain why infants have subdural hemorrhages and brain injury without having tears in the scalp and broken skull bones from blows to the head. It also explained to him why these injuries would be associated with the long-bone injuries he would find in the X-rays of injured infants: the abuser would injure the limbs as well as the head if he grabbed the infant by the limbs. It also explained to him why many of these infants had hemorrhages inside the eyes: the shakings would also cause the eyes to move back and forth and cause blood vessels to tear and bleed.

In addition to the Jaspers case, he reported many more cases of the "whiplash shaken infant syndrome" in articles published in 1972 and 1974. Other forensic doctors eventually became hooked on the idea with John Caffey. Sure, Caffey in his way had to admit that no one actually sees children shaken in a way that leads to his syndrome ("Usually there are no witnesses," he wrote), but he believed in its existence because assailants eventually admitted to violently shaking infants. He believed such admissions were "reliable."[2]

How reliable are the admissions or confessions of accused people?

We learned in Chapter 5: Good Cop, Bad Cop how the police get a confession. Here is what happens with child abuse and shaking:

- First, forensic doctors examine an infant and give a diagnosis of "child abuse" and "the whiplash shaken infant syndrome."
- Then police officers, who wholeheartedly believe forensic doctors, confront the alleged assailants with the doctor's diagnosis. Through questioning and accusing that involves *confirmation bias*, some of the alleged assailants admit that the doctor's theory of what happened was actually what happened.

What is confirmation bias? Here is one way to explain it. Let's say that I as a forensic doctor have a belief about what happened to cause the death or injury of an infant. If you were to agree with my belief, I would salute you, praise you, give you a "high five," and think that you are an all-around good person. If you were to disagree with my belief, I would not accept what you are saying. Instead, I would minimize the importance of what you say, avoid what you say, belittle what you say, and give you the "finger." If many other forensic doctors agreed with my belief, they would publish it in their journals and praise it for how well it explains what happened. If they were to disagree, they would criticize, minimize, and even ridicule my opinion. They would refuse to allow publication of my opinion.

This sort of thinking occurs in public discourse all the time with a wide variety of topics; however, it is particularly scary when forensic doctors, who are seemingly scientific people who seemingly should know better, engage in this kind of bias. It is even scarier when police officers who interrogate suspects believe these doctors.

Police officers who interrogate suspected child abusers believe the doctors and do not believe the people they interrogate. As a consequence, if what the suspect says agrees with the doctor, the police officers will compliment the suspect and say that he or she has done the right thing by confessing. If the suspect disagrees with the doctor, the police officers will not believe the suspect, so they will continue to interrogate until the suspect finally says something that agrees with the doctor's theory. If someone is in such a "no-win" situation, it is pointless for that person to try to defend himself. Defending oneself in such a situation does not persuade anyone.

In the early 1970's, most "assailants" did not confess, but that soon changed. Over time, more and more people confessed to shaking infants, and more and more of the people who confessed were males.[3] With more and more people confessing to shaking infants, particularly people who are stronger than what Virginia Jaspers might have seemed, the love affair with the notion of shaking grew more and more entrenched in the medical literature and the public consciousness. Shaking would not go away, nor does it look like it will ever go away. Doctors who act and think like Sherlock Holmes diagnose shaken baby syndrome, and nobody effectively and convincingly argues with Sherlock Holmes, particularly the people accused by Sherlock Holmes.

Caffey, in both his 1972 and 1974 articles, believed that even mild shaking of an infant could jostle the brain in such a way as to cause damage, even damage leading to mental retardation, cerebral palsy, and epilepsy. He thought that the whiplash shaking of infants was a widely practiced activity found in all levels of society. Giving children a "good shaking" was an activity that people had not suspected to be harmful, yet Caffey believed ordinary and casual shakings could kill and cripple children.

The notion that casual shaking of an infant could damage the brain changed in 1987 when a group composed of both medical doctors and scientific experts in *biomechanics* from the University of Pennsylvania published a study that demonstrated that it was *not humanly possible* to damage an infant brain by shaking.[4] They used dummies with instruments that measured acceleration in the dummy heads. They both slammed the dummies against surfaces and shook the dummies without slamming them. Using previously published acceleration levels known to cause various brain injuries in monkeys (taken from previous experiments performed in the 1960s), they found that impacts were well within the levels for brain injury but that the shakes did not even come close to a concussion ("knocking a person out"), let alone a subdural hemorrhage. Impacts had accelerations that were 50 times greater than shakes.

It is not hard to understand why impacts have higher measurements for acceleration than shakes. With an impact, the head makes a sudden stop—a sudden decrease in velocity over a very brief period of time. This causes a very high acceleration measurement (in physics, a sudden decrease in velocity is a high acceleration in the opposite direction of the motion of the head—a "deceleration"). On the other hand, the head does not come to a sudden stop with shaking: the stopping time is prolonged compared to an impact, and that prolongation greatly decreases the levels of acceleration. It is the sudden stop that brings about the head injury.

It was clear to these doctors and scientists from Pennsylvania that shaking could not cause brain injury. Still, they could not shake the feeling of shaking. At the end of the article, they wrote that shaking by itself could not cause any injury but it could be a part of the process. The doctors then proposed what they believed to be the "most common scenario": the child is shaken and then thrown against a surface where he hits the back of his head. The impact against a surface would then allow a "large, brief deceleration" sufficient to cause injury.

Notice the "most common scenario." If we were to analyze this scenario in the same way we analyzed the Brides in the Bath scenario, here is what we would have:

There are nine elements to this scenario, and we can number each from one to nine:

1. The abuser grabs the infant firmly by the arms or chest.
2. Then the abuser pushes the infant rapidly away from the abuser's chest.
3. Then he pulls her in rapidly toward his chest.
4. Then he pushes her away from his chest.
5. Then he pulls her in toward his chest.
6. Then he pushes her away from his chest.
7. Then he pulls her in toward his chest (repeat this as may times as you like).
8. Then she is thrown against a surface, striking the back of her head.
9. Then her brain is injured.

We flip the coin nine times and get "heads" every time, but we cannot stop there. Now imagine all of the people who at various times are imagined to have engaged in the "most common scenario." The number of people is countless, all doing the same thing to infants. We would have to flip the coin thousands of times and still get heads every time. Would this be likely or even "common"? Of course not!

Yet forensic doctors do not stop to think of this. The same Sherlock Holmes virus that infects the brains of detective fiction enthusiasts also infects the brains of forensic doctors.

In the years following that study, biomechanical experts became more and more involved in the shaken-baby discussion. Although the great majority of forensic doctors by this time were in the shaken-baby camp, most biomechanical experts had a hard time accepting the notion: the idea did not square with what they were measuring and observing.

One biomechanical expert, Dr. Faris Bandak, asked why these cases had no neck injuries.

I have spoken to Dr. Bandak personally. One illustration that he likes to use is what it would be like to kick a football so hard that it would fly to the moon. If any human were to kick a football that forcefully, his hip and knee joints would come apart. This would be more than straining a few ligaments or causing a little soft tissue damage: a person's knee and hip joints would completely separate from his body with such a forceful kick.

In a similar way, if any person were to shake an infant so rapidly and so forcefully as to cause brain damage and hemorrhage in the head, the shaker's shoulder and elbow joints would fall apart.

If adult limbs cannot withstand such forceful movement, what would happen to the neck of the shaken infant? What about that important structure in a tiny baby that all people who hold babies are told to protect?

Using the monkey data from the 1960s which measured how much acceleration it would take to tear blood vessels inside the head with just accelerating the head, Dr. Bandak demonstrated in an article in 2005 that these accelerations would be much higher than the neck could structurally withstand.[5]

This is not really that hard to understand. Many predators in the wild will kill small animals by grasping their heads and shaking them, breaking their necks. At least from what we can observe in nature, shaking tends to break necks.

What is often simple to understand is made more complicated by critics who are hooked on the shaking notion. Following that article, two different sets of doctors—most of them biomechanical experts—wrote letters to the editor that had the same criticisms: Bandak made mistakes in his calculations—"numerical errors."[6],[7] The results from proper calculations would have shown forces 10 times lower than what Dr. Bandak calculated. Had Bandak done his math properly, they claimed, he would have discovered that it is possible for infants to be shaken rapidly and not have their necks damaged.

Dr. Bandak responded.[8] The two sets of doctors who wrote letters claiming "numerical errors" used acceleration numbers for their calculations that were measurements of how rapidly a human could shake a dummy. Dr. Bandak used acceleration numbers from the monkey experiments of the 1960s for his calculations—where monkeys were accelerated so rapidly that blood vessels inside their heads were torn. Dr. Bandak and his critics used two different sets of measurements.

The 1960s experiments had monkeys strapped into a sled that was struck by a piston. This would generate accelerations much greater than what a human could generate with his hands. In order to test for the accelerations necessary to cause hemorrhages inside monkey heads, the monkeys' necks were "potted"—meaning that metal cylinders were placed around monkey necks to keep them from moving and from getting injured. On the other hand, the necks of so-called shaken infants are not potted.

The experts argue endlessly with each other, but none of this matters to doctors who testify, to jurors who listen, to judges who admit evidence, or to police officers who investigate. What matters to them is that a child has been harmed and someone should be brought to justice for this, regardless of whether or not the injury or death was caused by shaking or something else. The debate about shaking goes on, but it is all a waste of time. Science and scientists provide no solutions when confirmation bias reigns and when forensic doctors have reputations to maintain and livelihoods to protect. Shaking is not going away, regardless of the science, regardless of the human tragedy that continues to send innocent people to jail.

***

A short drive to the south of Kansas City on 71 Highway (Kansas Citians say "71 Highway," not "Highway 71") will bring you to the small town of Peculiar, Missouri. I recall driving by it and seeing from the highway a sign: "Welcome to Peculiar, where the 'odds' are with you."

I spent three and a half years of my life in Omaha, Nebraska, while I was in the Air Force several years before, so coming to Kansas City felt like coming home. I was reminded how wonderfully odd people in the Heartland of the United States could be. Most people are incredibly friendly and helpful, going out of their way to help a stranger, always being available to help when some need arose or disaster struck. The friendliness and helpfulness were sincere, without the kind of pretense I was accustomed to seeing while I lived near the east and west coasts of the United States. On the other hand, if someone did not like you, that person would often show that dislike openly, without pretending or trying to hide anything. I found that to be refreshing because I didn't have to guess too much about what someone was thinking.

Jackson County was generous in covering my relocation expenses. They put me up in a hotel for a couple of months while the rest of my family remained in Atlanta. Yara had several matters to take care of, including the sale of our home, but we were not accustomed to being apart for so long. During one of our telephone conversations, Yara told me what was happening with our 11-year-old daughter. She would sleep at night holding a paperweight with my initials on it close to her chest. "When I hold this, I feel close to Daddy," she explained. When I heard this, I realized I needed to get my family to Kansas City as soon as possible, even though we hadn't sold the house yet.

During that time without my family, I spent long hours at the office, not only during the day but also at night, traveling with the on-call investigator to death scenes and watching everyone do their work. My mentors instructed me not to make any changes in the office operation too soon but simply to observe how things work. This turned out to be great advice because I could see how every employee was worried about change. They thought that I would make sweeping changes that would upset everything, and several were worried that I would replace them with people I would bring with me from Georgia. Pathologist #2 was also worried. He did not want me to take his office—the larger of two doctor's offices—away from him, so he painted the walls pink, thinking this would work to keep me away from his space.

Pathologist #2 supplemented his income with several *locum tenens* hospital jobs in small towns in eastern Kansas and western Missouri. I wondered how he was able to do all of these jobs and still keep pace by himself with the autopsy load. He asked to do autopsies in the afternoons and evenings so that he could provide hospital coverage in the morning. I agreed to that for a short while.

Finally, I got to see what was behind the locked autopsy room door I encountered during my interview a few months before. The single autopsy table in the room was broken, not allowing it to be raised to accommodate my relatively tall stature. The room was small, not allowing more than one pathologist to do autopsies at a time.

That was not the only problem. Our operation was on the ground floor of Truman Medical Center, and we relied on the services of that hospital. Often, trash containers would overflow with biohazardous materials because housekeeping personnel did not want to enter the morgue. Radiology technicians operating portable X-ray machines were slow to respond to the morgue for gunshot-wound cases, blaming the demands of patient care for their slowness, often slowing down our work on busy days.

There were also problems with the police department. Medical-examiner investigators would often show up to death scenes only to be blocked out by police investigators and crime-scene technicians working on a homicide. Crime-scene technicians would also come to the morgue and remove all clothing and other items prior to the appearance of the pathologist. In many cases, it is important for a forensic pathologist to view items on the body, but the doctor was often left with only a naked dead body that the crime-scene technicians had cleaned. Eventually, police leadership and I had to meet with the prosecutor to iron out our differences. As heated as the discussions were, eventually we agreed to solutions that were mutually beneficial. Also, with the help of my boss, the Jackson County Executive, we finally managed to iron out our problems with the county hospital.

As annoying as these problems were, they paled in comparison to what I discovered shortly after starting the job.

While thumbing through the case records, I found several manila case folders with orange stickers. The secretary did not give me a straight reply why those stickers were present, but it did not take me long to discover the reason for myself: these folders had no autopsy reports. More than one hundred cases performed over the past year-and-a-half by Pathologist #2 were never finished, and several of these were homicides.

I informed the county attorney and the prosecutor's office of the situation. Pathologist #2 had to stop the moonlighting and complete these cases, but he was not willing to complete them. While I performed nearly all of the autopsies during the fall of 1995, he did little to fulfill his promise to finish the delinquent cases. Eventually I fired him in February of 1996, with the county's blessing. In spite of my best efforts, several of those cases could never be completed.

Months later, the new pathologist I hired discovered several brains in formalin fixative solution on shelves in the autopsy room. Often, a pathologist will retain a brain for examination at a later date following formalin treatment if the investigation and autopsy require it to be done. The case files demonstrated complete autopsy reports with detailed descriptions of the brains, but the containers held brains that had never been dissected. Pathologist #2 invented the autopsy findings: the items he described were not present when we finally dissected the brains. Investigations by the Missouri State Board of Registration for the Healing Arts and the Missouri attorney general led to the revocation of pathologist #2's medical license in Missouri. Years later in Florida, he would have his medical examiner appointment revoked for failing to complete autopsy reports.

During the next 11½ years until the end of December in 2006, the office relocated into a facility built for it within the same Hospital Hill medical center complex but outside of Truman Medical Center. Later, the medical examiner office underwent an additional expansion. The autopsy suites were state-of-the-art for that time, with walk-in morgues, rooms with special air handling, and carts that could be wheeled to multiple separate autopsy stations. We also obtained accreditation for the office twice by the National Association of Medical Examiners and operated a training program in forensic pathology. Years later in 2016, by the time I traveled to Texas for Deterryon Kelly's case, the office, under new leadership, occupied a new state-of-the-art facility that is no longer attached to the Hospital Hill complex. The office is worlds apart from the time I performed autopsies on a broken table.

Notes

1. The Boys Jeered Her. *Newsweek*, September 10, 1956;48(11):90.
2. Caffey J. The whiplash shaken infant syndrome: Manual shaking by the extremities with whiplash-induced intracranial and intraocular bleedings, linked with residual permanent brain damage and mental retardation. *Pediatrics* 1974;54(4)396–403.
3. Lazoritz S, Baldwin S, Kini N. The whiplash shaken infant syndrome: Has Caffey's syndrome changed or have we changed his syndrome? *Child Abuse and Neglect* 1997;21:1009–1014.
4. Duhaime A-C, Gennarelli TA, Thibault LE, Bruce DA, Margulies SS, Wiser R. The shaken baby syndrome: A clinical, pathological, and biomechanical study. *Journal of Neurosurgery* 1987;66:409–415.
5. Bandak AF. Shaken baby syndrome: A biomechanics analysis of injury mechanisms. *Forensic Science International* 2005;151:71–79.
6. Margulies S, Prange M, Myers BS, Maltese MR, Ji S, Ning X, Fisher J, Arbogast K, Christian C. Shaken baby syndrome: A flawed biomechanical analysis. *Forensic Science International* 2006;164:278–279.
7. Rangarajan N, Shams T. Letter to the editor. *Forensic Science International* 2006;164:280–281.
8. Bandak F. Response to the letter to the editor. *Forensic Science International* 2006;164:282–283.

8 The Emperor Wears No Clothes

Who are forensic doctors? Are they the doctors that most people see in hospitals and clinics?

The answer to the second question above is "Yes." Most forensic doctors practice in hospitals and clinics, but you may not recognize them as forensic doctors. Even most of these doctors do not necessarily recognize themselves as forensic doctors.

Any doctor who testifies in court as an expert witness is a forensic doctor. Any doctor who consults with police officers or attorneys regarding cases that may or may not go to court is a forensic doctor. Any doctor who offers opinions that may lead to someone being arrested for criminal behavior is a forensic doctor. Very few of these doctors are forensic doctors full-time. Most of them spend the majority of their time taking care of patients.

Several of the forensic doctors in the United States who practice full-time as forensic doctors are forensic pathologists. They have been around the longest as forensic doctors. The American Board of Pathology, an organization that accredits doctors who specialize in the study of disease, officially recognized forensic pathology as a subspecialty of pathology back in 1959. In truth, forensic pathologists have been around for a lot longer than that. Most full-time forensic pathologists work in coroner or medical-examiner offices, where they investigate why a person died. They perform many autopsies. Most autopsies in the United States are performed in coroner and medical-examiner offices; few are performed in hospitals anymore.

Currently, there are many forensic pathology training programs in the United States, but few of the trainees stay in forensic pathology full-time. The number of active full-time forensic pathologists is in the few hundreds—a small number compared to the many thousands of people who die violently, suddenly, unexpectedly, or mysteriously in this country.

Most of the few forensic pathologists that exist affiliate themselves with two forensic professional societies. They have been part of a section of the American Academy of Forensic Sciences (AAFS) since the inception of that organization in 1948. Most of the AAFS is composed of scientists who are not forensic physicians. Forensic pathologists share the Pathology/Biology section of the AAFS with forensic botanists (plant specialists), forensic entomologists (insect specialists), and other scientists who are not physicians.

Later in 1966, forensic pathologists formed their own professional society, the National Association of Medical Examiners. Although the term "medical examiner" is used in the name, other forensic pathologists who work for coroners or who are otherwise not affiliated with any medical-examiner office can, and often do, join.

These forensic doctors who work full-time are not involved in patient care, but they, at one time in training or past practice, participated in the care of sick people. The terms and strategies from this experience very much influence their ways of thinking and reasoning from evidence.

Another very small group of forensic doctors who practice forensic medicine full-time are child-abuse pediatricians.

Child-abuse pediatrics is a subspecialty of pediatrics and was recognized as an official subspecialty by the American Board of Pediatrics in 2010. Most child-abuse pediatricians are in academic settings: university hospitals and children's hospitals where advanced subspecialty medical care takes place. Ironically, inserting the words, "child abuse" in front of pediatricians—doctors who diagnose and treat diseases in children—puts a red flag on the confirmation bias that is so rampant among these practitioners. It is done this way without apology. They see as their mission to confirm child abuse. They see protecting children as their main function. One way to protect children is to stand between them and their abusing parents. Child abuse is a negative presumption, in which the worst is accepted about people before proof is offered. We have already seen in a previous chapter how presuming negatively about people does not lead to truthful answers; this applies to physicians as well as police officers.

Child-abuse pediatricians and forensic pathologists are only a small number of all the forensic medical practitioners that exist. The rest of them are found in numerous other specialties in medicine: internal medicine, pediatrics, surgery, neurosurgery, neurology, ophthalmology, psychiatry, radiology, anatomic and clinical pathology, orthopedics, emergency medicine, family medicine, etc. The number of doctors who stand ready to accuse people of criminal behavior is much higher than the few full-time forensic practitioners. These doctors may ask the child-abuse pediatricians to confirm their opinions, but they are more often the ones who make the initial diagnosis of foul play and provide medical evidence for it.

Yet, for the most part, none of these doctors, including child-abuse pediatricians, belong to any forensic-science society. There is no training for how to infer properly from evidence or how to conduct a criminal investigation. None of that is even considered. All that is done is to use the tools and techniques of patient care, of diagnosing and treating disease.

What works in the patient-care setting does not work for criminal investigation. The reasons for the confusion are amazingly simple and easy to understand; at least, they are easy to understand by anyone who is not a forensic doctor.

When we go to the doctor, we see this professional most often for a problem that exists in the present. We may have signs and symptoms from a present underlying condition that is often not readily seen or even understood.

The doctor initially interviews us in detail. She asks us what our main problem is (the chief complaint), and we describe what our symptoms have been over time (patient history). She asks us about medical problems we have had in the past and about previous surgeries (past medical history). We tell the doctor what other problems we might have with other parts of our body (review of systems), and we talk about other aspects of our life (family history, social history, occupational history).

Then the doctor examines us (physical examination).

Following that, the doctor offers an opinion of what might be wrong with us based on what she has learned so far. This opinion is called a *diagnosis,* but the doctor does not stop with a diagnosis. She may do one of two things: (1) she may treat our condition based on her diagnosis, or (2) she may order more tests. For the first, if the treatment seems to work and we are relieved of our signs and symptoms, then we are satisfied. If the treatment does not seem to work, the doctor considers why and orders more tests. She may do this to "rule out" other conditions that may be the cause of the signs or symptoms: conditions that are included in a differential diagnosis list. The doctor may watch us carefully over time to see what happens with the underlying condition that no one can readily see with his or her eyes.

In other words, medical care is a sophisticated form of trial-and-error, of "Let's try this and see if it works." The doctor looks at the "clues" from the history; the physical examination; and the clinical laboratory, radiologic and other imaging, and other clinical tests. She then guesses as to the internal "train of events" in our bodies that lead to the clues. So far, this is like Joseph Bell and Sherlock Holmes, but this is not all: the doctor treats the patient to see if the underlying condition that no one can readily see is made better or goes away.

Doctors are aware of what treatments work for a diagnosis—a category used to summarize the internal "train of events" going on in the body—by studying populations of people with the same diagnosis. If the treatment works for most people, the thinking is that the treatment will likely work for a particular patient. If everything works out, then…great! Problem solved! If it does not, then there may be more testing, treating, and waiting.

What about situations considered in a court of law?

Crimes are not ongoing internal problems that are not readily seen that lead to signs and symptoms. Crimes are external behaviors that readily can be seen by witnesseses. Crimes are not present conditions; they are past events. Present conditions can be tested through imaging, laboratory procedures, and other procedures in a hospital setting because they exist; but past events that occurred outside of the hospital and no longer exist cannot be tested that way. Furthermore, other events similar to the past events could be prevented from happening again, but past events cannot be treated and made to go away like a disease or other ongoing condition. Without successful treatment and a disease improving or being cured, there is no way to "prove" those past events with medical methods.

But there are ways to prove that crimes did occur. These methods are used in courtrooms and criminal investigations all the time, but the vast majority of forensic doctors do not understand this. It also seems that the vast majority of criminal investigators do not understand that the vast majority of forensic doctors do not understand this.

I mentioned the way to test for past events previously in this book. You may recall the Inferential Test:

> One can be reasonably certain if witness accounts of the past are consistent or not consistent with physical evidence in the present, but one cannot reliably surmise past events from physical evidence unless there is only one plausible explanation for that evidence.

Maybe by now, the wordy sentence above is making more sense to you. If not, there is always the simpler, more-easily-understood version:

> You can listen to an eyewitness with an open mind and see if what he says fits the clues, but you cannot make up a story from the clues and expect it to be true.

Now, consider a simpler, more-easily-understood version of the Inferential Test written for forensic doctors and other scientific professionals who look at cases with suspected criminal behavior:

> A forensic doctor can study eyewitness accounts and other types of memory evidence like audiovisual recordings to see if what is there fits the clues, but the doctor cannot from the clues summarize a "train of events" in a diagnosis of criminal behavior and expect it to be true.

What a forensic doctor can do reasonably and logically when approached by attorneys or the police is to reason forward:

1. Look at witness information from both outside and inside the hospital—from 911 calls, police records, ambulance records, and medical records—and compare them to physical evidence clues learned from the medical care setting and from the crime-scene investigation.
2. Express an opinion about whether or not the witness information fits or does not fit the clues.

3. If everything fits, the doctor can state: "According to what I know from evidence-based science, it all fits."
4. If even one point does not fit, the doctor can state: "According to what I know from evidence-based science, this particular point does not fit."

The forensic doctor should refuse to accuse anyone of doing anything criminal or even make such a diagnosis. They should simply point out to attorneys or investigators where things fit or do not fit, according to evidence-based science. Even if things do not fit entirely, it cannot be assumed that a crime has occurred—that "child abuse" is the "only plausible explanation." This is because "you don't know what you don't know": it is important for anyone to look at as much information as one can before making the leap—the very scary leap—of stating criminal behavior to be the "only plausible explanation." The "only plausible explanation" is taken from the original Inferential Test: "...unless there is only one plausible explanation for that evidence."

Besides, whether or not a crime is the only plausible explanation is up to a judge or jury to decide and not some forensic doctor. The judges or jurors are the ones who are presented with all the evidence for consideration; the doctor only has a limited view.

Do all forensic doctors reason forward all the time in the courtroom? No! Most forensic doctors are ignorant of the logic and the necessity of comparing witness accounts of the past to physical evidence clues in the present for consistency ("it all fits" or "it is possible") or inconsistency ("it does not completely fit" or "it is not possible").

I used the term, "evidence-based science," above. What is evidence-based science?

Evidence is something that is "evident": something that can be seen, heard, touched, tasted, smelled, or otherwise observed by scientists. Such observable and evident items can be called *facts*. Scientists have to observe numerous facts at numerous times and also learn as much as possible what others observed before concluding that a "train of events" is the "only plausible explanation" for a set of "clues."

All of this is in contrast to *beliefs*—items that are not observed that may or may not be true. Scientists may express beliefs about what they think could be going on. If those beliefs are "evidence-based" from what has been observed repeatedly by scientists and others, then those beliefs are more likely to be true than beliefs that are not "evidence-based."

Much of what is in the medical literature about "child abuse" is not evidence-based: it is belief-based. Doctors do not observe children being abused but they make scientific studies based on beliefs that they are abused—beliefs formed from clues found during hospital care and from "confessions."

They compile and summarize cases based on their beliefs and publish them in medical journals. Doctors who peer-review and publish these kinds of journal articles should recognize the error in what they do, but they do not recognize a problem. They simply confirm and have others confirm their beliefs and biases.

Hopefully, I have explained the problem in a way that you can understand, but I have bad news for you. The bad news is that it does not really matter whether or not forensic doctors understand the problem. The problem will not go away, regardless of understanding.

Consider the little story of "The Emperor's New Clothes," written by Hans Christian Andersen and originally published in 1837. Often, authors of children's stories intended them to be a form of political satire. Andersen's story appears to be no different.

In the story, two con men posing as tailors received money from the vain and fashion-inclined emperor to make an exceptionally wonderful set of clothes. In spite of their promise, the tailors never had the skill to make the clothes, so they convinced the emperor that they were sewing clothes for him by pantomiming the action of sewing clothes. The emperor's sense of wish fulfillment and fantasy allowed him to be conned, and he proudly displayed his imaginary clothes in a parade before the town's people. The crowd and the retinue accompanying the emperor were not willing to tell the emperor that he was naked, so they soldiered on—even when a little kid in the crowd yelled, "The emperor wears no clothes!"

As a satire for forensic doctors, consider Dr. Joseph Bell as a con man. He convinced medical students, including Arthur Conan Doyle, that he could observe physical evidence on a person and know from only those observations what that person did. Conan Doyle unwittingly perpetuated that con through his fictional writings, and each new generation of forensic doctors accepts it. Consider forensic doctors as vain emperors who testify in court like Sherlock Holmes, who continue to exert power and undue influence over the minds of judges, jurors, and the rest of society. These doctors are not con men. They are conned. They believe what they do really works. Consider the crowd to be the rest of society, who allow forensic doctors to tell them what to believe. We could consider the child as someone who has the audacity to point out something that should be obvious about forensic doctors.

The story abruptly ends after the child cries out, leaving it to the reader's imagination what would happen next. Of course it is not hard to understand what would happen next or why it would happen. Of course, the emperor, his retinue, and the people would ignore the child and continue on, continuing to pretend the emperor is wearing splendid apparel.

Everyone has something to protect. People want to make a livelihood. People want to prosper financially. People do not want to have to defend themselves against accusations. People do not want to stand out in a negative way. People for the most part want to "go along to get along" in their jobs and hopefully retire without major problems.

Take forensic pathologists, for example.

Forensic pathologists mean well. They officially recognize that it is important for a forensic doctor to be independent from law-enforcement agencies both in reality and in perception. According to autopsy standards accepted by the National Association of Medical Examiners (NAME), the very first standard is.

> A1.1 Medicolegal death investigation officers should operate without any undue influence from law enforcement agencies and prosecutors.[1]

NAME later emphasized that position in a position paper, stressing how important it is that medical examiners and forensic pathologists remain independent of "political influences from other agencies."[2] The intent may be good, but the reality is different. Rank-and-file medical examiners are civil servants with little political power and who are heavily affected by the powers-that-be, regardless of any desire to be independent from those political influences. Medical examiners may have tremendous influence like an emperor over jurors in the courtroom, but they do not have the political clout of an emperor. A medical examiner who wants to keep his job does not do well by offending politically powerful entities like law-enforcement agencies and prosecutors. In fact, most medical examiners do whatever they can to keep police and prosecutors happy and not offend them. If it were to be pointed out that a medical examiner had been drawing unreasonable conclusions like Sherlock Holmes, that medical examiner could very well become unemployable. Of course he would not admit to drawing unreasonable conclusions! He would choose instead to soldier on, marching naked, pretending and hoping that no one notices.

Do not look for currently employed medical examiners to stand up and point out any problems with the way things are being done. They have too much to protect.

Take child-abuse pediatricians as another example.

Child-abuse pediatricians make a living out of diagnosing child abuse. They rely on the respect and the admiration of their pediatric colleagues for what they do. Academic institutions and children's hospitals receive government and other extramural funding from the activity of child-abuse pediatricians: the more diagnoses of child abuse that are made, the more money the institution receives.[3] If it were pointed out that a child-abuse pediatrician had been drawing unreasonable conclusions like Sherlock Holmes, then much would be put into jeopardy. Vast sums of money would evaporate and so would the livelihood and reputation of the child-abuse pediatrician. The child-abuse pediatrician would have to go back to practicing general pediatrics or—even worse—have his medical license threatened. Of course, no child-abuse pediatrician would admit to drawing unreasonable conclusions! He would choose instead to soldier on, marching naked, pretending and hoping that no one notices.

For certain, do not look for child-abuse pediatricians to stand up and point out any problems with the way things are being done. They have too much to protect.

Now take the rest of the forensic doctors who "dabble" in legal medicine while continuing to see and treat patients as yet another example.

Most doctors rely on their clinical practices to make their living and not so much on their forensic activity. If these doctors were to learn that they had been drawing unreasonable conclusions like Sherlock Holmes, they would have good reason to fear that their ability to make a living as a clinical doctor would be in jeopardy because of a damaged reputation. Of course they would not admit to such a thing! They would choose instead to soldier on, marching naked, pretending and hoping that no one notices.

Do not look for any forensic doctor of any type to stand up and point out any problems with the way things are being done, particularly if they are currently practicing medicine. They have too much to protect.

I imagine that all who sit in prison because of the testimonies of forensic doctors would find excuses like "I have too much to protect!" to be pitiful and empty. Still for the most part, these inmates are not going anywhere. The rest of society places undue importance on the testimony of such doctors. Nothing will change as long as forensic doctors continue doing what they do.

***

On July 21, 1994, a 31-year-old African-American male planned and executed the great escape.[4]

He was serving time in the Municipal Correctional Institution in Kansas City for multiple minor traffic violations and stealing. For some reason, despite the relatively minor nature of his offenses, he thought he had to get out of there.

Several other inmates watched what he did. Two chain-link fences surrounded the compound. Coiled razor wire lay in the long grass outside the outer fence. The man first crawled through a gap in the inner fence, scaled the outer fence, and then fell into the coiled razor wire obscured by the grass. After extricating himself from the razor wire, he fled into the woods nearby. Ambulance personnel later found him by a road near the correctional facility.

Pathologist #1 performed the autopsy. The doctor determined that the man died from "multiple head trauma." Months later, after the county informed pathologist #1 that they would not renew his contract, the doctor alleged that the death may be a possible homicide that the police were covering up. He alleged that multiple guards had beaten the great escaper in the head and that the police were trying to suppress the doctor's findings.

As would be expected in such a situation, angry family members and citizens protested vehemently against the city and the police. The police turned to pathologist #2 for help. Police investigators saw the numerous cuts on the man's body, and they believed his death was due to blood loss. They cited as evidence a massive amount of blood staining the victim's clothing. Pathologist #2 supported their theory after reviewing the findings and changed the cause of death from head trauma to blood loss from sharp injuries.

The county attorney approached me in late July of 1995, shortly after I began my new job. By that time, the family asked the United States Department of Justice to investigate a civil rights offense. They called for the body to be exhumed and for another autopsy to be performed by another pathologist from outside of Kansas City. "Dr. Young," the county attorney kindly requested, "could you look at this case for us? Somehow we need to resolve this."

I looked at the autopsy report and the photographs of the autopsy and crime scene, but I needed to see more. None of the multiple sharp force wounds in the skin appeared to be in the vicinity of any major blood vessel in the body, and the report didn't describe any disruption of an artery or major vein. The autopsy report also disclosed no significant head trauma.

At my request, one of the medical-examiner investigators retrieved from the police the clothing they removed from the decedent before the autopsy. Unlike what police investigators claimed, only a few small bloodstains lay in the clothing. I also made a trip to the Institution, viewing the fences and the razor wire, viewing the field outside of the facility, and following a trail that led to the road where the decedent was found.

Medical-examiner investigators also retrieved for me the record from the ambulance call, a record known as the ambulance "trip sheet." Ambulance personnel described the man to be lying on his side and clutching his abdomen. He was in distress and in apparent pain, gasping for air. A short time later, he went into cardiac arrest and became unconscious. He was unable to be revived after aggressive cardiopulmonary resuscitation. The trip sheet did not mention any attempt to stop or treat blood loss or even any significant bleeding, although rescue personnel noted the sharp force injuries. All efforts were toward reviving the man from a cardiac arrest.

I invited the mother of the decedent to visit me at my office. When she arrived with several other family members, I had all the documents spread across my desk—documents not only from the autopsy and original investigation but also photographs of the clothing and death scene taken under my supervision. I also had the ambulance trip sheet. Much of the time, this kind of information is too graphic for most family members, but I knew this mother would want to see everything, no matter how graphic.

She was angry. Her countenance was hard and her words were biting. Still, we went over the evidence carefully, and I answered all of her questions.

I explained to her that her son's death could not have been from blood loss because hardly any of his blood was lost. The difficulty breathing and the heart stoppage happened because his heart could no longer withstand the stress he had put it through. Even though a heart may look normal at autopsy (as his did), situations of heavy exertion and fear can cause it to fail. I told her I was sure he was aware of the injuries he received from the razor wire—how could he not be aware of them? "Fear, pain, and running for your life can cause your heart to fail," I explained to her. Having a normal-looking heart and having it fail under extreme situations is something well described in the medical literature and something I learned from several of my previous cases.

At the end of our session, her angry face turned sad, and the tears came. "Dr. Young, you have no idea what I have gone through since I lost my son. You have no idea of the nights I haven't been able to sleep, of all of my prayers, all my anger, and all my pain. I thought you were just one more doctor who was going to give me some official line that would dismiss all the wrong I felt was done to my son, and I wasn't ready to accept anything you had to say."

"I want to thank you, doctor, for taking the time to show me what you have shown me and for answering all my questions. Everything you said makes sense to me. As sad as I am, I am at peace now. I can now die in peace."

"And Dr. Young," she finished, "when I die, I want you to do my autopsy."

Our session was complete. After she and those with her left the office, I fell back into my chair, both tired and amazed. She wanted me to do her autopsy! As morbid as what she said may have sounded, that may be the nicest compliment anyone has ever paid me as a forensic pathologist.

Notes

1. National Association of Medical Examiners. *Forensic Autopsy Performance Standards.* Approved by General Membership, including amendments, on August 11, 2011.
2. Melinek J, Thomas LC, Oliver WR, Schmunk GA, Weedn VW, NAME Ad Hoc Committee on Medical Examiner Independence. National Association of Medical Examiners Position Paper: Medical Examiner, Coroner, and Forensic Pathologist Independence. *Academic Forensic Pathology* 2013;3(1):93–98.
3. US Department of Health and Human Services. The Child Abuse Prevention and Treatment Act as Amended by P.L. 111-320, the CAPTA Reauthorization Act of 2010. https://www.acf.hhs.gov/sites/default/files/cb/capta2010.pdf. Accessed on November 6, 2017.
4. Penn S. Heart trouble blamed: New medical examiner gives third explanation for inmate's death. *Kansas City Star,* August 5, 1995.

Broken Bones in Babies 9

According to many forensic doctors, not only do cruel people shake and rattle baby brains, but they also break their bones. In fact, some people are so cruel that they do not break a bone or two: they break numerous bones in the same child.

Broken bones have been on the child-abuse radar for a long time. Radiologist John Caffey reported seeing multiple fractures of bones in infants with chronic subdural hematomas back in 1946.[1] A chronic subdural hematoma is a collection of blood beneath the dural membrane that has been around for a long time. When he reported these cases, he was not certain why chronic subdural hematomas and broken bones occurred together, but after Virginia Jaspers, that all changed. After Virginia Jaspers, Dr. Caffey believed that the fractures were associated with the violent whiplash-shaking event, just as the infant serial killer confessed. In Dr. Caffey's mind, the whiplash-shaken-infant syndrome was associated with the kind of long-bone fractures (arm and leg bone fractures) that he described in 1946.

Over time, however, long-bone fractures became associated less and less with the shaken-baby syndrome. They were replaced by rib fractures in the literature as an association; then fractures disappeared as a discussed association.

Still, for decades, broken bones have been associated with child abuse with or without other injuries.

Typically, health care providers discover infants with multiple fractures in their clinics. Parents bring their infants to the doctor for some other reason, but the healthcare providers notice something peculiar with the limbs of the child during the examination. The parents are often surprised when X-rays show multiple fractures, not suspecting that their child had all these broken bones.

The questioning then begins. The healthcare providers ask for an explanation for all the broken bones, but the parents or other caretakers are baffled. They offer their stories for what they think might explain what was found, but the stories typically do not explain the fractures. As a result, the parents or caretakers and their inconsistent stories raise suspicions for child abuse.

The healthcare providers do not wonder why the child is not in the kind of exquisite pain that people often have after an accidental injury when a bone is fractured. The infant fussiness may be there, but the infant is often easily consolable. No doctor questions why an infant who has multiple healing rib fractures does not have the kind of internal organ injury—lung or liver injuries, for example—that would be expected from great violence. These questions are never asked, it seems.

But in all fairness to these healthcare providers, they recognize that there may be something wrong with the bones themselves that may lead to all the fractures, so they admit the child to the hospital for the big workup. The doctors go through their differential diagnosis list, ruling out conditions that are not found in any of their diagnostic testing.

One of the conditions tested for is *osteogenesis imperfecta*, a rare, inherited condition that could lead to bones that are easily broken. Tests for this rare condition often do not disclose it because—after all—it is a rare condition. Other tests are also run. Vitamin D, a vitamin associated with the incorporation of calcium into bones, is tested for, and so is parathormone, a hormone that is part of the body's way of handling calcium. Of course, if the fractures occurred in the past, blood levels for these items in the present may not explain why the child had fractures in the past.

Items having to do with the body's handling of calcium are often tested for in such cases. This is because our bones are made up of calcium and phosphate salts. It is the deposition of calcium and phosphate salts in bones that hardens them, and that hardness prevents them from being fractured. The incorporation of these minerals into bones as the infant develops becomes a point of interest.

Doctors do not only look for mineralization problems with laboratory tests for minerals, vitamins, and hormones. Radiologists will look at the X-rays to see if they can see signs of decreased mineral content. If there is very little mineral content in the bones, some doctors might think that the X-rays would show darker, less radiodense bones, but most of the X-rays in children who have all these fractures do not show this finding. Radiologists and other doctors may look for signs of rickets (a condition brought about by a lack of Vitamin D), scurvy (a condition brought about by a lack of Vitamin C), or even copper deficiency, but radiologists and other doctors typically do not find evidence for these conditions in multiple unexplained fracture cases.

At the end of a large and expensive workup in which both laboratory testing and X-rays are performed, when all the tests do not disclose any reason for the fractures, the doctors conclude that the fractures had to be due to child abuse. After all, they have ruled out everything else!

Have they really?

Beginning in 1985, medical doctors discovered cases in which infants would break bones in the hospital setting. An infant in a hospital is highly unlikely to be the victim of child abuse because numerous trained individuals observe infants around the clock in such a setting. Fractures occurring in settings where child abuse is not likely began to crop up in the medical literature, and none of these fractures could be explained after a "million-dollar" workup.

One physician, Colin Paterson, from Scotland published multiple articles about infants with fractures—often multiple fractures—that occurred in non-child-abuse settings. Dr. Paterson and a colleague in one relatively recent article studied the findings of 104 patients between the years 1985 and 2000 who had 976 fracture or fracture-like lesions. There were "disproportionate numbers" of infants born prematurely or as multiple infants in a single pregnancy. Most of the fractures occurred in the first six months of life and entirely within one year. Most of the breaks did not lead to symptoms, especially rib fractures and those labeled as "metaphyseal lesions" near the growth plates of long bones. Few infants had bruising, and none had any evidence of inflicted injury consistent with the fractures. Doctors examined 22 patients in clinics for physical problems unrelated to fractures. Several of the fractures took place while the infants were in the hospital.[2]

Dr. Paterson assigned a name to this "condition" occurring within infancy: temporary brittle bone disease. Unfortunately, doctors, particularly forensic doctors, like to assign names to conditions and situations that they know very little about. Often giving a name to something and calling it a "disease" or a "syndrome" seems to indicate that we know much more about what is going on then we actually do. Also, it seems to suggest to many that there is one underlying cause, so it is simply a matter of finding that one underlying cause.

But if we recognize that infant growth and development changes over time and that it is more complicated than we can even imagine, those recognitions can explain why broken bones in babies can be both temporary and unexplained.

Consider that a human being goes from a clump of dividing cells to a highly complicated system. Everything develops in a complicated order over time, and one thing going wrong can make growth and development not work as well as it should.

For example, consider infant bones. The bones are first made of cartilage, and the cartilages grow in both width and length. Over time, these soft cartilages receive calcium and phosphate salts that make the bones firm. The minerals are received through the placenta when the fetus is in the womb and received from the diet after birth. Also, certain vitamins and other substances are important for mineralizing to work well.

Besides these factors, the fetus has to push his little arms and legs against the walls of his mother's uterus. Stress placed on bones stimulates bones to mineralize. Without that kind of "exercise," the bones will not develop properly as they should. For example, if the mother took drugs that made the fetus sluggish, then that fetus will not push very hard and his bones might not mineralize right away. In a pregnancy with multiple fetuses, one fetus might find it hard to move among other squirming fetuses.

In spite of problems that could delay mineralization of the bones, nature manages to find a "work-around." The bones eventually become mineralized but it may take longer.

For example, let's say that an infant is born premature. He is removed from that "exerciser" called mommy's uterus and is now placed in an incubator and put on a respirator that breathes for him. He may not absorb and receive the nutrients as well as when he was inside the womb, and he may not move as much because of problems affecting his brain and other parts of his body.

So it should not be a surprise that minor handling of such an infant can lead to broken bones. It also should not be a surprise that such easy "breakability" is temporary. As the premature infant grows toward maturity, his bones eventually mineralize as they should so that they are not as "breakable."

In spite of the problems that come with labeling something as a "diagnosis," a "disease," or a "syndrome," Dr. Paterson did us all a great service by bringing such a situation to light. His observations were clearly "evidence-based"—based on factual observations rather than fanciful beliefs. People actually saw that handling a child in a hospital setting could lead to broken bones in infants.

However, too often "no good deed ever goes unpunished," as the famous proverb goes. Authorities in the United Kingdom removed Dr. Paterson's license to practice medicine. He was—as the British say—"struck off" by the General Medical Council, the authority regulating the practice of medicine in the UK, in 2004.

The British Medical Journal reported the decision.[3] The doctor had failed to fulfill his responsibilities as an expert in two different trials. One judge in one of the trials described Dr. Paterson's evidence as "woeful."

Eileen Shaw, chairwoman of the professional conduct committee of the General Medical Council, claimed that the doctor was entitled to believe however he wanted, even if very few doctors throughout the world shared his belief in temporary brittle bone disease. Still, in spite of that entitlement, he was not permitted to behave recklessly in court. Dr. Paterson failed to apply consistently his own diagnostic criteria for the condition he discovered: he failed to take into account the bruising seen in the infants in those cases—something he claimed didn't occur with temporary brittle bone disease. By ignoring significant clinical evidence at variance with his published views, he acted as an advocate for his beliefs rather than as a scientific expert. "You risked misleading the court and undermining the confidence which the judiciary is entitled to place in medical expert witnesses," Mrs Shaw claimed.

In all fairness, there are often two sides to any argument. Much goes on in these proceedings that the media does not report. Still, by now, you may have noticed the big elephant in the room, the one that sits in the corner munching peanuts, the one that nobody seems to acknowledge or be aware of.

That big elephant is the notion that a doctor can diagnose child abuse. Inventing stories about something no one ever saw is incredibly weak, as I have demonstrated so far in multiple ways in this book. The General Medical Council in the United Kingdom may accuse Dr. Paterson of promoting his own medical theory, but they fail to recognize that accusing someone of child abuse based on clinical observations and a diagnosis is also highly theoretical. Furthermore, unlike Dr. Paterson's theory, conclusions of child abuse are not "evidence-based." They are "belief-based" and demonstrably highly unlikely to be true. Mrs. Shaw may criticize Dr. Paterson advocating for his belief, but prosecution experts advocate for their belief that child abuse occurred every time they testify.

There are also a few more items made evident in this media report.

One is the claim that only a few doctors around the world believed in the existence of this condition. It is not clear how anyone testifying against Dr. Paterson would know this, but there is one thing that should be clear: any doctor who publicly agreed with Dr. Paterson would be in similar danger as Dr. Paterson of losing his ability to practice medicine or being discredited in other ways. Very few physicians are willing to run that kind of risk. Very few are willing to speak out.

Mrs Shaw claims that expert witnesses should not behave as advocates, but forensic doctors who diagnose child abuse are advocates in the worst way. Expert witnesses should explain science to a judge or jury and not accuse people of crimes, but our system now operates with forensic doctors as the chief accusers. Mrs Shaw does not see this or does not want to admit that she sees this.

Mrs Shaw also felt that Dr. Paterson was also guilty of "undermining the confidence which the jury is entitled to place in expert medical witnesses." Truthfully, that confidence should be undermined: forensic doctors who reason like Sherlock Holmes are blind guides and should not be trusted by anyone, let alone a judiciary who feels "entitled."

Finally, Mrs Shaw and the General Medical Council felt that Dr. Paterson and his evidence-based testimony posed "an unacceptable risk to the safety of children."[4] Forensic doctors who reason like Sherlock Holmes are the ones who pose "an unacceptable risk to the safety of children." Taking infants and children away from loving parents and placing them in a system of foster care—with people who do not have the emotional and biological connection with the child—is not only unjust and unfair, but it also harms the well-being of children.

But this is not understood. It is not accepted. And the same mistakes are made year after year with seemingly no end in sight. When will enough be enough?

***

During my 11½ years as the Jackson County medical examiner, I had the privilege of hiring and working with a succession of four deputy medical examiners. The first three deputies served with me as the second pathologist in the office for a period of time, but the fourth deputy, after completing our accredited fellowship program in forensic pathology, expanded our staff to three pathologists. The county provided funding for the expansion of our staff to meet the demands of an increasing workload.

The husband of the second doctor wanted to move back to the east coast, so in the summer of 2002, I had to cover the office by myself when she left with her husband. I was already appointed to be the medical examiner for three additional counties on the Missouri side of the Kansas City metropolitan area, so the office was quite busy. We announced our open position, performing a nationwide search, but available forensic pathologists were in short supply at that time—just as they are now. We needed someone who was board certified in forensic pathology, but those who applied had inadequate credentials. The county executive and the prosecutor by that point realized the importance of properly trained doctors.

Finally, I invited one doctor—a doctor with boards not only in forensic pathology but also in brain pathology (neuropathology)—to come to Kansas City for an interview. His credentials were terrific, but he had some problems. He was quick to share those problems with me at the time of the interview.

Many years before, this doctor served for 15 years as a neuropathologist at a teaching hospital affiliated with a medical school, but he was let go in 1992. He then accepted a position as a coroner's pathologist in Indianapolis, Indiana, in 1993, without having done any training in forensic pathology. On his way to work in 1994, the police arrested him for driving under the influence of alcohol. Indiana suspended his medical license, and the coroner's office dismissed him from his job.

Indiana maintained the suspension of his license until he successfully completed a Physician Diversion Program—a program for recovering alcoholic physicians—in California. His arrest marked the last time he ever drank any alcoholic beverage. During his time in California, he completed a fellowship in forensic pathology at the Los Angeles County Coroner/Medical Examiner Office and successfully passed the examination for board certification in forensic pathology.

The pathologist went to work in northern California, joining a group of forensic pathologists who provided services to several northern California counties. One of his cases involved a prominent physician in one of the smaller northern California towns. This physician reported his alcoholic wife to be dead in the yard in the morning, claiming that he had found that she committed suicide by submerging her head in a bucket of water. Police at the time did not consider the case to be anything suspicious, so they collected no evidence and took no photographs. The pathologist, however, found injuries in the face of the woman that appeared suspicious to him. After consulting with several of his colleagues from Los Angeles who all agreed with him, he called the death a homicide.

The prosecutor realized that the lack of evidence in the case made a forensic pathologist with an alcoholic past his star witness. The doctor was short, rail-thin, and soft spoken, not exuding the kind of Bernard-Spilsbury-like confidence the prosecuting attorney was looking for in his star witness, so the attorney hired a speech consultant to help the doctor with his delivery from the witness stand. Prior to the trial, the defense attorney obtained several videotapes of sessions with the speech consultant. The defense attorney alleged that the pathologist's testimony had been extensively coached, even to the point of perjury.

Trial attorneys consider it good practice to prepare a witness for his testimony, and this is what the state attorney general concluded upon investigating charges brought by the defendant. They found no evidence of perjury or other wrongdoing. Both the prosecutor and the pathologist were let off the hook, but the case never went to court. Following that spectacle, the pathologist had his casework greatly limited by the pathology group; he was not allowed to perform autopsies for several counties.

This was why he was looking for a job in Kansas City. Several of his colleagues wrote strong letters of recommendation for him and spoke of him in glowing terms, recognizing that a fine doctor was being treated unjustly.

I informed the county prosecutor and my boss, the county executive, of all I knew about this doctor. They were not thrilled with the prospect of hiring someone with such a checkered past. Because of the shortage of qualified individuals willing to relocate to Kansas City, they reluctantly accepted my request to hire the doctor, warning me that they would hold me fully responsible if the county encountered any problems prosecuting their cases because of him. I accepted the responsibility and hired this doctor—doctor #3—in September of 2002.

Doctor #3 remained in the office for four years. Although all the deputies I had hired had their strong and weak points, this doctor's strong points exceeded his weak points. He was hardworking, honest, and humble. The office staff and several of the assistant prosecuting attorneys who worked with him praised him for his job knowledge and his work in the witness stand. At no time did anyone ever see him under the influence of alcohol. None of the office staff ever saw the doctor impaired while on the job. Doctor #3 remarked to me that he had no choice but to be honest about everything in his life; if he were anything but honest, he would find himself back in the hell he had finished crawling out of. At no time did any assistant prosecutor have any problem trying a case because of the doctor's past.

Sometime after I hired doctor #3, the county executive appointed a new prosecutor to fill the vacancy of one who accepted an appointment as a judge.

This new prosecutor was ambitious, frequently appearing before television news cameras when there was breaking news of a sensational crime, commenting on the charges and the prosecution. Prior to the summer of 2004, I had never met the new prosecutor, although I saw him frequently on television.

That all changed in the summer of 2004.

This prosecutor faced his first election, and he had stiff competition from two other attorneys: a seasoned assistant prosecutor and a federal prosecutor. The greatest challenge would be to succeed in the primary election in August because he would face only token opposition from the opposing party in November.

A few weeks prior to the primary election, an investigative reporter from a local news channel came to the medical examiner's office with a cameraman, demanding to know about doctor #3, his alcoholism, and his controversial case in California. At the same time, I received a hand-delivered letter signed by the ambitious prosecutor and his fellow prosecutors from adjacent Missouri counties, demanding that I prevent doctor #3 from performing autopsies on victims from any of their court cases.[5]

From that point on, we had our own descent into hell. The news coverage of doctor #3 was anything but sympathetic, portraying him through sensational reporting and slick editing as someone evil and incompetent. I had to write a letter to the county legislators defending the doctor. In a meeting with all the area prosecutors, I explained to them that I understood their concerns but that I couldn't physically comply with what they wanted. One may not know if a case is a homicide until after an autopsy is completed. I would not be able to run a busy office and give them what they asked for. Still, I offered to help them by agreeing to testify as a witness to doctor #3's good work and behavior if any of their cases demanded that kind of support.

The ambitious prosecutor won the election, and the situation died down for the next two years. Under the Jackson County Charter, prosecutors are not allowed to influence the hiring practices and management of a medical examiner's office, so doctor #3 remained in the office for two more years—all without any problem with any court case. During that time, we added our fellow to our staff of doctors.

But in 2006, the prosecutor ran for the county-executive position. He faced only token opposition in both the primary and general elections. He would become my supervisor, so doctor #3 and I realized that our days were numbered. We needed to look for another job prior to his taking office. We interviewed for several jobs in various parts of the country, but the soon-to-be county executive provided negative references to the prosecutors in the places we interviewed.

I realized that it was not going to be possible for me to find a job as a medical examiner in another office. Hoping to settle our differences, I attempted to contact the prosecutor, but he never returned any calls or emails.

Finally, I wrote the following in an email (I substituted "doctor #3" for the doctor's name):

After multiple unsuccessful attempts at trying to contact you to speak with you in person, I realize that the only way I will be able to communicate with you is in writing. This is risky because frequently issues are misunderstood when expressed only in writing. I will do my best to communicate clearly, and I apologize in advance for any misunderstanding.

I recognize that you have not been happy with my decision to allow doctor #3 to perform autopsies on homicide cases. I understood at the time your concerns about losing cases because of doctor #3, but even if I had wanted to comply with your wish and the wishes of other area prosecutors, I would not have been able to do so physically. I would not be able to be on call to do every homicide autopsy because I would never be able to take a weekend off or a vacation. I also would not have the time to testify in every homicide case and still manage a busy office.

Still, I thought the issue had resolved itself successfully. After 4 years of doctor #3's tenure in Kansas City, his sad past experiences have never had an impact on a single court case. Doctor #3 has negatively affected not one of your cases or the cases of any area prosecutor. On the contrary, doctor #3 has done well and continues to do well in court. I thought we turned a corner until this last spring, when you and the other prosecutors communicated to me through the media and through a legislator how displeased you were with the job I was doing. The message to me was clear at the time: "Dr. Young has got to go."

I recognized at the time—not only I but others as well, both in my office and on the legislature—that I needed to look for other employment. I informed the county executive of this last July so that no one would be taken by surprise. After several months of inquiring about job offers, I discovered that you had been providing negative references about me to the prosecutors in the jurisdictions where I applied.

At this time, I am thoroughly confused. On the one hand, you and others communicated to me your displeasure and your desire for me to leave, but now you are engaged in the kind of activity that prevents me from leaving. I can only think of two explanations for this:

- You really don't want me to leave after all, or
- You are so angry with me that you want to destroy my career and reputation.

So it all boils down to this question: Do you want me to stay or do you want me to leave?

If you want me to stay, I would be happy to stay, but I need a clear answer from you one way or the other very soon.

That answer never came. On December 1, 2006, I tendered my resignation, providing the county a month's notice. The pathology group in northern California that doctor #3 left accepted him back. Our former fellow and most recently hired deputy medical examiner found employment in Tennessee. I stayed in Kansas City. We all left our jobs prior to the new county executive assuming office on January 1, 2007.

I was on call for my final weekend on December 31, 2006. As I prepared to perform the autopsies that Sunday morning, I admired our most recently completed expansion, walking through the halls of our well-appointed office area into a separate brightly lit autopsy building. The facility smelled fresh because of the air handling. The well-waxed seamless floors shined. The stainless steel autopsy tables and stations reflected light from multiple bright surgical and ceiling lamps. On-call investigators in a quiet office adjacent to the multi-stationed autopsy room watched the aide and I complete the autopsies for the day through multiple broad windows.

After saying farewell to the on-call staff that Sunday and wishing them the best for the future, I slowly walked out of the office into the parking area. The weather was chilly and cloudy, typical for Kansas City on New Year's Eve, as I walked to my car, opened the door, sat in the driver's seat, and wept over the steering wheel.

Notes

1. Caffey J. Multiple fractures in the long bones of infants suffering from chronic subdural hematoma. *Radiology* 1946;194:163–173.
2. Paterson CR, Monk EA. Clinical and laboratory features of temporary brittle bone disease. *Journal of Pediatric Endocrinology and Metabolism* 2014;27(1–2):37–45.
3. Dyer O. GMC strikes off proponent of temporary brittle bone disease. *British Medical Journal* 2004 Mar 13;328(7440):604.
4. BBC News. Child injury "expert" struck off. March 4, 2004. http://news.bbc.co.uk/2/hi/uk_news/scotland/3533487.stm. Accessed on October 28, 2016.
5. Pflaum N. Cuts both ways. The deputy medical examiner gets probed. Pitch.com, July 22, 2004.

The Unified Hypothesis 10

On the way to becoming experts at diagnosing and treating disease, student doctors learn several pithy sayings in medical school.

One comes from a medieval cleric, William of Ockham (1287–1347). His "law of parsimony" has as a basic idea that if you have two possible hypotheses, you select the one that is the least complicated. That makes sense. If a hypothesis has "fewer moving parts," then there is a higher probability of it being true: calculations of probability would tell you that. Think of the flipping-a-coin-and-getting-heads examples that I have used repeatedly in this book.

Another is to "think horses and not zebras." If you have two possible hypotheses, you select the one that is the most common. It makes sense because if something is more common, then there is a higher probability of it being true.

Maybe those approaches work for diagnosing and treating disease, but they do not work for understanding what happened in the past. The truth about what happened in the past in any particular case is unique and amazingly complicated, occurring in a way that has never occurred before or will ever occur again in exactly the same way.

There is, however, one pithy saying that might work not only for medical students but also for forensic doctors. Medical students learn the story of Willie Sutton (1901–1980), a career bank robber. As the story goes (it is not certain that this account is even true), a reporter asked Sutton why he robs banks. Sutton replied, "Cause that's where all the money is."

This is another saying with kind of a dumb-smart ring to it, but it does seem to make sense to go to the best source for answers if you want to learn the truth.

What is the best source for answers about what happened in the past? Is the best source the hypotheses of forensic doctors who think like Sherlock Holmes: who look at physical-evidence "clues" and determine the "train of events" that took place in the past? If you have been paying any attention up to this point, you might sense that this approach does not have much going for it.

On the other hand, if what happened in the past was witnessed or even recorded on a voice recorder or video camera, don't those memories or records seem like a better source of information for what happened?

Of course they are! Why speculate about unique and complicated past events when you can listen to someone who can recite the complicated and unique "train of events" from what they saw or when you can see a recording of those events!

Then the arguments from naysayers come: "You can't believe these people! Witnesses lie all the time! You can't believe recordings! People splice and alter recordings all the time!"

Really? Do you really think so? On what basis does any naysayer determine that someone is lying or telling the truth?

The truth is that everyone lies, though some may do it more than others. When we lie, we often become nervous. Why?

Because there is evidence out there—other witness accounts or physical evidence "clues"—that can unmask our lies. If that is the case, doesn't it seem reasonable that the best way to find the truth is to listen to what an eyewitness says the "train of events" were and then compare what he or she says not only to other witnesses but also to the physical-evidence "clues" that scientists may find? Wouldn't that be where the money is?

In spite of that kind of simplicity, forensic doctors still insist on doing things the hard and less-straightforward way, continuing to invent "trains of events" in the form of scientific-sounding "hypotheses." They continue to think like Sherlock Holmes.

Consider, for example, what happened to Dr. Jennian Geddes, a brain pathologist from the United Kingdom.

Dr. Geddes was active in her practice in a major London hospital during the early 2000s. In the United Kingdom, coroners in large metropolitan centers perform investigations of violent and suspicious deaths. This is unlike the United States, where mostly medical examiners do this work in populous metropolitan areas. In performing their investigations, the non-physician coroners would often ask for help from medical specialists like Dr. Geddes. In her practice, she would often perform or be made aware of autopsies of infants who were suspected to have died violently and also of fetuses and infants who died from natural causes in the hospital setting. In this kind of practice, it would be easy for her to compare the two sets of cases with each other.

Dr. Geddes saw the same changes in the shaken-baby cases as she saw in fetuses and infants dying of the complications of natural disease. In fetuses, for example, she would often find the same thin subdural hemorrhages declared as shaken-baby cases. She would also find them in infants who died stormy natural deaths while on a respirator—a breathing machine.

Also, in both the natural and shaken-baby deaths, she would find brain swelling with frequent changes related to a lack of oxygen or a lack of blood flow to the brain. Not only were there thin subdural hemorrhages—hemorrhages below the dural membranes—in both kinds of cases, but there were also hemorrhages of the dural membrane itself. She thought the source of the thin collections of subdural blood was leakage from bleeding dural membranes.

Prior to that time and even now, believers in the shaken-baby syndrome thought that shaking would tear veins that bridge from other veins on the surface of a moveable brain to non-moveable, fixed, large dural blood channels attached to the skull bones. Since "bridging veins" cross the subdural area, the tears from shaking or head impact were thought to allow leaking blood to form the subdural hemorrhages. Bridging vein tears did not seem to fit the situations with fetuses or with respirator-bound infants who had no head trauma at any time. It seemed to Dr. Geddes and others with her that there was some unifying event that explained the bleeding in both kinds of cases. She believed that the unifying event was a lack of oxygen or blood flow to the head: that was the cause of dural bleeding that led to thin subdural blood collections. She also believed that the brain swelling and the retinal hemorrhages—the other two findings often described with the shaken-baby syndrome—could also be explained by a lack of oxygen or blood flow to the head.

This idea made sense from what scientists know about the importance of oxygen delivered to complex functioning tissues in the body. Blood vessels that need oxygen to function properly could become leaky if they are not supplied with oxygen for a period of time. Blood clotting, a process that also needs oxygen, might not work very well when oxygen is not adequate. Massive brain swelling was already a well-known result of a lack of oxygen: this condition had been observed many times by doctors in hospitals. If tissues are deprived of oxygen or blood flow and the death is immediate, then an autopsy would disclose no bleeding; it takes blood flow and blood pressure for bleeding to occur. On the other hand, if tissues are deprived of oxygen or blood flow and the death is *not* immediate—if there are periods where blood flow is restored to tissues—then hemorrhages (blood leaking out of blood vessels) could occur. With fetuses and infants who, at an early stage of growth, have numerous primitive veins in the dura that later disappear, subdural bleeding could become a problem if those veins became leaky from a lack of oxygen. Blood would ooze from the leaky blood vessels once blood flow was restored, and that ooze would leak out of the membrane and form subdural collections. Also, because the veins that drain blood from the retinas in the backs of the eyes pass through the same space in the head as the swollen brain, the swelling of the brain could impede drainage of the blood. The back-up of the blood flow combined with the lack of oxygen could bring about retinal hemorrhages.

Well…so far so good, but Dr. Geddes and her colleagues took a bridge too far: they invented a hypothesis for a train of events that nobody ever saw and called it the "unified hypothesis." She offered this hypothesis in an article published in 2003. According to that article, a lack of oxygen was the main factor in both trauma and non-trauma cases, but she and the other co-authors thought the movement of the neck with shaking would injure the lower portion of the brain that controls breathing: the brainstem. If this portion of the brain is injured from shaking, she thought it could cause the infant to stop breathing ("apnoea"), which then could lead to a lack of oxygen to the entire brain ("global hypoxia") and horrible brain swelling as a consequence of a lack of oxygen.[1]

Amazing! One hypothesis explains it all! It is all unified and has seemingly few moving parts! Now there would be no need to deal with traumatic ruptures of veins to cause bleeding that would need excessively high accelerations. Now, just simple damage of the brainstem from a lack of oxygen can explain all the complications, including all the bleedings.

Stop for a moment and look at how many steps are in the "train of events" for this hypothesis: the shaking back and forth several times leads to brainstem injury, which then leads the infant to stop breathing and then the infant for some reason to start breathing again, which then leads to brain swelling and to damage of immature blood vessels in the dura and retinas. We would have to flip the coin and get "heads" for every step, then we would have to get the same "heads" for the same "train of events" happening in the same way for every case. This is not just unlikely; this is ridiculously unlikely.

But forensic doctors who reason like Sherlock Holmes do not see this. They are too used to floating hypotheses in the form of diagnoses, so this kind of speculation feels very comfortable to them.

Nevertheless, this new hypothesis of how infant shaking could lead to shaken-baby syndrome led to serious concerns by those who relied on doctors to diagnose child abuse in courtroom testimony.

In many cases where forensic doctors eventually diagnose shaken-baby syndrome or abusive head injury, parents and other caregivers would notice the infant to stop breathing suddenly and unexpectedly. The child would be resuscitated, only to die later in the hospital while on a respirator. Medical practitioners recognize that this can happen in the medical literature; they call such a cessation of breathing an apparent life-threatening event (ALTE). About half of the time, the cause for such an event is not discovered after a medical evaluation.

If non-traumatic events like ALTE with a temporary lack of oxygen can cause the same findings as shaken-baby syndrome, wouldn't that call into question the ability of these doctors to diagnose abuse? Doctors would then lose their credibility in the courtroom, and prior judgments might be called into question. Something had to be done about that.

So prosecutors in the United Kingdom took the issue up at the Court of Appeal in 2005. Dr. Geddes offered sworn testimony in court regarding her hypothesis. She admitted that she didn't think she had the hypothesis "quite right;" she never intended it to be offered as evidence in a trial. She was not happy to think that cases could be thrown out of court by considering her hypothesis to be factual.[2]

The court then declared that because the unified hypothesis is not reliable as a cause for the triad in shaken-baby syndrome, the established theory remains unchallenged and prior convictions based on that theory remain safe. Case closed.

It would be understandable for Dr. Geddes to have misgivings about floating a hypothesis as sworn testimony in a courtroom. This is because a hypothesis is unproven: all scientists know this. In science, numerous hypotheses are considered all the time but very few of them turn out to be true after further scientific experimentation and testing. With past events that no longer exist, hypotheses cannot be proven by the usual scientific and diagnostic/treatment methods.

All of those shaken-baby convictions were deemed to be safe, but once again, there is the elephant in the room, the one that sits quietly in the corner eating peanuts, the one that anybody would notice if they happened to turn their eyes in the direction of the elephant. We have already discussed him.

The unified hypothesis is a hypothesis, but so is shaken-baby syndrome: if the judges threw out one hypothesis, they should have to throw out the other as well. This would have overturned many convictions; that is something that judges do not want to do. Judges want to stare straight ahead and avoid the gaze of the large elephant.

Regardless of judicial rulings, scientists do not throw out hypotheses that seem to them to have great explanatory power. The unified hypothesis still lives on.

Several years following the Geddes hearing, pediatric experts recognized that controversy about the shaken baby syndrome label caused problems in court cases, so they proposed their own "unified hypothesis." Although they did not eliminate shaking, they decided to include it under a new rubric of "abusive head trauma."[3] The improved and broadened diagnosis included both shaking cases and cases with evidence of blunt head impact. The experts also acknowledged newer concepts about spinal cord injury and the secondary global hypoxic injuries described by Dr. Geddes. By broadening the concept of pediatric head trauma, they hoped to avoid the kinds of physiologic mechanism arguments among experts that would prevent abusive parents and caretakers from receiving their just due.

Ever eager to instruct other doctors in the abusive head trauma hypothesis, one child abuse expert wrote an instructional guide entitled "Understanding Abusive Head Trauma: A Primer for the General Pediatrician."[4] In it, she describes abusive head trauma (AHT) as "a well-recognized constellation of injuries" caused by the infliction of head trauma on infants and children. To her work, I add my own much shorter "primer" to describe the trauma AHT has inflicted in the courtroom, entitled "Understanding Doctors Who Diagnose Abusive Head Trauma: A Primer for Anyone Who Cares." Here it is:

- Doctors have never seen anyone inflict AHT: they simply imagine it happens after finding injuries in infants and children.
- The "well-recognized constellation of injuries" of AHT are accepted by most doctors without question—except for a few "skeptics" who offer their own alternative hypotheses. Child abuse experts and many other

doctors recognize that—for whatever reason—errant defense experts oppose ideas that go against recent advances in scientific understanding, recent biomechanical research, new techniques in neurological imaging, and perpetrator confessions.

- Rather than the police alerting doctors, doctors more frequently alert the police after recognizing the "well-recognized constellation of injuries" in infants and children they see in hospitals and clinics. The doctors order additional diagnostic tests to bolster what they already consider as "well-recognized." They also perform screening for other occult injuries. Doctors alert social service agencies to protect children and ensure their safety. These agencies often not only remove the injured child from the care and custody of parents but also remove other children from the home. Foster parents replace the biological parents based on the strong beliefs of doctors.
- The police believe doctors are as smart as the arrogant Sherlock Holmes, so they obtain confessions that agree with what the doctors believe. Any review of interview transcripts where these confessions are documented discloses that the police typically are the ones who introduce the idea of AHT and how it was perpetrated, not the alleged perpetrators.
- Caregivers eventually confess to frustration and exhaustion that culminates in violent shaking and head impact, even though they stated at first that the child became unresponsive and they didn't know why. Despite emergency telephone call transcripts that document caretakers saying the child became unresponsive and they didn't know why, the police typically believe what the caretakers eventually confess in the interrogation and ignore what was stated and documented at first.
- In court, doctors successfully convince jurors, prosecutors and judges that the accused caretakers committed crimes no one ever saw them commit. Doctors imagine crimes nobody sees, and their arrogant insistence under oath that what they imagine is true persuades everyone.
- Doctors add the convictions to the medical literature as further evidence for AHT, further emphasizing what is already "well-recognized."

Modern-day court cases involving abusive head trauma are never-ending, repeated circular arguments. Doctors, police officers, judges, and jurors accept as a premise the very thing they eventually conclude which is, by definition, a circular argument. They accept the premise that a doctor can diagnose abusive head trauma in an infant or child at the outset, so it is no surprise when a jury concludes the same after courtroom deliberation. All the while, none of the doctors, police officers, prosecutors, defense attorneys, judges and jurors realize that they have been conned by Sherlock Holmes. They fail to recognize the trap of backward reasoning by surmising complex past events from injuries identified in an infant and child. They fail to recognize that by paying attention carefully to what eyewitnesses saw and heard at first and by comparing what was seen and heard to the injuries for consistency or inconsistency—"reasoning forward" according to Sherlock Holmes—they would avoid the never-ending, repeated circular argument trap.

If forensic doctors were to pay close attention to eyewitness accounts, finally considering them with an open mind, they would discover something that would be startling to them. They would realize how the past events that eyewitnesses describe are not only highly complex but also unique, never occurring the same way twice. They would also realize that one event occurring after another in a vast number of ways will often lead to a final common pathway of injury characterized by a lack of oxygen and blood flow. They would also realize that a lack of oxygen and blood flow to organs and body systems, which can explain strokes and heart attacks in adults, could also explain findings in infants that are characteristic for their immature level of growth and change.

If these forensic doctors were to pay close attention to eyewitness accounts, they would finally realize that inventing simple and simple-minded hypotheses for vastly complex past events is unspeakably crazy and something that they should have never done in the first place.

Midway through December of 2006, prior to my leaving employment as the Jackson County medical examiner, I set up an LLC, a limited liability company. I was and still am the sole proprietor and employee of Heartland Forensic Pathology, LLC. Anyone who needs the services of a forensic pathologist can contact me.

This was a major step. Since medical school, I had received a check every two weeks from some type of government. Now I was on my own, bereft of that precious paycheck. Living without automatic biweekly deposits to my checking account can be scary, particularly at the beginning when not much business flowed in.

Much has changed for me since January of 2007 when I embarked on this new journey. No longer did I need to drive to work downtown; my commute is simply walking downstairs to my small basement office. No longer did I have access to state-of-the-art autopsy facilities; the occasional autopsies I performed took place on embalming tables in funeral homes until I stopped doing them altogether in 2011. No longer was I under the beck and call of some prosecutor somewhere to testify in court; defense attorneys are the ones who now contact me for criminal cases. The list could go on because nearly everything changed.

Well…not everything.

One thing never changed for me. At no time did I ever play fast and loose with the truth. I have given my life to God every morning since I was 17 years old, asking Him to guide me, to help me make good choices, to do always what is right. I do nothing to compromise my relationship developed over many years with Jesus Christ.

In other words, it is not necessary for anyone to have me "swear or affirm to tell the truth, the whole truth, and nothing but the truth, so help me, God." This is something I have done publically and privately, professionally and personally, for my entire adult life. I had no interest in 2007—nor do I have any interest now—in massaging any case to help a client. In fact, I am now much more free than I was as a medical examiner: no one can fire me if they don't like what I say.

And I have grown accustomed to saying many things that few people like.

Since 2007 and even for many years prior to leaving my old job, I noticed something horribly wrong with forensic pathology and forensic pathologists. Often at national meetings during case presentations, doctors offer opinions that vary markedly from one another. Even seasoned professionals rarely agree with each other. I imagined that if forensic pathologists were in charge of the National Aeronautics and Space Administration (NASA), they wouldn't have agreed reliably enough to get a rocket one inch off of the ground, let alone to the moon. It did not seem that what we were doing was reliable in the least.

For years, I have wondered what we were doing wrong. As I encountered work performed by doctors outside my office, the problem and the reason for it gradually became apparent to me. The problem did not simply involve forensic pathologists but doctors everywhere who reason backwards, who hypothesize what happened in the past based on their scientific or medical examinations and observations. As I studied cases in greater detail as a consultant, I found that hypothesizing like this did not work: the totality of the facts in any case pointed out the problems.

Then it became apparent to me what did work.

For years as a medical examiner, I had always believed in the importance of seeing the death scene. You might recall what I wrote earlier about the "scene being the thing." As it turned out, as important as the scene is in the investigation of any death, it is not "the thing." It is not "where all the money is" (thank you, Willie Sutton).

The "money" is in the accounts of eyewitnesses—people who were present to see what happened and who provide the kind of information needed for the court to determine who was responsible for what happened.

I began to write about the problem. My first attempt was an article I submitted to the *Journal of Forensic Sciences* at the end of 2007, entitled "Forensic Science and the Scientific Method."[5] The editor did not accept it, so I published it on my website. In that article, I claim that the scientific method, an approach that has worked for centuries for scientific discovery, does not work for past events because past events are items that no longer exist for observation or experimental manipulation by scientists. Courtroom cases analyzing past events needed an alternate method—the "Forensic Scientific Method"—in which witness accounts of the past events are compared to present physical evidence for consistency or inconsistency. It was apparent from the editor's comments supporting the rejection of my manuscript that he did not understand my argument.

In 2009, I wrote down what I believed in a statement. You may recall it:

> One can be reasonably certain if witness accounts of the past are consistent or not consistent with physical evidence in the present, but one cannot reliably surmise past events from physical evidence unless there is only one plausible explanation for that evidence.[6]

At first I called this "Young's Postulate." A postulate is statement that is not proven but is instead assumed to be true. I assumed it to be true because it has worked out for all the cases I have ever analyzed as a forensic pathologist. Putting my name in front of it indicated that this was my assumption.

I discovered later after reading a college-level logic textbook twice that what I proposed as a postulate is not a postulate. I discovered that it is a theorem of deductive logic that can be proven. Perhaps you recall what a theorem is from high school geometry, and you may recall what it is like to write a proof. I took the statement that I now call the Inferential Test and proved it with symbolic statement logic. I published the proof on my website in 2011.[7]

After failing to get other items on the topic of inference published in any peer-reviewed journal, I knew that no forensic pathologist had enough exposure to statement logic to understand the proof I offered nor even the inclination to learn about it. Earlier, I had tried to persuade the president of the National Association of Medical Examiners to set up a committee in which we could discuss inference in forensic cases. Only a few people agreed to join, but even with a few people, the Association cancelled the committee days later.

I wanted some feedback on the proof and truth tables, so I contacted a professor of philosophy at one of our local Kansas City universities, a person who is a teacher of logic. The professor never found any problem with the proof or the truth tables, but she claimed I was naïve in my approach. "The issues go beyond this kind of deductive logic," she said. "What you need to do is to approach the problem with Bayes' theorem."

Scientists and philosophers use Bayes' theorem in statistics and probability theory. Using a deductive theorem is passé among logicians and philosophers because none of us can be certain of anything, the professor claimed, so we need to see how probable an inference could be, given the conditions for the inference.

So I tried probability theory and Bayes' theorem.[8] What I found was incredibly amazing and ridiculous at the same time. Past events are exceedingly complex, with one event following another in split seconds, with each new event dependent on the event that happened a split second before. Offering theories about such highly complex and variable past events—essentially writing "detective fiction"—is doomed to fail, no matter who tries it. A lying witness is just as unlikely to invent a story that fits all the physical evidence as any scientist, doctor, or prosecuting attorney.

On the other hand, a witness or group of witnesses who offer accounts that fit all the physical evidence are able to do something that no lying witness or any other person (including a scientist, doctor, or attorney) is clever enough to do. Detailed witness accounts compared to consequent physical evidence are like fingerprints or DNA at a crime scene compared to their sources—highly complex data that work amazingly well for comparisons.

I discovered something that has been the reason for my success as a consultant forensic pathologist. No longer do I have to advertise my services on websites with expert listings: all of my cases come from referrals. Clients now see what the mother of the great escaper saw back in 1995: that what I say makes sense. There is no need for me to come up with a theory that will help an attorney client; all I do is listen to what witnesses say, then I tell the attorney how those accounts fit or don't fit the physical evidence, according to what I know as a scientist. The words of truthful witnesses make sense scientifically; all I do is to point it out.

Unfortunately, what I found has been a two-edged sword for me. Yes, it has provided a living for me, but it has also put me at odds with my colleagues and with so many others in the forensic science community. I keep trying to help my colleagues understand, using ridiculously simple examples—like "2 + 2 = 4" and a person getting heads every time after flipping a coin numerous times—to illustrate something that to me is so incredibly and ridiculously obvious.

In spite of the simplicity of the concept, it is clear that one cannot persuade people who do not want to listen. My colleagues repeatedly have rejected abstracts I have submitted for presentation at national meetings, so I stopped submitting them.

Finally, I had an abstract accepted for presentation at an international meeting, and I traveled to South Korea to present it in 2014.[9] I spoke to about a half-dozen people sitting among numerous empty seats in a vast auditorium.

Notes

1. Geddes JF, Tasker RC, Hackshaw AK, Nickols CD, Adams GG, Whitwell Hl, Scheimberg I. Dural haemorrhage in non-traumatic infant deaths: Does it explain the bleeding in 'shaken baby syndrome'? *Neuropathology and Applied Neurobiology* 2003;29(3):14–22.

2. Crown Prosecution Service. Crown Prosecution Service response to Judgements in Four Appeals involving Shaken Baby Syndrome Issues. CPS.GOV.UK, July 21, 2005. http://webarchive.nationalarchives.gov.uk/20160302134730/http://www.cps.gov.uk/news/latest_news/137_05/. Accessed on November 3, 2017.
3. Christian CW, Block R. Abusive head trauma in infants and children. *Pediatrics* 2009;123(5):1409–1411.
4. Deutsch SA. Understanding Abusive Head Trauma: A Primer for the General Pediatrician. *Pediatric Annals* 2020;49(8):e347–e353.
5. Young TW. Forensic Science and the Scientific Method. http://www.heartlandforensic.com/writing/forensic-science-and-thescientific-method. February 13, 2008.
6. Young TW. An Inferential Test for Expert Testimony. http://www.heartlandforensic.com/writing/an-inferential-test-for-experttestimony. April 5, 2009.
7. Young TW. The Inferential Test is Always True. Think of it as a Law. http://www.heartlandforensic.com/writing/forensic-inference/theinferential-test-is-always-true-think-of-it-as-a-law. September 11, 2011.
8. Young TW. Diatoms, Retinal Hemorrhages and Other Forensic Tests: A Logical Assessment Using Probability Theory. http://www.heartlandforensic.com/writing/diatoms-retinal-hemorrhagesand-other-forensic-tests. August 29, 2012.
9. Young TW. A Little Lesson in Logic. *Presented at the World Forensic Festival, International Academy of Forensic Sciences*, Seoul, South Korea, October 16, 2014.

Failing the Infamous 11

Up to this point, you might have thought that flawed forensic thinking only involved child protection issues with children seen in hospitals and clinics. Nothing could be further from the truth. The work of forensic doctors has affected the investigations of all kinds of crimes and the outcome of all kinds of court cases. If I were to write about all of the forensic doctor follies that have occurred not only throughout history but also occurring currently, there would not be enough space in libraries to contain it all.

For now, you will have to be satisfied with the few examples I give in this book to help you understand how forensic doctors fail you daily.

If anyone were to search for news reports that illustrate reasoning backward as done by forensic doctors, they would not be hard to find. What will follow are some of the relatively recent sensational stories that have involved flawed thinking by forensic doctors. These stories do not cover the forensic doctors who are already considered to be the "bad apples." These stories instead demonstrate the flawed thinking of doctors who, to this day, are held in high esteem and are thought to be doing good work by most of the public.

Daily Mail, June 11, 2012: The Dingo DID Do It: Lindy Chamberlain in Tears at Verdict after 32 Years[1]

This is one of the most famous cases in Australian legal history—one that I described in this book's introduction. Books have been written and movies made about this case. It is a tragic example of how the work of forensic doctors and other backward-reasoning forensic scientists can damage lives, but the authors and filmmakers writing and filming about this case pay no attention to backward reasoning.

You may recall some of the story in the Introduction. In 1980, the family of Michael and Lindy Chamberlain vacationed at Ayer's Rock (Uluru) in the Northern Territory of Australia. They spent an evening at a campsite with Greg and Sally Lowe, a couple they had only recently met. During that evening, the Lowes saw Lindy rocking her 10-week-old baby, Azaria, to sleep. When the child fell asleep, Lindy and her oldest child walked to the family tent and placed the infant in a bassinet.

Later in the evening, the Chamberlains and Lowes heard a baby cry. Lindy returned to the tent and saw a dingo, a wild Australian dog-like animal, exit the tent. She went inside the tent and found the baby missing. There was blood in the bassinet. Several people at the campsite noted paw prints by the tent flap. The family and others at the campsite searched frantically but they did not find the child.

A week later, portions of plastic diaper, an infant jump suit, a singlet, and infant boots were found six kilometers west of the camp. The jump suit and singlet were bloodstained. A matinee jacket with pale lemon yellow edging that the child was wearing at the time of disappearance was not found.

Several people witnessed the events of this case, yet the police insisted on inventing a theory of what happened rather than focusing on witness accounts. According to the theory, the dingo did not take the baby; instead, Lindy murdered her. Police investigators believed that the mother killed her infant child days before the disappearance and that the mother, the father, and other witnesses of the events of that evening came up with an elaborate story to conceal the crime. The police invented a conspiracy theory: multiple witnesses worked together to cover up for a murderous mother. Complex conspiracy theories are highly unlikely to be true; but the Australian police, media, and public did not understand that.

Multiple forensic science tests performed on several items of evidence supported the theory. There were no dingo hairs, dingo saliva, or teeth marks in any of the clothing items. Experiments performed with dingoes in a zoo using a kid goat dressed in baby clothing fueled skepticism of the dingo account because these captive dingoes did not leave findings similar to Lindy's case.

So far, the police invented an elaborate theory, and the forensic scientists provided the kind of evidence useful for supporting that theory; however, the worst was yet to come.

A professor of forensic medicine in London, England—the forensic doctor described in the Introduction—examined the clothing evidence and concluded that (1) there was a bloody handprint from an adult female, and (2) the child's neck had been cut with a sharp instrument, consistent with scissors or a knife.

Wow! Imagine being able to determine that from halfway around the world! This professor must have been really smart like Sherlock Holmes. Who would want to argue with Sherlock Holmes?

Lindy Chamberlain was tried and found guilty of murder. She was released from prison five years later when the matinee jacket with the lemon edging was found in a dingo lair on the opposite side of Ayer's Rock—a place where it would not have been possible for Lindy to have gone.

In spite of this, the case did not go away. It went back and forth in the courts in Australia. Many Australians to this day still accept the conspiracy theory, but in 2012, after 32 years of torment for the Chamberlain family, the Northern Territory coroner finally acknowledged the dingo as the reason for the death.

This case, of course, represents one more forensic science tragedy, supported in large part by the testimony of a forensic doctor. In spite of flawed conclusions from evidence, most forensic doctors do not recognize anything to be wrong.

Radar Online, June 8, 2016: Natalie Wood Coroner Dodges Lawyer's Attempts to Bring Robert Wagner to Justice[2]

Over one year after the disappearance of Azaria Chamberlain, top Hollywood actress Natalie Wood and her also famous actor husband, Robert Wagner, sailed together on the *Splendour* off of Santa Catalina Island near Los Angeles.

According to both Wagner and the ship captain, Robert Wagner and Natalie Wood had a heated argument, allegedly about an extramarital affair Wood was having with another Hollywood star. "The last expression I saw on her face," according to the ship captain, "was pure humiliation as she stormed off to her stateroom."[3] The following morning, the police recovered Natalie Wood's body on the beach. A small inflatable dinghy also lay nearby the body.

Dr. Thomas Noguchi's book—the one I found in the bookstore years ago—described in great detail the final events in Natalie Wood's life. She put the dinghy in the water to ride away from the *Splendour*, only to slip and fall into the ocean. She was unable to climb into the dinghy due to her drunken state, so she succumbed to hypothermia and drowned. Dr. Noguchi's description was as if he recorded all the events with a video camera.

Thirty years later, in 2011, the authorities reopened the case after the ship captain alleged that Robert Wagner was responsible for her death, an allegation that held up after polygraph ("lie detector") testing. The ship captain saw the couple argue, but he never saw the murderous event he claimed took place. Still, a new investigation led Dr. Noguchi to back off of his determination of accident for manner of death, claiming that he now thinks it is undetermined. The article cited above expressed the frustration of an attorney and former federal prosecutor when the former coroner/medical examiner refused to discuss the case. The current coroner/medical examiner changed the cause of death from "accidental drowning" to "drowning and other undetermined factors."

The remarkable thing about this case is that an accidental determination was changed to undetermined without new information or evidence. No one claimed to have seen anyone kill anyone. Having a heated argument is not the same as killing someone. Neither Robert Wagner nor the ship captain—the only living witnesses on the boat—saw anything homicidal, so the original determination of accident should remain. Accident essentially means a violent event *without evidence of destructive intent*—either self-destructive or other-destructive. Given the witness accounts, accident remains as the only plausible explanation, even though we may not be able to describe Natalie Wood's final events in any detail.

Unfortunately, a change of the manner to undetermined leaves a stigma on Robert Wagner and his family, one that is not deserved. This is all thanks to forensic doctors who prefer to theorize rather than listen to and test the accounts of eyewitnesses.

ProPublica, July 5, 2011: Casey Anthony Trial Shows the Limits of Forensic Science in Proving How a Child Died[4]

This story came out shortly after an Orlando, Florida, jury found defendant Casey Anthony not guilty of killing her two-year-old daughter, Caylee. This case was a media sensation throughout the United States, and the not-guilty verdict angered many in the public at the time it was rendered.

After Casey's mother reported her grandchild, Caylee, to be missing in 2008, Casey lied to police detectives about why the child was missing, including lies indicating the child had been kidnapped by a nanny and that she was too frightened to notify police authorities that her child was missing.

The child's body was found in the woods near the Anthony home six months after her disappearance. Plastic bags covered the remains, and duct tape stuck to the child's skeletonized head. Following an autopsy, Orange County chief medical examiner Jan Garavaglia, the star of the program "Dr. G: Medical examiner" on the Discovery Health Channel, concluded that the cause of Caylee's death was "homicide by undetermined means."

Following that conclusion, prosecutors composed an elaborate account of the child's disappearance: Casey Anthony used chloroform to drug her daughter, then she put duct tape around her mouth and nose to suffocate her. A rancid smell and the finding of a strand of decomposing hair in the trunk of her 1978 Pontiac Sunfire allowed prosecutors to allege that Casey hid the child's dead body in the trunk before placing the remains in the woods.

A highly respected forensic doctor—one who was even featured on a television program—declared that the child had been killed by another person based on...based on what? Witness accounts? No. Based on clues found in a wooded area near the home of the Anthony family. From those physical evidence clues, prosecutors weaved together an elaborate and complicated account that by its complicated nature was highly unlikely to be true.

All the while, this case was called a *circumstantial evidence* case. A circumstantial evidence case is where the criminal act is not witnessed but there is a lot of evidence to indicate what happened. In the case of Caylee Anthony, the final lethal act may not have been witnessed, but the State of Florida considered both the witness and physical evidence to be so plentiful and overwhelming that the only plausible explanation was murder.

Although there were doctors and scientists to comment on the physical evidence clues in the courtroom, the witness accounts were nonexistent. Good circumstantial evidence cases have abundant witness accounts leading up to and away from the lethal act, but this case had no witness accounts to support the state's accusations. All it had was a past event theory cobbled together like a Sherlock Holmes story.

Casey Anthony was implicated as a murderer because she was demonstrably lying. This overlooks a great irony: everyone lies at some point in time and some may even lie to law-enforcement officers, but very few people murder their children. Even if a person is readily shown to be a liar at a later time, the probability of that person being a murderer is still very low.

Even highly regarded forensic doctors do not seem to understand these things. Instead of appropriately calling the manner of the death "undetermined," Dr. Garavaglia's homicide determination plunged the entire nation into a big mess, compelling prosecutors to try to prove the unprovable "beyond a reasonable doubt."

Bustle.com, September 16, 2016: Who Is Werner Spitz? The Forensic Pathologist Has a JonBenet Ramsey Theory[5]

One pathologist highly critical of the work of Dr. Garavaglia in the Casey Anthony case was Dr. Werner Spitz. Dr. Spitz participated in that case as a defense expert. He described Dr. Garavaglia's autopsy as "shoddy" and insufficient.

Dr. Spitz is a doctor with long experience. Unfortunately, that experience has not prevented him from being ensnared by the Sherlock Effect.

Dr. Spitz provided his own form of backward reasoning in a recently released documentary about the unsolved mystery of JonBenét Ramsey. Jon Benét was a six-year-old beauty queen found dead in the basement of her Boulder, Colorado, home on the day after Christmas in 1996. An autopsy at that time allegedly disclosed evidence of ligature strangulation, blunt head trauma, and sexual assault.

Since that time, numerous experts and nonexperts have weighed-in with theories about what happened in this highly sensational case. Dr. Spitz was one of those experts. The article in Bustle.com reports on a documentary reuniting several investigators who consulted in the case. The article reports on Dr. Spitz's vast experience as a forensic pathologist, including his role in many celebrity cases, including the Kennedy assassination. The report mentions his textbook in forensic pathology, one used by many forensic pathologists, including myself.

Dr. Spitz suspected that a flashlight found in the kitchen of the Ramsey home could have been the object used to cause JonBenet's skull fracture. The venerable pathologist tested his theory by striking the corpse of another child with a similar flashlight to see if it would cause wounds similar to those in JonBenet Ramsey. From this test, he concluded that the flashlight could have been the weapon, but there was not enough evidence to conclude that with certainty.

Bustle.com also reported an interview of Dr. Spitz with the *Fort Wayne Journal Gazette* in 2006. The doctor stated his belief that the little girl was killed by "somebody in that house," presumably one of the family members. The Bustle.com article claimed that the parents and the brother were "exonerated by DNA evidence" in 2008 and that all family members denied any involvement in the murder.

The article came out following a CBS documentary on the Ramsey case that featured Dr. Spitz. In it, Dr. Spitz is one of several experts offering past-event theories. All of the experts are heavy-hitters: retired FBI supervisory special agent Jim Clemente who was one of the original case investigators, forensic scientist Dr. Henry Lee, former Boulder District Attorney chief investigator James Kolar, retired FBI agent James Fitzgerald, behavioral analyst Laura Richards, and statement analyst Stan Burke.[6] The forensic experts studied the evidence, including a bowl of pineapple with milk. They performed an experiment not as gruesome as Dr. Spitz's experiment but more painful: tasering a police officer.

Studying crime scene evidence and using experiments to support or deny a scientist's complex theory of past events are a waste of time. Any complex past-event theory invented by scientists, attorneys, or police officers is already highly unlikely to be true, regardless of the results of any such analyses.

Following the documentary, Burke Ramsey, JonBenét Ramsey's brother who was nine years old at the time of her death, filed a lawsuit against Dr. Spitz for defamation.[7] The suit alleges that Dr. Spitz's theory accuses the nine-year-old boy of bludgeoning, strangling, and sexually assaulting his sister. According to the article reporting the lawsuit, Dr. Spitz was quoted as saying, "If you really, really use your free time to think about this case, you cannot come to a different conclusion. It's the boy who did it."

Burke Ramsey claims to have done no such thing. If I were to bet money on who is correct, I would place my wager on a witness who knows what he did and didn't do and not on a forensic doctor who doesn't know what anyone did.

The New York Times, July 13, 2013: Zimmerman Is Acquitted in Trayvon Martin Killing[8]

Another highly publicized case from Florida even elicited comments from United States President Barak Obama. It ignited racial tensions at the time, and it still does to this day.

The State of Florida charged the defendant in this case, George Zimmerman, a "Neighborhood Watch captain," with murdering 17-year-old Trayvon Martin by shooting him with a handgun. *The New York Times* article reported Mr. Zimmerman's claim of self-defense: the teenager knocked him to the ground, punched him, and repeatedly slammed his head into the sidewalk. The jury agreed with Mr. Zimmerman's account of what happened on February 26, 2012, finding him not guilty of murder or manslaughter, accepting his justification for self-defense based on his fear of great bodily harm.

Prosecuting and defense attorneys found forensic doctors to bolster their respective arguments. In our court system, this is appropriate; however, in spite of disagreements between these doctors, it is still possible to tell which testimonies from forensic doctors are reliable and which are not. This is easy to demonstrate.

Another news article from ABC News reported the testimony of a prosecution expert.[9] Medical examiner Valerie Rao testified that George Zimmerman was struck as few as three times in the fight that night and may have only been slammed once on the concrete. She also called the wounds "insignificant" and "non-life-threatening." This, of course, contradicted Zimmerman's account of his head being repeatedly slammed into the concrete numerous times in a life-threatening struggle. The injuries were minor and consistent with severe force, according to the doctor: "If you look at the injuries they are so minor they are not consistent with grave force. If somebody's head is banged with grave force I would expect to see a lot of injuries. I don't see that."

Dr. Rao formed her opinions from physical evidence clues only and made no reference to any witness account. Her testimony could contradict the defendant's assertion if she had taken Mr. Zimmerman's claims into account, but she made no reference to that account: Mr. Zimmerman did not claim "grave force." Dr. Rao apparently did not consider that the injuries in the head could also be consistent with multiple blows as claimed by the defendant. By necessity, witness accounts must be compared to physical evidence for consistency or inconsistency, but Dr. Rao offered no such comparison.

On the other hand, the defense expert witness made comparisons to a witness account for consistency or inconsistency. An article from the *Los Angeles Times* reports the testimony of Dr. Vincent DiMaio.[10] Regarding the head injuries, Dr. DiMaio claimed that the medical evidence was consistent with the defendant's statements of what happened. The doctor found two head lacerations (tears in the tissue), two wounds in the temples, and wounds in the nose and forehead of Mr. Zimmerman. These were consistent with his head being repeatedly slammed into the sidewalk. The prosecution expert might not agree with that opinion, but at least the defense expert offered one that was deductively valid and not hypothetical, reasoning forward from witness account to physical evidence rather than backward from physical evidence to a hypothesis of insignificant force.

Dr. DiMaio further testified about the gunshot wound in Trayvon Martin. He said that the powder marks in the skin and the soot on the clothing indicated that the muzzle was in contact with the clothing but two to four inches from the skin of Martin's chest. According to Dr. DiMaio, "This is consistent with Mr. Zimmerman's account—that Mr. Martin was over him, leaning forward at the time he was shot."

Dr. DiMaio admitted on cross examination from the prosecutor that he focused on the statement offered by George Zimmerman to the police and on the statement of Zimmerman's neighbor, John Good, who saw Trayvon on top of Zimmerman. The doctor admitted to not considering the accounts of several witnesses who claimed that Zimmerman was the aggressor in the struggle. He also said that rolling on the concrete with Trayvon could have caused the injuries.

Certainly, failing to take into account the other witness statements is problematic—something a defense expert might fail to do—but at least there was a reference to witness accounts. Too often, forensic doctors do not make mention of witnesses. Instead, they become magicians who look like Sherlock Holmes and pull a rabbit out of the hat in the courtroom, speculating about events that may or may not have happened (and probably did not happen) using physical-evidence clues only.

Dr. Vincent DiMaio also testified in the Phil Spector murder trial in Los Angeles.

Billboard, May 29, 2007: Coroner Provides Graphic Details at Spector Murder Trial[11]

This was another widely reported sensational case involving a famous record producer and a Hollywood actress. Lana Clarkson was found dead in Phillip Spector's mansion from an intra-oral (inside-the-mouth) gunshot wound. The single witness for the case was Phillip Spector's chauffeur who heard Spector say, "I think I killed someone." During two different trials, the defendant claimed that Lana Clarkson shot herself in the mouth.

The first trial in 2007 ended in a mistrial because the jurors were not all in agreement. Jurors found Spector guilty in a second trial in 2009. He is in prison to this day where he works on getting his conviction overturned.[12]

The story from *Billboard* reports on the testimony of the forensic doctor investigating the case for the Los Angeles County Medical Examiner Office. Dr. Louis Pena in sworn testimony claimed that someone forced the barrel of a gun into Lana Clarkson's mouth, causing a bruise in her tongue before the gunshot killed her. He did not testify about that in the earlier trial, but the prosecutors asked him to go back and examine the evidence. He discussed the evidence with his colleagues prior to reaching his conclusion. "The bruise is very unique and is consistent with blunt-force trauma. Something struck the tongue," Dr. Pena claimed. That something struck the tongue before the gun was fired, and that gunshot blew her top front teeth out of her mouth.

The testimony was lurid. The news account mentions how the doctor powerfully described the moment that Lana Clarkson died.

Dr. Pena offered graphic details in his testimony that no one ever saw but that he somehow knew to be true. It reads like detective fiction because it is detective fiction: nobody ever saw the events depicted by a medical examiner who thinks and speaks like Sherlock Holmes. He showed this case to his colleagues before making his conclusion, but none of them saw anything wrong with cobbling together a complicated story.

Dr. DiMaio testified about several items that made it clear to him that it was a suicidal gunshot wound. He claimed that from his experience, about 98% of such wounds are self-inflicted. Dr. DiMaio didn't compare his findings to any eyewitness account of the gunshot because there were none.

There is one basic problem that no one at that time brought up: Dr. Pena cannot claim that his complicated past event story is true. His story of someone inserting a gun deep into someone else's mouth against her will, bruising her tongue before firing the gun, then firing it has too many "moving parts." Claiming that such a story is true is not reliable in the least, yet this is what he did on the witness stand. He claimed to know the combination of a combination lock without ever learning the combination from someone who knows it.

We imprison people frequently based on fanciful claims made by forensic doctors.

***

The morning of September 19, 2016, was clear and bright—a typical beautiful autumn day in Kansas City. Attorney Richard Hurlburt traveled north to visit with me about two weeks prior to the trial of Deterryon Kelly. Often I will meet with a client at the hotel where they are staying. His choice was the

Hilton Garden Hotel on College Boulevard in Overland Park, Kansas, a short drive from my home office.

As I walked into the lobby, I noticed him seated at a table just off of the lobby. He dressed casually and comfortably with shorts and a baseball cap. In spite of his relaxed appearance, all of the papers on the table and his laptop computer showed him to be hard at work.

After greeting each other, he told me his concerns. He puzzled about the video recordings and about all of the injuries found in the child. I spoke to him the last time in December of 2014, but it did not seem that much of what I said to him at that time registered in his mind.

At a time prior to our meeting, the nurse-attorney who was helping him, Kandi Ash, studied the child's medical records, noting that the mother had taken the child to the doctor over 30 times in his short life. She also noted that 27% of the child's estimated blood volume—blood estimated to be in the child's blood vessels—lay in his abdominal cavity, the space inside the abdomen surrounding the stomach, intestines, and other organs. Usually children do not die from blood loss until they have lost over half of the total amount of blood in their blood vessels. The mother also gave her child many prescription drugs; could too many drugs have contributed to the child's death?

"No," I said flatly. "The medications are not the problem."

He was surprised at my immediate response, even taken aback. How could I seem so sure about this?

"Your client has already told you what the problem is. You should listen to him."

Unfortunately, doctors are not the only ones under the spell of the Sherlock Effect. Prosecuting and defense attorneys everywhere invent backward-reasoned theories about past events. Because of this, courtrooms everywhere have become theaters of absurdity, with attorneys heatedly arguing back and forth about their invented theories, leaving jurors and everyone else totally confused. All the while, the defendant sits in the courtroom and listens to the arguments. He is also completely confused, wondering why no one—not even his own attorney—believes him.

"Mr. Kelly said he found the child trapped between the nightstand and the bed. That sufficiently explains everything in this case. It doesn't matter how many medicines he was taking; being trapped that way will kill a child."

A Marshall Police Department crime scene investigator dismissed the notion of entrapment because, according to his measurements, there were only a little more than 3 inches between the nightstand and the bed, certainly a space too small to allow a child of Ja'Keen's size to fall through. Unfortunately, just like his two-dimensional crime scene diagram, police officers too often think in two dimensions rather than three—something akin to thinking the earth is flat instead of like a ball. Sure, there were only three inches between the top of the nightstand and the bed, but the top of the nightstand jutted out as a ledge from the rest of the nightstand. The nightstand below the top was greater than 3 inches from the mattress. The top of the mattress was also slightly lower than the top of the nightstand. All of this could be seen in the crime scene photographs I examined. If the child moved around in the bed as he was described as doing, he could have easily moved to the edge of the mattress next to the nightstand. That mattress edge could be pushed down by his weight, allowing his body to slip quietly into the space below the ledge formed by the top of the nightstand. The elastic mattress would then push against the chest of the child once he slipped into the space, making it difficult or even impossible for him to move his chest to breathe. Since he would be unable to breathe, he would not be able to cry out to alert his mother and her boyfriend.

The rest of what happened inside the child's body is easily explained by what is already known by medical doctors and scientists. A lack of breathing leads to a lack of oxygen. While the heart may have raced at first from the fear and excitement of being trapped, over time the heart will contract slower and slower. This is what the heart does to preserve whatever oxygen is left in the blood: a slower heart rate uses less oxygen, allowing the child's vital organs to receive blood flow for a longer period of time. Eventually the heart slows to a standstill. The electrical activity of the heart on an electrocardiogram may remain, but there is not enough oxygen to allow enough energy for the heart muscle to contract: electrical activity of the heart without heart muscle contraction for pumping is known in clinical medicine as pulseless electrical activity (PEA).

One of the first responders who arrived to the scene detected what he thought was a faint pulse at first, but it went away. Electrocardiograms at the scene and in the emergency department where the child was transported detected PEA.

Deterryon Kelly felt the child's legs sticking out beyond the nightstand while it was still dark in the room. When he found the child, he said he quickly extricated the child's body and began aggressive, adult-style cardiopulmonary resuscitation (CPR). He told the police he might have performed the chest compressions too hard.

CPR is an aggressive and traumatic maneuver, even when performed properly. With it, the liver is squeezed repeatedly at about 100 times per minute between the lower part of the ribcage and the spine that juts into the abdominal cavity. With several minutes of CPR lasting from when they were started by Deterryon until the child was pronounced dead, the liver could very well have been squeezed vigorously over 1,000 times. This is sufficient to explain the gaping tears in the liver noted at autopsy.

Chest compressions from CPR are not nearly as efficient for pumping blood as an adequately functioning, pumping heart, no matter how aggressively the

CPR is performed. The liver has a rich network of blood vessels going to and from it. If the heart was functioning normally, then the child could easily have lost more than half of his blood volume into the abdominal cavity over a short space of time.

On the other hand, if there was no heartbeat, there would barely be any blood loss from a torn liver: maybe about 5% to 10% of the total amount of blood would end up in the abdominal cavity from the CPR, if that much.

In this case, both the nurse and I calculated 27%. If the child still had a small amount of heart activity at the end, just as the first responder noted, then 27% would fit.

In fact, everything fits. "What about all the bruises?" attorney Hurlburt asked. Well…they fit too.

We are accustomed to seeing what someone looks like when they are beat up, but typically people who are beat up breathe adequately and receive adequate oxygen. Hypoxia—the medical term for "lack of oxygen"—changes all of that, making injuries look much, much worse. Blood vessels become leaky when they don't receive enough oxygen. The blood does not clot properly because clotting cells need oxygen. Also, oxygen-starved blood vessels and other tissues release enzymes that dissolve blood clots that may have formed to staunch the bleeding.

So when there is aggressive handling while trying to resuscitate a child who has been oxygen deprived, there may be extensive areas of bruising and bleeding beneath the skin, particularly when the heart hasn't stopped yet.

What Deterryon Kelly said fit all the available scientific evidence. If he were lying about any of this, he would have been a lying genius who thought to place the child in between the nightstand and bed prior to Jameshia noticing him do it, who knew what the electrocardiograms and autopsy would show before being made aware of them, and who could conjure up the right explanation to offer to investigating officers at the spur of the moment. This is like guessing the correct combination to a complicated lock or the correct complicated computer password. For him to lie and be correct would be like him reciting the winning lottery number prior to the balls being cast. No one is either that lucky or smart.

"What about those suspicious videos?" attorney Hurlburt asked. I told him I had not seen them yet; they did not open on my computer or on a computer at the local public library. Looking at those surveillance videos would be something I would have to do when I arrived in Texas.

"Regardless of what the videos show or how they were interpreted," I assured him, "they will not explain this death. They will not explain the findings at the autopsy and the circumstances as described by Mr Kelly. The only thing that makes sense is the defendant's account."

"Mr. Hurlburt," I told him, "you will see that as the trial gets under way, we will learn more that will not only support what your client saw but will also show how ridiculous the State's case against your client is." I was able to tell him this because of all the court cases I have seen in which the evidence is consistent with the defendant's account.

Richard Hurlburt later told me, "Before our meeting in Overland Park, I had only spoken to you over the phone and didn't have a really good idea of what caused the child's death. I felt stronger about the case after our meeting in Overland Park based on the lower amount of blood loss, the PEA rhythm being present at the hospital and the facts surrounding 'hypoxia' which explained bruising. Also, the injury was consistent with rigorous CPR attempts."

But he felt the jury would not easily dismiss the videos. This was because those videos gave jurors the opportunity to see the events with their own eyes—as if they themselves were witnesses to the crime.

Notes

1. Daily mail.com. The dingo DID do it: Lindy Chamberlain in tears at verdict after 32 years. *Daily Mail*, June 11, 2012. http://www.dailymail.co.uk/news/article-2157971/Azaria-Chamberlain-case-Dingo-DID-baby-rules-coroner.html. Accessed November 11, 2017.
2. Radar Staff. Natalie Wood coroner dodges lawyer's attempts to bring Robert Wagner to justice. Radar Online, 8 Jun 2016. http://radaronline.com/celebrity-news/natalie-wood-mysterious-drowning-investigation-robert-wagner-suspect/. Accessed on November 11, 2017.
3. Radar Staff. Skipper of Natalie Wood's death boat DEMANDS immediate arrest of Robert Wagner! Radar Online, April 18, 2016. http://radaronline.com/celebrity-news/robert-wagner-natalie-wood-death-mystery-splendour-skipper-dennis-davern-polygraph-test/. Accessed on November 11, 2017.
4. Shahani A. Casey Anthony trial shows the limits of forensic science in proving how a child died. *ProPublica*, July 5, 2011. http://www.propublica.org/article/casey-anthony-trial-shows-the-limits-of-forensic-science-in-proving-how-a-c. Accessed on November 11, 2017.
5. Millstein S. Who is Werner Spitz? *The Forensic Pathologist Has a JonBenet Ramsey Theory*. Bustle.com, September 16, 2016. https://www.bustle.com/articles/184271-who-is-werner-spitz-the-forensic-pathologist-has-a-jonbenet-ramsey-theory. Accessed on November 7, 2017.
6. Cowen TW. "The case of: JonBenét Ramsey" trailer shows original investigators reuniting to try and solve murder. Complex.com, August 17, 2016. http://www.complex.com/pop-culture/2016/08/case-of-jonbenet-ramsey-trailer-shows-original-investigators-reuniting-try-solve-murder. Accessed on November 11, 2017.
7. Raven B. JonBenet Ramsey's brother sues Michigan pathologist with murder theory. MLive.com, October 7, 2016. http://www.mlive.com/news/detroit/index.ssf/2016/10/jonbenet_ramseys_brother_sues.html. Accessed on November 11, 2017.

8. Alvarez L, Buckley C. Zimmerman is acquitted in Trayvon Martin killing. *The New York Times* July 13, 2013. http://www.nytimes.com/2013/07/14/us/george-zimmerman-verdict-trayvon-martin.html. Accessed on November 11, 2017.
9. Tienabeso S, Gutman M. George Zimmerman jury told his injuries were 'insignificant.' *ABC News*, July 2, 2013. http://abcnews.go.com/2020/george-zimmerman-jury-told-injuries-insignificant/story?id=19552856. Accessed on November 11, 2017.
10. Muskal M, Susman T. Martin was leaning over Zimmerman when shot, expert says. *Los Angeles Times*, July 9, 2013. http://articles.latimes.com/2013/jul/09/nation/la-na-0710-zimmerman-trial-20130710. Accessed on November 11, 2017.
11. Coroner provides graphic details at Spector murder trial. *Billboard*, May 29, 2007. http://www.billboard.com/articles/news/1051865/coroner-provides-graphic-details-at-spector-murder-trial. Accessed on November 11, 2017.
12. Vituscka J. Shocking appeal! Phil Spector files to overturn conviction for murdering girlfriend—read the court documents. radaronline.com, August 31, 2015. http://radaronline.com/celebrity-news/phil-spector-appeals-overturn-conviction-murdering-girlfriend/. Accessed on January 5, 2016.

12 The Deadly Bed

Ja'Keen Sanders was not the only victim of an unsafe sleep environment. According to doctors, many infants are also victims of unsafe sleep environments, particularly when their parents share the bed with them. Bed sharing or—as doctors now refer to the practice—"co-sleeping" can be a killer of infants.

One public radio station in Milwaukee, Wisconsin, reported on the problem and what is being done about it.[1] At the time of their report in December of 2013, they had already had 16 possible co-sleeping deaths for the year. The public health department had been trying to discourage co-sleeping for some time, but clearly, not enough had been done.

In 2011, the city released several startling images in an advertisement. One image displayed a baby lying down in an adult bed next to a butcher knife. Sleeping with a baby, the advertisement seemed to claim, is as dangerous as sleeping with a butcher knife. Still, in spite of an ad campaign that sought to encourage parents to place their children on their backs in cribs to sleep, little progress had been made. The number of co-sleeping deaths remained around the same: about 15 deaths per year for the last five years.

Dr. Geoffrey Swain, medical director for the Milwaukee Health Department and professor of family medicine at the University of Wisconsin School of Medicine and Public Health, admitted that he thought the problem would be easy to fix at first, but people have been accustomed to sleeping in the same bed with the baby for generations. He admitted that it is difficult to change such ingrained behaviors, so they had to be in this fight for the long run.

For most of the cases, babies who died suffocated on pillows, blankets, and other soft items of bedding. A few of the deaths were linked to a co-sleeping adult's use of alcohol or drugs. One bill circulating through the state legislature aimed at making it a felony to sleep with an infant while intoxicated.

The news report also detailed the efforts of Jackie Sevallius, a nurse in the neonatal intensive care unit at Wheaton Franciscan's St. Joseph Campus in Milwaukee. She offered her patients' parents pack n' plays, tight-fitting crib sheets, a swaddle sack—all the items needed for a safe sleep environment for the baby. Room sharing is okay, she said. You may sleep in the same room as the baby, but you should never sleep in the same bed as the baby.

Sevallius is sympathetic to parents who are tired, who remain awake to take care of a newborn baby at night, but she can't understand why tired parents would be willing to run the risk of co-sleeping. She is frustrated with the problem and why it continues in her community.

Co-sleeping, according to Dr. Swain, is only a part of a larger problem with infant mortality. About 10 out of 1,000 babies in Milwaukee die before their first year of life, and most of the deaths are due to prematurity. About three times as many of these deaths occur in black babies as compared to white babies. Still, Dr. Swain was happy to report that most of the deaths are preventable. In addition to encouraging women to get adequate prenatal care, public health officials need to keep sounding the gong about the benefits of safe sleep.

Infant deaths in Wisconsin are not much different from infant deaths everywhere else. It used to be in the olden days that death in a bed or crib—something that also occurs with "co-sleeping" and "unsafe sleep environments"—was called "crib death." About one percent to two percent of live births will have infants die like this. Back in the days of crib death, the cause or causes for these deaths were unknown.

Then came the medical doctors. They put their heads together to see if they could find the answer for why babies die in their sleep; however, in order to study this problem, they had to come up with a definition that says more than just "crib death."

They got together and developed a consensus. Crib death became sudden infant death syndrome, commonly known as SIDS.[2] SIDS, according to doctors, involves an infant under one year of age who is found dead after being put down to sleep. Autopsies on these children are negative, demonstrating no explanation for the their deaths. Frequently these autopsies show no disease or injury at all. SIDS deaths are the most common kinds of infant deaths investigated by a coroner or medical examiner.

Of course, now that doctors have defined the condition, now it is simply a matter of finding what causes it. Right?

So far, dear reader, if you have been paying attention to what I have been writing, you may have spotted a problem by now. I have already demonstrated how using the word "syndrome" to explain past events that no longer exist in the present does not lead to reliable and truthful answers. Using a term that all doctors unanimously accept does not mean that the term reflects what is really going on.

There is a way to illustrate the absurdity of being unanimous. A long-running television variety program broadcast in South Korea set up a game with seven cast members. The writers for the program called it "The Unanimity Race."[3] The seven members were locked in a building and were told that they could not come out until they won enough contests in which they all agreed with each other, until they were unanimous. For one of the contests, each member was given a box, each containing a red ball and a blue ball. The members could reach into their boxes to grab a ball, but the design of the box prevented them from looking inside the box. At the count of three, they were all supposed to pull out balls with the same color.

The members tried as hard as they could three times, somehow trying to convey which ball needed to be picked through telepathy, by sending mental messages to each other. For the first attempt, four members pulled out blue balls and three red. For the second attempt, two members pulled out blue balls and five red. For the third attempt, four members pulled out blue balls and three red. When they failed to be unanimous after the third time, men dressed as red devils ran into the room with howitzer-like water guns and drenched the seven cast members. Such was the punishment for failing to be unanimous.

Think carefully about this now: What would be the probability of all seven members removing the same colored ball? The first member would have to pull out a red ball (or a blue ball), AND the second member would have to pull out a ball of the same color as the first member, AND the third, fourth, fifth, sixth, and finally the seventh would all have to pull out the same-colored ball. Since there are only two possible colors, that would be like flipping a coin. It would be 0.5, divided by two, divided by two, divided by two, divided by two, divided by two, and finally divided by two. The answer? 0.008 or 0.8%. The probability of all of them *not* pulling the same colored ball would be 99.2%. With that kind of probability, the seven cast members should have brought seven raincoats with them!

If we were to think of the developing human as a black box—one with innumerable "moving parts" that pass in time from a glob of a few cells to an amazingly complicated organism—we would realize how seriously crazy it would be to come up with a single, unanimous cause for everything that could cause a sudden infant death, even if the presentation—an infant found dead in bed with a negative autopsy—looks the same. The use of the term, syndrome, indicates a single underlying cause, but is it really possible or reasonable to conclude that the deaths of numerous infants found dead in a crib throughout history had the same cause? What is the likelihood of that happening? How many times would we need to flip a coin before figuring that out?

When doctors who think like Sherlock Holmes get together, such things become possible. It becomes possible to reach a consensus that there is a single cause for a mysterious event like crib death—or at least reach a consensus for what may cause it "most of the time." After the consensus is reached, red devils with high-powered water guns do not rush into the room to punish these doctors for getting the wrong answer. Instead, the ideas are wholeheartedly accepted and made a matter of public policy.

The cause for SIDS changed over time. Many years ago, crib deaths were thought to be due to a thymus that was too large. The thymus is an organ in the chest cavity found over the heart and trachea of an infant; it shrinks over time as the infant develops into an adult. Perhaps that organ impaired breathing or heart function because it was too big. As time went by, however, doctors found many infants who had very large thymuses to do well and many infants who had small thymuses to be found suddenly and unexpectedly dead. The big thymus theory did not work. Still, this did not prevent many infants from having doctors shrink many large thymuses with radiation from the 1920s to the 1940s.

A wide variety of other possible causes of SIDS were brought out. Since African-American babies have a higher incidence of SIDS, doctors floated the idea that sickle-cell trait, a condition that is more common in black babies, may have been the culprit. Unfortunately for that idea, many children found suddenly and unexpectedly dead do not have sickle-cell trait, and many with sickle-cell trait do not die in infancy.

Some thought that overwhelming infections or extreme allergic reactions were what caused these infant deaths. Unfortunately for those ideas, infants found suddenly and unexpectedly dead are in seemingly good health before being found dead. In the vast majority of cases, none of them appear sick or to be getting sick—something that would be anticipated with overwhelming infections or severe allergic reactions.

In the 1970s, doctors considered that an apnea spell (a cessation of breathing) due to prematurity, an apparent life-threatening event, or some other condition might be responsible.[4] For a while, children were sent home with apnea monitors intended to detect some cessation of breathing or heart rate in the child. If the alarm went off, the parents or caretakers would be alerted to arouse the child. That idea did not seem to pan out either. In the vast majority of cases, none of the infants have any problems with breathing prior to being found dead. Apnea monitoring to detect SIDS was no longer recommended by the mid 1980s.[5]

Many ideas have been floated over the years, but none of them panned out.

In the 1940s and even before, doctors thought that infant deaths may have been in large part due to suffocation—a condition that may lead to no findings at the autopsy. That idea was discarded back then, but in this modern age it has returned in a slightly different form.

In the mid 1980s, doctors noted that infants in Hong Kong were routinely placed on their backs to sleep. The cases of SIDS in such situations were found to be lower than elsewhere. Other population studies from the Netherlands and Australia found decreased numbers of SIDS cases when infants were put down to sleep on their backs and not on their tummies. In 1994, the Back to Sleep campaign was launched, and to this day, parents everywhere are instructed to place their babies on their backs to sleep. Doctors speculated that infants were not able to breathe properly because of the sleeping position and the bedding environment.

Doctors eventually added more "moving parts" to SIDS: more than one situation or condition occurring in an infant at the same time that could explain the results of these studies. In addition to the sleeping environment, the infant's age and immature development combined with some sort of problem with the arousal mechanism of the brainstem might cause vulnerable infants to die. Thus was born the triple-risk model or hypothesis.[6]

From that point until now, it is widely accepted not only by doctors and other scientists but also by the public at large that the cause of many of the SIDS deaths is due to unsafe sleep environments—environments that include fluffy bedding and others sleeping with the infant (co-sleeping). In many places and in many cases, medical examiners have replaced the SIDS term with "suffocation," "smothering," or "asphyxiation," thereby lowering the number of SIDS cases.[7]

Now, more and more people are accused of suffocating, smothering, or asphyxiating their babies. Crib death in several situations has now become criminal behavior, thanks to forensic doctors who think like Sherlock Holmes.

Consider the story of the Texas Sharpshooter.

One day while firing a gun absent-mindedly and randomly into the siding of his barn, a farmer noticed that the randomly shot bullet holes formed clusters. There were clusters of bullet holes that were much closer together than other bullet holes. Noticing that, the farmer became excited. He ran to the shed, grabbed a brush and a bucket of red paint, and drew target circles around the clusters of bullet holes. Excitedly, he showed the townspeople all the targets, declaring to them that he was a Texas Sharpshooter!

We would be foolish to hire such a man to become the sheriff based on the information presented from the barn siding, yet somehow when numerous Sherlock Holmes-like physicians present similar information—where targets are drawn around clusters of cases without any visible demonstration of how these cases came to be—we accept that as gospel and guide our lives according to it. We accept one hypothesis without observable proof, then cobble onto it another hypothesis without observable proof. After years of doing this, doctors have developed a monster like the one made by Dr. Frankenstein. They have made a house of cards that can be destroyed by a slight gust of wind. Whenever doctors take past events that cannot be witnessed and build oversimplified explanations and scenarios around them, we cannot expect to have anything near the truth. The truth for any situation may be highly variable, highly complex, and involve something we do not know that we do not know.

Even on the face of it, there are problems with the unsafe sleep environment hypothesis.

First, crib death is not common, really. It involves about one percent to two percent of live births. Now it is even less than it was a few years ago due to fewer cases being called SIDS. On the other hand, unsafe sleep environments are highly common, in spite of all the public health campaigns that have been launched over the years. People commonly sleep with their babies and put them to bed in unsafe sleep environments, despite the public health measures. If unsafe sleep environments were the cause, crib deaths would be more common than they are. Actually, I could say that unsafe sleep environments might prevent SIDS because more children survive in unsafe sleep environments than die. Since doctors draw targets around bullet holes, what is to prevent me from drawing that target?

Secondly, children who die suddenly and unexpectedly in the bed or crib often die at about two to three months of age, and some live on for at least a year—at least according to the target that has been drawn by doctors when they define SIDS as extending to a year. Up to those several days and months, an infant often sleeps in the same unsafe environment. Since the child survived the unsafe environment more often than died in it, couldn't we also argue that a child is more likely to survive in an unsafe sleep environment than die in it?

Most importantly, we should not take complicated successions of past events—in which one event led to another and then led to another—and a complicated developing human—in which there are so many moving and developing parts that could fail—and think that we could come up with a simple hypothesis that could explain even "many" or "most" of the deaths. We certainly wouldn't think it wise to go to Las Vegas and bet hard-earned money with those kinds of poor odds; what makes us think that we should do this in matters of public policy and criminal justice?

What about crib death? Will we ever get any answers?

Consider the claim of the wannabe Texas Sharpshooter: How can we test the shooting ability of the Texas farmer? The answer to that is easy. First, we set up a target before any shot is fired. We then hand the farmer a rifle, have him stand some set distance away from the target, and watch him fire at the target. We can then look at the bullet holes in the target to see if he is good at shooting. Pretty simple.

Unfortunately, crib death is not that simple. We would need to monitor the vital signs, brain-wave activity, oxygenation, heart rhythms, and other bodily functions of many infants. We would have to monitor each child remotely, and we would need to think of all the possible things that could go wrong in order to select our monitoring equipment. We would have to deal with all the problems that come with this technology, including false positive and negative readings. Then, somehow, at the right time, we would have to detect a problem with the infant's functioning at the time the infant dies. We would have to take a past event situation and turn it into a present-day, observable situation.

In spite of the sophistication of the kind of monitoring that is currently available, we are not even in the remotest ballpark of doing this. Even if we were able to monitor several functions, we still could not be sure of our findings because we do not know what we do not know.

When it comes to science and crib death, the answer to "Will we ever get any answers?" is not presently known; however, from a forensic aspect, there are some things we can know right now.

We can know that infants and even older persons can die suddenly and unexpectedly in an unknown fashion: though this is relatively infrequent, it is not rare. We can know what infant caretakers saw simply by listening to them. We can even use a doll to represent the baby, allowing the caretakers to show us what happened—this is called a "doll re-enactment." We can examine the physical evidence clues at the scene and autopsy. Forensic doctors can compare the eyewitness accounts with the clues and readily say what "fits" and "does not fit." We have enough information to reason forward like that.

If an infant dies suddenly and unexpectedly, if the eyewitnesses describe such a sudden and unexpected death without anything violent in it, and if the autopsy and other investigation do not disclose any reason for the death, forensic doctors can and should know that such unexplained deaths can happen. They should explain that there is nothing to implicate any person of a crime or foul play.

On the other hand, if items of evidence do not fit each other, forensic doctors can know something is not right. Forensic doctors can point out the problems and the police can continue to investigate.

Forensic doctors, however, should not behave like Sherlock Holmes: a person who thinks he knows everything he needs to know to put people behind bars.

***

The Harrison County Courthouse, a four-story square building that houses several county offices, lies to the west of the town square of Marshall, Texas, west of the old historic county courthouse situated within the town square. After entering the doors and passing through a metal detector monitored by a few sheriff deputies, a short elevator ride to the second floor and a trip down a long hallway lead to the courtroom of the 71st District Court. Upon entering that courtroom, a wood panel on the right surrounds the two rows of chairs where 12 jurors and two alternates would carefully consider the evidence in *State of Texas v. Deterryon Tyrell Kelly*. The district attorney and defense tables, the judge's bench, and seating areas for the court recorder, the clerk, and the bailiff lay in front of the jurors and in front and slightly to the right of the courtroom entrance.

The audience for the trial that began on Monday, October 3, 2016, was larger than most audiences typically seen in court cases; they sat to the left of the courtroom door on benches that resembled church pews, to the left of the short wall—the "bar"—that separates the onlookers from the participants in the slow-moving drama that would last the rest of the week. Deterryon's family attended the proceedings, but the family of Jameshia Cooks and Ja'Keen Sanders outnumbered them. About 20 people attended the trial on most days, and this number swelled from 35 to 40 on the final day.

Multiple paintings of prior judges for the 71st District Court seemed like silent onlookers, keeping watch from the paneled walls on the participant side of the bar. The elected district attorney, Coke Solomon, and his assistant, Kristin Kaye, sat at the prosecutor's table. Books, papers, and computer equipment covered the table surface, and a television monitor to the right of the table and in front of the jury would eventually display the video evidence. Further away from the jury panel was the defense table. Attorney Richard Hurlburt sat at the right side of the table, to his left sat Investigator Michael Reinhart, and defendant Deterryon Kelly sat to the left of Mr. Reinhart. Nurse and attorney Kandi Ash sat in a chair behind the table. When I arrived in court on Wednesday, I occupied the chair where Mr Reinhart usually sat while I passed notes with my observations and suggestions to Mr Hurlburt during much of the trial.

Juror selection occupied most of the day on Monday, and opening statements from both prosecuting and defense attorneys followed this. The prosecution then presented witnesses for their case. Several prosecution witnesses testified on Tuesday.

Pete Patel, manager of the Best Western Executive Inn in Marshall, Texas, described hearing a loud noise while in his apartment above the vending machine room on the evening of May 5, 2014. He asked the front desk night clerk on duty, Wilma Laywell, to find out what caused the loud noise. Later, after speaking to her, he entered the lobby and spoke with the defendant. He saw the child with the defendant, next to the computer desk and on the chair.

> "Was there anything unusual about that kid?" asked the district attorney.
>
> "Something didn't—didn't seem right with the kid," responded Mr. Patel.
>
> What do you mean 'didn't seem right'?
>
> I think he was losing consciousness maybe. Because his eyes were opening and closing. And if I remember correctly, he was making some sort of noise. I cannot tell you exactly what noise.
>
> Did he look like he was asleep, or did he look like there was something else wrong?
>
> Something—something was wrong.

Attorney Coke Solomon asked Mr. Patel if he asked the defendant about the condition of the child. Mr. Patel responded:

> Yes, I did ask him. I was like, is everything okay with the child? And he said, yes, everything is fine. I think he said, yes, we're just waiting on his mom.

Pete Patel testified that the defendant carried the child out of the lobby. The child did not look right when Deterryon Kelly carried him out: he looked "floppy." On cross-examination, the witness agreed that the condition of the child did not prompt the witness to call 911.[8]

Next came Wilma Laywell, the front desk night clerk on duty. She heard "banging noises," and this prompted her to examine the monitor for a closed-circuit television camera.

> It was like something was hitting up against something. It was just like bang, bang. You know, once I went looking, I saw a gentleman inside of the room where the vending machines are, and I was looking at the camera so I could see the gentleman going from side to side through the window.
>
> So I thought that there was someone in there fighting because it sounded like someone might have been pushing someone up against one of the machines in there once I saw what was going on, on the camera.

Attorney Kristin Kaye asked her what she did after checking the camera.

> I went out the back door so that I could peep through the window to see what was going on and what I needed to do from there.

Ms. Kaye asked the witness, "Were you worried that you might need to call 911?" The witness replied that she was. She saw the defendant going from side to side on the camera, so she thought someone might have been fighting.

She encountered Deterryon and the child when she went to the vending machine room. "He said something about having issues getting something out of the vending machine, but he didn't really complain or anything. As we were standing out there, he asked me if I had anything in the office that I could give them, and I told him that I had a banana, I believe. And I went…"

> "Let me slow you down," Ms. Kaye interrupted. "Take a breath. When you got out to the vending machine room, you saw the defendant, and you saw the baby?"
>
> Yes, ma'am.
>
> What did the baby look like? Where was he in the room, and what was he doing?

The child was in the room beside the vending machine, "on the floor close to the trash can." He was "laid up against the wall sitting." The child was not moving around or making noises.

Ms. Laywell went to retrieve a banana from the office. While there, she looked at the camera monitor and noted Deterryon throwing the child into the air. After speaking with Mr. Patel on the telephone, she went back outside to give Deterryon the banana. She then described what Deterryon did after entering the lobby: "He laid the child across two chairs, and he got on the computer."

Attorney Kaye further inquired, "Were you concerned about the baby, the way he looked when he was lying on the chairs?"

> Yeah, because it was kind of—when he was holding the child, it's just the way the child's head would flop from—you know, if the child was more this way, the head would flop over this way. And then—but—or if it was this way, it would flop, you know, like it—he didn't have no control over it, I could say.

To her, the child "didn't seem right"; however, she admitted under cross-examination that she had told the investigating officer at the time that the child "looked kind of sleepy like when my grandson gets sleepy." She also told the officer that the child did not seem upset or even distressed. She did not think at the time that the child was in any danger.

Jameshia Cooks testified after Wilma Laywell. Ms Cooks was Ja'Keen's mother, Deterryon's girlfriend, and the one pregnant with Deterryon's unborn child. When Deterryon and Ja'Keen returned to the hotel room, she had just finished her bath. Ja'Keen laid against Deterryon's shoulder with his eyes closed. He put the child down on one of the beds and put the covers over him. "Ja'Keen would make a noise like we were disturbing him or something because we were talking," she observed, so both the man and the child's mother stepped outside of the motel room. While sitting on steps outside of the room, Deterryon watched the child through the door that was left slightly open, but she did not watch the child.

Attorney Kaye further inquired, "Did you ever—from the time that Deterryon brought the baby back into the hotel room while you were in bath until y'all went to bed—did you ever touch Ja'Keen or pick Ja'Keen up or check on him at all?"

> No. He seemed as if he was asleep.
>
> So Deterryon did all of the taking care of Ja'Keen from the time he brought him back from the vending machine until y'all went to sleep?
>
> Yes.

Later, Ms Cooks described checking on Ja'Keen when she got up to use the restroom several times during the night. She never touched him, according to her testimony, and she never checked to see if he was breathing. The child was covered. When she got up again to use the restroom, she did not see the child in the bed. It was dark in the room, but Deterryon told her the child was on the floor between the two beds in the room. She claimed the child was not between the bed and the nightstand. Deterryon said the child was cold, and that was when he started doing cardiopulmonary resuscitation.

On cross-examination, attorney Hurlburt reminded Ms Cooks about what she told the police during their interview with her:

> Do you recall on the first interview that you gave that—I think you said that Deterryon had tucked the child in, and when you got up to pee, he was outside the covers. Do you recall telling them that he was outside the covers?
>
> Yes.
>
> Then you said later you actually saw him tossing and turning. Do you remember telling them that you saw him tossing and turning?
>
> Yes.
>
> So he wasn't asleep; he was—he was moving around, correct?

She agreed.

> Obviously, you didn't think anything was out of the ordinary because you would have checked on him and carried him to the ER or called the doctor, would you not?
>
> Yes.

Jameshia admitted on cross-examination that Ja'Keen looked sleepy after they returned to the motel room, that she saw the child's eyes open after Deterryon put him to bed, that the child made noises as if the adults were disturbing his sleep, and that Deterryon asked to go outside because he did not want to disturb the child further.

Also, she did not question Deterryon's account of finding the child between the bed and the nightstand at that time. She didn't doubt Deterryon until he was arrested, until video surveillance showed Deterryon Kelly hitting her son.

> "So it was that video that made you believe that he killed Ja'Keen?" queried Ms Kaye.
>
> "Yes," responded Jameshia Cooks.
>
> And if he murdered your son, would you want to see him found convicted of capital murder?
>
> Yes.

Notes

1. Toner E. Co-sleeping deaths persist in Milwaukee. *WUWM Milwaukee Public Radio*, December 4, 2013. http://wuwm.com/post/co-sleeping-deaths-persist-milwaukee#stream/0. Accessed on November 11, 2017.
2. Beckwith JB. Defining the sudden infant death syndrome. *Archives of Pediatric and Adolescent Medicine* 2003;157(3):286–290.
3. Running Man (런닝맨), Episode 178. Dramafever.com https://www.dramafever.com/drama/3970/178/Running_Man/?ap=1, October 4, 2015. Accessed on November 2, 2016.

4. Steinschneider A. Prolonged apnea and the sudden infant death syndrome: Clinical and laboratory observations. *Pediatrics* 1972;50(4):646–654.
5. American Academy of Pediatrics Policy Statement. Apnea, sudden infant death syndrome, and home monitoring. *Pediatrics* 2003;111(4):914–917.
6. Filiano JJ, Kinney HC. A perspective on neuropathologic findings in victims of the sudden infant death syndrome: The triple-risk model. *Biology of the Neonate* 1994;65(3–4):194–197.
7. Moon RY, Hauck FR. SIDS risk: It's more than just the sleep environment. *Pediatrics* 2016;137(1):e20153665.
8. Reporter's Record, The State of Texas vs. Deterryon Tyrell Kelly, Trial Court Cause No. 14-0275X, Court of Appeals No. 06-17-00001-CR. Volume 4.

Failing the Numerous Not-So-Infamous 13

Maybe by this point in the book a horrible thought has darkened the transom of your mind. "Maybe," you might think, "this problem with forensic doctors is worse than I thought."

Well...yeah. It is. I do not think even at this point you can imagine how bad it really is.

So far in this book, we have considered the impact of the opinions of forensic doctors on individual court cases and with public health issues like infants found dead in bed. What if we were to discover that the problem with forensic doctors involves a vast number of people who use government services daily to manage important legal issues beyond the criminal and public-health realm? Is it possible that for so long we have trusted the wrong methods and the wrong people to get the right solutions?

Sometimes, problems persist for so long that we get to the point where we cannot perceive the problems anymore. Perhaps we may sense that there is a problem, but we cannot put our finger on it or even know how solve it. Maybe some problems that persist year after year call for expensive solutions that in the end do not work.

Maybe this news article presents one of those problems:

The Charlotte Observer, September 21, 2015: State Budget Boosts Pay, Training for Medical Examiners[1]

> The newly minted $21 billion state budget doubles the pay for North Carolina's medical examiners and, for the first time, sets aside money for mandatory training.
>
> The spending plan tries to address some of the shortcomings in the state's dysfunctional system for investigating suspicious and violent deaths, officials said.
>
> Medical examiners—mostly doctors and nurses who look into deaths in their spare time—are supposed to determine the cause of deaths that happen under mysterious circumstances.
>
> But unlike states and counties with leading medical examiner systems, North Carolina requires no training for hundreds of on-the-ground investigators.

North Carolina pays medical examiners $100 for each case, no matter how much or how little work is involved. Under the new budget, the fee will rise to $200 per case beginning Oct. 1.

An Observer investigation last year found that medical examiners routinely skip basic investigative steps, raising questions about the accuracy of many rulings. Medical examiners fail to go to death scenes in 90% of the cases they investigate and sometimes don't even look at the bodies.

In response to the Observer series, legislative leaders and Gov Pat McCrory vowed to focus on the problems. The General Assembly's special oversight subcommittee last year found "serious and significant performance issues" with the current system.

Shelly Carver, a spokeswoman for Senate President Pro Tem Phil Berger, said the new budget is a step forward.

"The final budget makes substantial investments throughout the medical examiner system to ensure that our county medical examiners are better trained and better paid," Carver said.

The changes come more than two years after the system's failures played a role in the death of 11-year-old Jeffrey Williams of York County in a Boone hotel. He died two months after a Washington state couple were found dead in the same room at a Best Western. State officials took about six weeks to produce the toxicology tests in the first case, which involved a test that experts said could be completed in less than 20 minutes. Even after the state medical examiner's office learned that Shirley Jenkins of Longview, Wash., had a lethal level of carbon monoxide in her blood, authorities did not alert local police or fire investigators until after the poisonous gas killed Jeffrey in the same room.

State Sen Jeff Tarte, a Mecklenburg County republican, worries that this year's reforms fail to address many of the system's problems.

Tarte introduced a bill that would have traded the roughly 350 part-time medical examiners for a staff of trained, full-time death investigators. Tarte wanted to phase out the current system over a five-year period and hire 40–60 professional death investigators stationed across the state. His proposal would have required investigators to visit most death scenes.

But General Assembly leaders balked at the cost of Tarte's proposal, an estimated $80 million over the next 10 years.

Tarte said he's pleased lawmakers took some steps but feels the changes don't go far enough.

Medical examiners still won't be required to visit death scenes, which experts say is key to finding out how someone died.

"Right now, we have still got it (the investigative process) backwards," Tarte said.

Experts say a competent system is important to grieving families, who depend on timely death investigations to close estates and collect life insurance payments after relatives die. Police need accurate reports to help solve crimes. The Observer found four recent cases where medical examiners failed to detect homicides.

The new state budget provides:

- $100,000 a year for mandatory training.
  State Chief Medical Examiner Dr. Deborah Radisch has said training is vital to improving consistency in death investigations. It remains unclear how the state will conduct the training, a challenge since medical examiners are spread across the state. A spokeswoman for the state Department of Health and Human Services, which oversees the medical examiner's office, did not return phone calls.
- 250,000 a year to pay for two forensic pathology fellowships, with one performing autopsies at East Carolina University, the other in Winston-Salem.
- Nearly $2.2 million to replace and upgrade the medical examiner's information system, which contains a database with details about each case the state investigates.
  State officials say medical examiner funding will now rise from $8.6 million in fiscal year 2015–2016 to $10.4 million the following year.
  But North Carolina still provides less money than states and counties with accreditation from the National Association of Medical Examiners, which sets standards for the profession. They typically spend about $3 per capita, according to a study, while North Carolina usually spends less than $1 per capita.
  Last fall, North Carolina administrators laid out a list of needs for the system that tops $50 million.
  Lanier Cansler, DHHS secretary under Gov. Bev Perdue, said convincing lawmakers to make that kind of investment won't be easy.
  "There is not a lot of political pressure," Cansler said. "Unless there is something that causes (bad) publicity, it is not a priority. These things don't get day-to-day attention unless there is a problem."

Unless there is a problem?

Well…there is a problem, but to understand the problem with medical examiners and medical examiner systems, we have to go back to the beginning.

When the United States became a governing entity a few centuries ago, we adopted the British coroner system for investigating violent and suspicious deaths. At the outset, coroners were not medical people but simply elected officials without medical training.

At a later time, the idea that medical people should take charge of death investigation took hold. On the surface, it seems to make sense. Who is seemingly better qualified to look at the structure and function of the human body and apply that information to why a person died? Earlier in United States history, there were also issues with corruption among coroners, but it was thought that good and upstanding men like physicians would be immune from such corruption. Physicians have always been trusted, so why not trust them with an important governmental function like death investigation?

Massachusetts was the first state to replace coroners with "medical examiners" in 1877. Since that time, other states and jurisdictions employed physicians as medical examiners, replacing elected lay coroners.

Currently, we have a mishmash of death investigation systems in the United States. Some states retain the same lay coroner system brought to this country from England. Some states require elected coroners to be physicians. Some states have mixed systems—with medical examiners in larger metropolitan areas and coroners in more rural counties. Some states have appointed district coroners that are physicians, and some states have appointed district medical examiners that are physicians. Some states—like Massachusetts and North Carolina—have statewide medical examiner systems, in which the people performing death investigations from top to bottom are physicians.

When the National Association of Medical Examiners (NAME) formed in the 1960s, the goal was the eventual "medicalizing" of death investigation—essentially replacing lay coroners with physicians. Now, that goal is not so prominently stated, and it is clear that it is not even close to being achieved. Instead, NAME seeks to coexist with coroners, trying to get along rather than take over.

Political realities do not allow a total medical examiner takeover. On the contrary, there are jurisdictions and even some states—California, for example—that are replacing medical examiners with coroners. It seems like there may be a good reason for the resistance to adopting forensic doctors as death investigators. That reason becomes clear when one looks at the news headlines over many years.

According to the headlines, which type of death investigation system do you think has the most problems with scandals and mistakes? Surely, it must be the states with all lay coroners running the show. Right?

Wrong. The most scandal-plagued and problematic death investigation systems in the United States are state medical-examiner systems. Looking at the headlines makes this painfully obvious.

North Carolina is only one state under the gun. Other states with problems recently reported in the media are Massachusetts (where it all began), Oklahoma, New Jersey, Delaware, and Rhode Island—all state medical-examiner systems.

One great irony becomes apparent in the newspaper article from North Carolina printed above. There is a call for training in death investigation for forensic doctors and the expenditure of a lot of money, but aren't those doctors already supposed to know what to do? Isn't that why states with a statewide medical-examiner system appointed forensic doctors in the first place—because they already know more than the lay investigator?

Often when reporting the problems, the media reports back-and-forth discussion about what to do and how much money to spend. Often there is mention of a shortage of forensic doctors available to do the work, the need for more training of pathologists and other forensic doctors, the need for more standardization and accreditation of death investigation offices, and even the need for more "science" in what forensic doctors do. The same solutions are offered—solutions having to do with more training and money—but the same problems persist year after year with no end in sight.

All the while, lawmakers overlook something that to many of you might seem obvious by this time as you read this book.

Think about it this way: What if we, as hypothetical lawmakers and public leaders, decided to appoint Sherlock Holmes as the leader of our death investigation system?

His resume would certainly look good. His academic background as a forensic doctor would be terrific. He would have a lot of experience. He would speak impressively, using words of his profession that few lay people would understand.

On the other hand, he would have these nasty habits of accusing people of crimes after examining the clues and failing to compare those clues fairly and open-mindedly to the accounts of eyewitnesses. He would float theories for past events that are currently in vogue among other forensic doctors. He would diagnose a death like he diagnoses illnesses. He would not leave the confines of his office, clinic, or hospital to visit a death scene and look at other factual data—particularly the statements of those who actually saw what happened. He would think that ordering an X-ray or a laboratory test within his office, laboratory, or morgue would be better than finding out what really happened outside of his office.

Furthermore, he would have the kind of ego that Sherlock-style forensic doctors have. If he already knows what he already knows and he doesn't know what he doesn't know, how will anyone teach him anything better—particularly when he is unable to recognize when something really is better.

The kind of thinking and attitude of Sherlock Holmes does not work in real life, so if we were to hire Sherlock Holmes to run our death-investigation agency, we would certainly have problems.

That is not all. What if we were to hire numerous doctors who thought like Sherlock Holmes and placed them throughout the entire system? What if our system has more forensic doctors than any of the other systems? Could we expect to get better results than the other systems?

Do I need to answer that question? The answer by now should be painfully obvious.

But lawmakers do not realize any of this. They believe solutions require more money and maybe asking the people who really know what to do—people, for example, from the National Association of Medical Examiners:

The Charlotte Observer, October 2, 2015: As N.C. Struggles, Nation's Top Medical Examiners Meet in Charlotte[2]

> As North Carolina's medical-examiner system struggles to overcome problems, members of a national group focused on improving investigations into suspicious deaths have converged on Charlotte for their annual conference.
>
> Meeting at the Westin hotel from Friday through Tuesday, more than 400 members of the National Association of Medical Examiners (NAME) will attend an array of educational sessions, ranging from "sudden death in the young" to "the explosive effects of lightning."
>
> An Observer investigation, published last year, found that N.C. medical examiners routinely skip crucial steps when they look at suspicious deaths, raising questions about the accuracy of many rulings.
>
> North Carolina's system isn't accredited, but the conference comes as the state seeks accreditation from NAME for the main medical examiner office in Raleigh. That would mean it would have to meet minimum operating standards.
>
> It also comes less than two weeks after lawmakers approved a state budget that increases pay for the state's part-time medical examiners from $100 to $200 per case, and for the first time, sets aside money for mandatory training.
>
> Dr. Gregory Schmunk, a past president of NAME who is in town for the conference, said the changes approved by the legislature are an improvement. But he predicts that problems will persist if the state continues to rely on part-time medical examiners who aren't required to visit death scenes.
>
> "Do you want people who remove your appendix or perform heart surgery doing it on a part-time basis?" asked Schmunk, who serves as chief medical examiner for Polk County, Iowa, which includes Des Moines. "Wouldn't you rather have someone who is full-time and continually trained?"

So far, according to Dr. Schmunk, solutions include requiring doctors to visit death scenes and using only full-time forensic doctors with more education. These are expensive solutions that are beyond the reach of any state government.

The article later reinforces the call for "vast knowledge":

> Despite the grim nature of their work, medical examiners routinely show their senses of humor. In a raffle to raise money for NAME's non-profit foundation, the prizes on display Friday included the "chop shop"—a bag of candies shaped like body parts.
>
> But their jobs are no joking matter. Through their investigations, medical examiners often help catch killers, identify health threats and ensure that families get life insurance payments.
>
> Dr. David Fowler, who serves as NAME's vice president and as Maryland's chief medical examiner, said the association's conferences are crucial to helping examiners attain the vast knowledge required of their profession.

> "If you take every disease process known to man—and layer on it all the ways people can die an unnatural death—that constitutes the body of knowledge and the type of cases we investigate on a daily basis," Fowler said. "...We have a very specific set of skills. But we must have broad knowledge to base our conclusions on."

These are the kinds of responses that forensic doctors would be expected to give. In modern medicine, more subspecialty training is required to consider longer lists of differential diagnoses. Specific subspecialized knowledge is often the key to diagnosing and treating complicated diseases in diagnostic medicine.

But what many forensic doctors overlook is that they would learn more by listening to eyewitnesses than they would by obtaining a vast body of knowledge from other forensic doctors who reason backward. They would even learn more from listening to eyewitnesses than they would from visiting the scene of death and looking at it.

Over time, it becomes apparent to some of us who are paying attention how little all of us actually know and how often what is considered to be true changes over time. Although much knowledge is required to do a good job as a forensic doctor, too often what many forensic doctors deem as knowledge is speculative and not reliably tested.

It is painful to consider how often defendants and other eyewitnesses disclose information that is never considered by forensic doctors and scientists prior to a trial; yet many of these witnesses now wrongfully sit in jail, thanks to the vast information offered as testimony by Sherlock Holmes-like forensic doctors. Too often, forensic doctors are blind guides who add little to solving thorny public problems and even contribute to them. Problems persist and no one becomes wiser with the passage of time.

***

In 1989, 20th Century Fox released the movie, *Weekend at Bernie's*. This black comedy featured two men who drag around a dead body for an entire weekend, covering up the fact that the body is dead by pretending it is alive. The propped-up dead body is exposed to many people in the film, but none of these people notices a problem.

Perhaps this is funny and entertaining to some, but how likely is it in real life that anyone could ever get away with such a trick, especially with a body that has been dead for even a few hours?

Dead bodies do not behave the same way live bodies behave. Dead bodies don't breathe. They don't move voluntarily. They purge fluid, stomach content, and feces from mouth, nose, and anus, especially when jostled around. The muscles become stiff, and they don't conform to any natural position after they have been moved. They even start to smell bad.

None of what happens to dead bodies should be a mystery. What is a mystery, however, is how detectives and forensic doctors could believe that someone could cover up a murder by pretending a dead body was alive.

Shortly after my arrival in Longview on the evening of Tuesday, September 4, 2016, I drove a rental car to attorney Richard Hurlburt's office in downtown Longview prior to checking into a motel in Marshall. Mr. Hurlburt, Investigator Reinhart, and I viewed the multiple surveillance videos that I was not able to open on my computer.

The images were captured at night, so the images of Deterryon and Ja'Keen outside the building were silhouettes rather than detailed images—silhouettes formed by indirect lighting from lamps not directly shining on them. The subjects in the surveillance video appear further away than what is typical for a video camera. Also, as is characteristic of many monitoring systems, the motion on the video is not continuous and smooth. Some surveillance systems capture fewer images per second than typical video cameras in order to optimize computer memory and disc space. Reducing the images per second causes the activity in the video to appear jerky. Off in the background, headlights from cars travelling down Highway 59 do not move smoothly; instead, the images of the headlights jerk several times a second as they move down the road.

We also hear no sounds on surveillance videos. There is also no talking, no crying, no laughing, no loud sounds, no soft sounds—no sounds. All is silent. We also cannot detect smells in videos.

One camera shows Deterryon and Ja'Keen leaving their ground-floor motel room. The silhouette of the man leaves the room first, followed by the silhouette of the child. The silhouette of the child is covered and superimposed by that of the man at one point. Then the man raises his arm and suddenly swings it downward toward the child. Admittedly, it looks bad. It seems like the man is energetically striking the child, but there is a problem: the silhouette of the child never moves. It remains superimposed over the silhouette of the larger man, even though the arm swings rapidly. The swinging arm is at the level of the child's head, but we never see the child's head move. We never see the child fall down. We only see rapid motion of the man's arm moving toward what we know to be the superimposed silhouette of the child.

Then we see the man pick up the child and twirl him around like a baton twirler twirls a baton around his shoulder. All of this is stunning to look at, particularly with the jerky motion of the images.

From another camera, we see the man and the child enter the vending machine room. There is a window on the door to the room, but the lighting only allows the viewer to perceive silhouette images on a white background. We see the man pick up the child and seat him on something to the left of the window. Then we see the man make violent, punching motions toward the left at the level of the child.

Another person walks to the door of the vending machine room and then walks away. Shortly after that, we see the man and the child leave the vending machine room. The child does not stand or walk when put down—he appears to collapse—so the man then carries him. We then see the man outside the vending machine room throwing the child high into the air. The child extends his arms and legs outwardly in a natural fashion while being thrown upward.

Another video camera shows the man carrying the child into the lobby of the motel. The lighting in the lobby allows us to see clearly what is happening. We see Ja'Keen lying on the chairs, Deterryon at the computer, and a male manager speaking to Deterryon.

Later from another camera, we see Deterryon sitting on the stairs outside of the ground-floor motel room. He is holding the child, but it is not clear what he is doing with the child. The child flops around rather than sits up. We then see Deterryon taking the child into the motel room after the door opens. Later, Deterryon and Jameshia are seated on the steps outside the room.

The surveillance videos, of course, conform to the account offered by Deterryon Kelly. The swinging arm portion of the video looks suspicious, but Deterryon insisted that he did not strike the child. The autopsy report and photographs disclose no injuries—even minor injuries—of the head and neck.

Deterryon said he seated the child on the washer and dryer, and then he hit and rocked the vending machine next to the washer and dryer as he tried to dislodge the candy. The silhouette images through the window support that account. The account also explains how the person outside of the vending machine room came to see what was going on: the woman manager responded to the loud noises from Deterryon's manhandling of the vending machine.

The images support Deterryon's account of how the child was sleepy and whiny, refusing to walk or stand. They support Deterryon's account of trying to amuse the child by throwing him high in the air.

The activities in the lobby are consistent with Deterryon's account of a sleepy child, Deterryon's use of the lobby computer, and his conversation with the male manager about the ruckus he caused with the vending machine.

The video of the subsequent activities outside of the motel room supports Deterryon's account of trying to feed a fussy and sleepy child a banana and the attempts of adults trying to get the restless child settled into sleep.

Unfortunately for Deterryon Kelly, his account did not conform to the autopsy pathologist's findings.

Sergeant Daryl Griffin served as the lead investigator. He testified how the investigation changed once they learned the results of the autopsy:

> Because the autopsy came back that the baby died of blunt trauma, watching the video of different incidents happening in the vending room and outside of the room led us to the conclusion that it wasn't just a baby's death.[3]

The detective provided commentary to the jury for the video footage, first with what happened after Deterryon and the child came out of the motel room:

> First thing he did, the baby walks out, Mr Kelly walks out behind it. He walks behind the baby and gets into a position to where he can grab the baby on one side with one arm to hold him up, steady him, so then he can hit him upside the head with the other arm to keep him from falling in the parking lot.

The man's non-swinging arm theoretically prevented the child's head from moving after he was so viciously struck. This is how the state explained why the silhouette of the child never moved and remained superimposed over the silhouette of the man.

Attorney Kristin Kaye followed up that comment with a question:

> Now, the fact that he places his hand on the child to brace him, does that indicate to you, through your training or experience, an intentional act—that he's planning to hit this child, that he wants to brace him?

Detective Griffin responded: "Yes, ma'am. He's wanting him to feel the whole blow."

Reads like detective fiction, doesn't it? Badly written, cheesy detective fiction.

The detective then described the baton-twirling-like maneuver with the child:

> Mr Kelly grabs him by his arms and swings him up the first time this way, and then he flips him back this way and flips him back over his shoulder like a sack of potatoes, throwing him up on his shoulder.

"Is that the kind of act that a person should know could harm a child, through your training and experience?" queried Ms Kaye.

> I don't see too many parents or people that will grab a child that way. Because of a child's small arms, injuries can be caused by grabbing and jerking him. Swinging him over a shoulder can cause injuries to his chest.

The video commentary continued:

> Mr Kelly is in the vending machine room, and he's bent down delivering what looks like a blow at a downward angle...
>
> It looks like Mr Kelly puts his hands on both sides of the baby. Where it looks like he has the baby seated on the washer or the dryer, he's got the child with both hands, and he's leaning down and saying something to him. You can see another blow coming...
>
> He grabs the baby by one arm and takes him off the machine and places him on the floor...

> Once he delivers a blow, he grabs the child and goes right back by the door...
>
> He places the baby on the ground trying to stand him up, but the baby's head is slung back, and his body falls like a wet noodle. He holds the baby for a second time trying to get him to stand up on his own, and then the baby's head falls back again. He then grabs the baby and picks him up.

Ms. Kaye then asks, "Through your training and experience, the child that we are seeing in this part of the video falling to the ground, does he appear to be a healthy child, or does he appear to be deceased?"

"He walked in that vending room and never came out alive," Detective Griffin grimly observed.

The prosecutor and police took what was not clear in the surveillance video images and "filled in the blanks," inventing a story that would support a homicide. That story had Deterryon Kelly inflicting blows on the small child in the vending machine room, causing him to bleed from his abdominal injuries. The child shortly died after those blows, as they believed the video demonstrated, because the child would not stand or walk. They had Deterryon throwing a dead child high into the air, maybe as an attempt to get him to recover from his fatal injuries. Then the prosecutor and police had Deterryon Kelly carrying a dead child into the lobby and placing him on two chairs while Deterryon used the computer. Neither the woman who came to the vending machine room nor the male manager in the lobby noticed that the child was dead or dying.

Certainly, Ja'Keen's mother—a parent obsessed with her child's health—noticed nothing strange in the supposedly dead body Deterryon brought back to the motel room, even while they put the supposedly dead child to bed. Although the mother allegedly got up several times to use the restroom, she noticed nothing odd—not even an odd smell.

But none of that mattered to the prosecutor, the police, and eventually to the jury. The only thing that mattered was that a forensic doctor declared the cause of death to be from "blunt impact injuries" and the manner of death "homicide." The prosecutor and police theory had to support the opinions of that brilliant doctor, no matter how far-fetched they were.

I have one final note for this chapter.

The surveillance videos were not the only video images in this case. There were also videos that—unlike the surveillance videos—left little to the imagination.

Deterryon used Jameshia's cellular phone that evening and following morning to capture images of their sexual tryst. Unlike the surveillance videos, the motion was continuous and smooth, even though Deterryon's filming technique was jerky. There were also sounds to accompany the lurid sights.

Deterryon recorded the videos in three files, labeled 0505142358.mp4, 0506140001.mp4, and 0506140008.mp4. The labels correspond to the dates and times (24-hour clock) of the videos: 0505142358 for May 5, 2014, at 2 minutes before midnight, 0506140001 for May 6, 2014, at 1 minute past midnight, and 0506140008 for May 6, 2014, at 8 minutes past midnight. The first two videos capture the lovemaking, and the final video captures activities after the lovemaking. The items not involving sexual activity were admitted as evidence in court and available to the jury for their viewing.

Several items around the motel room are seen in the final video. We see the digital display on the air-conditioning unit that reads "66." We also see young Ja'Keen in the other bed. He wears an orange tee shirt and dark blue shorts with an orange stripe on the side: items of clothing that Dr. Lyon described at the autopsy. There is no blanket covering him. He lies on the white sheet of the bed on his right side with his right arm extending in front of him against the bed sheet and his left arm curled up against his chest. His eyes are closed and his lips slightly parted. Ja'Keen looks comfortable and his position is natural, as if he were fast asleep.

Ja'Keen's clothing is clean and dry: there is no soiling. The underlying white sheet is also clean. There is no fluid or gastric content exuding from his nose or mouth.

The orange tee shirt over the child's abdomen barely and faintly moves in and out, as if he is breathing while asleep.

Notes

1. Clasen-Kelly F. State budget boosts pay, training for medical examiners. *The Charlotte Observer*, September 21, 2015. www.charlotteobserver.com/news/local/article35913318.html. Accessed on November 11, 2017.
2. Alexander A, Clasen-Kelly F. As N.C. struggles, nation's top medical examiners meet in Charlotte. *The Charlotte Observer*, October 2, 2015. http://www.charlotteobserver.com/news/local/article37365939.html. Accessed on November 11, 2017.
3. Reporter's Record, The State of Texas vs. Deterryon Tyrell Kelly, Trial Court Cause No. 14-0275X, Court of Appeals No. 06-17-00001-CR. Volume 5.

The Double Dip 14

Impressive and emphatic forensic-doctor experts with great credentials are in tremendous demand.

Lawyers need them and love them. Such forensic experts are desperately sought after because the outcomes of many cases depend on their testimonies.

The media also love them, particularly visual media like television. The appearance of a world-renown forensic doctor can add to the weight of any news broadcast. If they look good, sound good, and look professional and professor-like, then more people believe them.

Most in society do not have the ability to think critically: to know when something could be true or cannot be true. That is not hard to believe because many—if not most—forensic doctors cannot think critically either.

Most jurors do not have the ability to think critically, so they have to evaluate medical experts not from the confusing things they say but from their résumés. How much medical training does she have? How many live patients does he see in a clinic? How many autopsies has she performed? Is the doctor licensed to practice medicine? How many professional societies does the doctor belong to? How many years of experience does he have? Has the doctor been involved in high profile media cases? How many peer-reviewed journal articles has she written and had accepted for publication?

Finding the right expert is often like observing women in a beauty contest where the "prettiest" one wins. Is the expert on one side more impressive than the expert on the other side? Who seems to know more? Which doctor is from around here and which is from some other place? If the expert is from some other place, how can we trust this person?

Such experts who have lots of positive attributes and nothing negative in their past are highly prized, but where can you find them?

Take, for example, forensic pathologists.

Attorneys need forensic-pathology experts for a wide variety of criminal and civil court cases in which the stakes are high and the rewards and punishments are great. There are numerous court cases but very few forensic pathologists. Most forensic pathologists are already trying their best to finish the paperwork for all the autopsies they have performed—to keep their heads "above water," so-to-speak.

Still, the demand for their services is overwhelming. Among the many telephone calls that forensic pathologists get to answer are from attorneys looking for help with their cases.

This situation presents an almost overwhelming temptation, particularly for the seasoned forensic professional.

The chief medical examiner is often the one member of the medical-examiner staff who has practiced the longest and has the most experience. The chief is also paid the most, yet he does the fewest autopsies. This is because administrative matters supposedly fill the hours and days of the chief, so the autopsy workload for this doctor has to be less. In very large offices, the chief may not do any autopsies.

But the chief is often distracted by the tempting calls of attorneys who are willing to pay top dollar for his services.

The chief will consult on his off-hours, when he is not on duty for his government day job. He is not allowed to earn money during duty hours. That would be "double dipping": earning both outside income and government income for the same time. He is also not allowed to use the instruments and equipment provided by the government to earn private money.

To take care of these outside demands while remaining on the job, the chief keeps track of his hours, doing private work after hours or while on vacation, using his own instruments and equipment.

In truth, such a division of time and resources between public and private is great in theory but it is not real. The day job is what enables the forensic doctor to be "beautiful" for the night job. The aura of one meshes with the aura of the other, and, in reality and over time, the resources of one will eventually mesh with the activity of the other.

This public/private problem also leads to peculiar behavior from the impressive and emphatic forensic doctor who is also a chief medical examiner. The doctor often does not look at his consultation cases the same way he does his day-to-day cases. Often, the expert will jump to conclusions—reasoning backward like Sherlock Holmes—in a way that he would never do on his day job. Of course, the master is different for each activity: the doctor will be biased for the state or county government during duty hours, and he will be biased for the outside client in his consultation cases.

"But doctors are not supposed to be biased!" you might say. "Aren't doctors supposed to be scientists who look at the facts and apply science to them, allowing jurors to understand the science?"

Too often, that is not how it works.

If doctors were to listen to witnesses and use physical evidence clues and their knowledge of science to test those witness accounts, then it would not matter if a doctor is biased or not. The emphasis is factual—on what a witness said and what the clues show—and not on belief—on what a forensic doctor believes the train of events were that led to the physical evidence clues. It is not easy to argue with facts because everyone can see and know the facts. On the other hand, if a doctor crafts a theory for complicated past events, then bias will lead the doctor to accept one complicated theory over another. The forensic doctor will accept the complicated theory that will help the person paying him.

Often it is the chief who keeps track of his own time. The government ignores what the chief is doing as long as there is no problem; however, when there is a problem, everything changes.

Look what happened to Dr. Richard Callery, formerly the Delaware Chief Medical Examiner.

The News Journal (Wilmington, DE), October 2, 2015: Ex-Chief Medical Examiner Gets Probation[1]

Delaware's former chief medical examiner was sentenced to about a year probation Friday for using state workers and equipment to run his private consulting business.

Dr. Richard T. Callery, who headed the state Office of the Chief Medical Examiner for two decades, also must pay $100,000 in restitution for using the employees and supplies to run a private consulting business that did work in Rhode Island and other states. Callery, 62, spoke for nine minutes during the hearing, first thanking state police and prosecutors for treating him well during the investigation—despite prosecutors having asked that he receive prison time.

He also apologized to his wife and three sons, who were in the courtroom, as well as friends and former employees who were affected by his misconduct.

"I am remorseful," Callery said at his sentencing hearing. "I was sloppy, and I didn't use common sense."

Callery, who was prepared to pay the restitution Friday, was advised by his attorney not to comment following the hearing. But his attorney, Dan Lyons, said, "it was a fair sentence."

Callery also will tender his medical license, but the state medical board will decide if he keeps his license, Lyons said.

Over a four-year period ending in December 2013, Callery used several state employees, including an administrative aide, histologist, medical transcriptionist and at least one morgue assistant, as well as his state car, histology slides, histological equipment and paper, prosecutors said.

A state police probe that begun in early 2014 found Callery engaged in a pattern of behavior that "constituted the criminal misuse of state personnel and resources," prosecutor Joseph Grubb wrote in court documents, but poor

> record-keeping hampered the state's ability to determine the extent of his misdeeds.
>
> Instead, the state found that Callery committed the lesser crime of official misconduct because he illegally "performed official functions in a way intended to benefit his own property or financial interests."
>
> Grubb wrote Callery "failed to properly segregate his personal and professional business."
>
> "Delaware always came second to his private practice," Grubb said during the Friday hearing, in which he asked Superior Court Judge Fred S. Silverman to exceed the sentencing guidelines and imprison Callery. Silverman declined to imprison Callery, saying that if prosecutors wanted him to go to prison they should have worked that into the plea agreement or charged him with something else.

At this point in the story, there is a question that may pop up in your mind: If Dr. Callery had been doing this for four years and had been doing it as badly as claimed, how is it possible that government officials in Delaware did nothing about this? Who was supposed to be overseeing the activity of Dr. Callery?

Well, government officials, particularly prosecutors, are happy with the impressive and emphatic chief as long as everything is running smoothly and there is no hint of a scandal. On the other hand, if it is discovered that under Dr. Callery's watch there was widespread theft of illicit substances from the evidence room—substances that were supposed to be used as evidence in court for drug cases—then everything changes.

> Callery lost his $198,500-a-year state job as a state probe focused on thefts of painkillers, heroin, cocaine, and other illicit substances from the drug laboratory's evidence room. He was not involved in the thefts from the drug lab that has left the state court system reeling.
>
> The state has spent $1.6 million to send drug evidence to an out-of-state lab and prosecutors dropped or reduced charges in 700 cases. Yet because oversight and controls were lacking, the state has been unable to hold anyone directly accountable for the thefts and tampering. Two lab employees were charged with felonies, but pleaded to lesser misdemeanors and had other charges dropped.

That impressive chief with the outstanding reputation and credentials may be so consumed with his private practice that he overlooks the mundane administrative matters of his day job—mundane matters like exercising oversight and control, writing and enforcing office policies and procedures, and holding employees accountable for workplace activities.

Dr. Callery is not the only chief to double dip. Consider the next news story involving a former chief medical examiner of the State of Georgia.

The Atlanta Journal-Constitution, October 3, 2015: Outside Work Challenges Medical Examiner's Credibility, Judgment[2]

Dr. Kris Sperry took the witness stand, exuding the full authority and credibility of the state of Georgia.

Without hesitation, the chief medical examiner testified that Henry Glover died from a bullet to the back, fired by a high-powered rifle. "Any competent forensic pathologist," Sperry said, would see the evidence the same way.

But Sperry hadn't examined Glover's body. He hadn't studied the bullet, because none was found. And his opinion, like a surprising number of others he presents in court, was far from unanimous.

Sperry wasn't even testifying in Georgia. On Aug. 29, 2013, he was in New Orleans, appearing as an expert witness against a former police officer accused of murder after Hurricane Katrina. For stating his opinion that day, Sperry earned a fee of $5,000.

It was one of more than 500 cases since 2003 in which Sperry acted as a paid forensic consultant—all while employed full time by the Georgia Bureau of Investigation.

Sperry's role as expert-for-hire doubles his $184,000 state salary and often takes him out of the medical examiner's office at GBI headquarters. It also exposes him to conflicts of interest and, at times, undermines his medical and scientific judgment, an investigation by The Atlanta Journal-Constitution found.

The newspaper examined court filings, depositions and trial transcripts from more than five dozen cases. Time after time, lawyers and other adversaries accuse Sperry of tailoring conclusions to suit his paying customers.

"He's a hired gun," said Rick Simmons, the defense attorney in the New Orleans case.

"It's about money," said George McGriff, another lawyer who challenged Sperry.

Sperry, 60, the chief medical examiner since 1997, oversees investigations into thousands of deaths each year: homicides and suicides, as well as those from accidents or natural causes. An opinion from Sperry or one of his 13 deputies can have profound consequences. Whether a killer faces charges or whether an insurance company pays a deceased person's beneficiaries may hinge on the medical examiners' conclusions.

Sperry, though, gives the impression of a detached, somewhat eccentric scientist lost in his work. He indulges an academic fascination with tattoos and sports facial hair invariably described as walrus-like. And yet he is so aware of his status as an expert witness that he can immediately cite how many times he has testified in court (704 on Oct. 31 last year, for instance).

Sperry is "a doctor of national reputation and accomplishment," said his boss, GBI Director Vernon Keenan. "He operates on an extremely high plane of expertise."

Sperry declined to be interviewed.

In a memo to Keenan about the Journal-Constitution's inquiry, Sperry said he remembers few details about his work outside the GBI. When those cases conclude, he told Keenan, he shreds his files.

Keenan dismissed criticism of Sperry as "the back and forth of professionals."

But in the New Orleans case, for one, four other pathologists attacked Sperry's conclusions as relying on supposition, not sound forensics. One called his theories on Glover's death "junk science."

"Are there people who go out and stretch the truth for the benefit of their private business? Yes," said Dr. Vincent DiMaio, the longtime medical examiner in San Antonio, Texas, and the author of several influential forensic-science books, who criticized Sperry's work in New Orleans. "Usually, these are not people who are employed as medical examiners."

For reviewing documents and writing reports, Sperry bills his clients $500 an hour. Depositions run at least $1,500. For courtroom testimony, he charges $7,500 a day, (up from $5,000 two years ago), plus travel expenses.

No professional organization or government agency regulates such rates. But interviews with other pathologists suggest Sperry's fees—like his caseload—rank among the highest in the country.

"Some people make a lot of money because they're good," said Dr. Steven Karch, a pathologist in Oakland, California, and a frequent expert witness. "Some make a lot of money because they hustle and do a lot of cases."

Either way, Sperry's private caseload rivals that from his state job.

He appeared in court 13 times as the state medical examiner between 2010 and 2014—and 42 times as a private expert. He performed 208 full autopsies for the medical examiner's office while accepting 158 outside cases for review.

Sperry is like any other hourly worker in state government, Keenan said: he puts in 40 hours each week, "either actually at work or in a combination of work and leave."

"After that," Keenan said, "it's his free time."

At times, however, Sperry conducts private business on the public's time.

The Journal-Constitution examined Sperry's weekly time sheets for the past five years. On 67 days, Sperry reported working at least eight hours for the state when, according to other documents, he spent time out of the office giving depositions or testifying in court for private clients.

On 13 of those days, Sperry recorded a full day at the GBI but actually was in court out of state.

For example, Sperry testified as an expert witness in Charleston, West Virginia, on Jan. 10, 2013. But his time sheet showed nine hours at his state job: 8:30 a.m. to 6 p.m., with 30 minutes off for lunch.

A GBI review prompted by the Journal-Constitution's inquiry found numerous inaccuracies in Sperry's time sheets, Keenan said last week. The agency docked Sperry 226 1/2 hours—about 5 1/2 weeks—of vacation time and other accumulated leave to make up for the discrepancies.

> Sperry signed the time sheets beneath a warning that false statements violate the law. The penalty is one to five years in prison.
>
> Keenan said Sperry often filled out the forms late and from memory. "I have no doubt this was a result of sloppy record keeping."

Six days following that article, the Atlanta Journal-Constitution released a follow up article, announcing the abrupt retirement of the chief.[3] Georgia Bureau of Investigation Director Vernon Keenan remarked about how "acutely embarrassed" and "remorseful" Dr. Sperry was. Keenan said that the decision to retire was Sperry's. "I respect his decision, of course," remarked the director.

What are we to make of this? Here is what I think.

The fascination with Sherlock Holmes and colorful characters like him lives on. We all want someone smart to tell us what happened, so we willingly listen to and accept double-dipping forensic doctors who prey on that need, who provide past event theories from physical evidence clues as if they are reading tea leaves. We continue to be impressed by their credentials, without understanding the content of what they say and why they say it. We continue to be drawn by personalities and not by facts.

Isn't it time to wake up and see what is going on? Shouldn't judges and government leaders recognize the overarching importance placed on the theories and testimonies of blind guides?

No one can claim to be unbiased. Being biased is part of being human. Still, there has to be logic and science correctly applied at all levels of the justice process; otherwise, injustice will abound.

Now, it is time for my personal "I Have a Dream" statement.

I have a dream that one day the following words will be displayed on courtroom walls in plain sight of all judges who admit evidence and all scientific witnesses who offer testimony:

> *The Inferential Test:* One can be reasonably certain if witness accounts of the past are consistent or not consistent with physical evidence in the present, but one cannot reliably surmise past events from physical evidence unless there is only one plausible explanation for that evidence.

I dream that forensic doctors, attorneys, and judges will understand these words. If they were understood, there would be a whole lot less injustice than what we have today. Unfortunately, not many seem to understand—particularly double-dipping forensic pathologists who find it necessary not to understand.

***

The State of Texas introduced their star witness on the morning of the third day.

To his credit, Dr. Robert Lyon, the pathologist who performed the autopsy on Ja'Keen, did not behave like a flamboyant and pompous Spilsbury-like witness. He looked serious, careful, and methodical.

He seemed uncomfortable on the witness stand. I can understand that. The witness stand is not a comfortable place to be, even for an expert. Also, Dr. Lyon may have been aware that I was sitting at the defense table next to the defense attorney by that time. If I were Dr. Lyon, knowing that another forensic doctor was sitting next to the defense attorney and taking notes would also make me uncomfortable.

The district attorney took Dr. Lyon through all the initial steps all experts go through while on the witness stand: The doctor stated his name for the record, explained what he does and where he works, how long he had been doing what he did, his education, his advanced degrees, his specialized training, the examinations he passed, his board certification as a forensic pathologist, his prior work experience, his memberships in specialty organizations, and his published works.

Following all of that, he described his autopsy of the body of Ja'Keen Sanders.

District attorney Coke Solomon inquired:

> When you perform an autopsy and prepare a report, what do you use to make a final determination of the cause of death?[4]

Dr. Lyon responded:

> I take all of the information available to me, including the circumstances of death, the scene of death, and additional studies such as toxicology, looking at glass slides under the microscope, and microbiology. I consider the initial background information provided by someone who knows some information.

Who provided that information? Not any eyewitness:

> A law enforcement officer attended the autopsy and provided me with some information that, as I recall, included that this child was found dead in a motel room with his mother and her significant other.
>
> The child was in bed, and his death looked suspicious. There was a question about whether or not the child became wedged between a table and a bed. The child had eaten a banana. Child deaths are suspicious until proven otherwise.

Attorney Solomon continued:

> So is it general practice to always treat a child death as a suspicious death, to make sure something didn't happen to the kid, to just over-investigate it?

"Yes," Dr. Lyon replied.

I agree with Dr. Lyon about that general practice. Forensic pathologists and other forensic doctors are often taught to "think dirty" about child deaths: to presume negatively until that negative presumption is removed by additional evidence. For centuries, English-speaking courts have afforded the accused a presumption of innocence, but at the outset of his investigation, Dr. Lyon afforded the defendant a presumption of foul play. That doesn't work. As described previously in the chapter "Good Cop, Bad Cop" a *negative* presumption is *not* a good place to start. The logic is simple, but Dr. Lyon and many forensic doctors do not understand logic.

Dr. Lyon described the myriad of injuries he found at autopsy, and all of those findings confirmed his suspicions of foul play and child abuse. There were bruises in the deep tissues of the scalp, bruises beneath the skin in the torso, extensive areas of bleeding in the deep soft tissues of the limbs, a gaping tear in the liver, and blood in the abdominal cavity. His report described the injuries in 11 paragraphs. All of these pointed to abusive blunt trauma as the cause, according to Dr. Lyon.

There were photographs of the injuries. Mr Hurlburt objected to several of these photographs—as defense attorneys often do—because the images were too graphic, too repetitive, and too inflammatory to the jury. The judge overruled that objection—as judges often do—so all photographs were admitted and shown to the jurors.

Personally, I have never had a problem with showing graphic photographs to a jury. The matters they consider are serious, so they should be afforded the opportunity to look at everything that is available, in my opinion. Unfortunately, jurors all too frequently misinterpret what they see and basically draw the same conclusions as forensic doctors.

Dr. Lyon described bruises in the chest in the second paragraph of the "Injury" section of his report. He described a six-by-six-centimeter zone of multiple bruises in the front of the ribcage, each "roughly circular" bruise ranging from "about a half a centimeter to about one and a half centimeters" in diameter.

"Would CPR cause those bruises?" Attorney Solomon asked.

"In my opinion, these bruises are not caused by CPR," Dr. Lyon replied.

> Because the child was dead at the time?
> Yes. And CPR bruises don't have that configuration. CPR bruises, in my experience, are not that numerous, are not scattered like that.
> So these are not just one area where an individual is putting pressure; these are scattered over the chest?
> Right. Right. There are multiple bruises.

According to the doctor, these multiple circular bruises clustered in the center of the chest and even some distance away from the center of the chest cannot be consistent with untrained, "bystander" cardiopulmonary resuscitation or CPR, with perhaps over 1,000 aggressive compressions delivered over 10 minutes by the shifting fingertips and palms of Deterryon Kelly's hands. If they were consistent, that would go against the State's and Dr. Lyon's theory of the death: a theory that had the child dead at the time the CPR was rendered.

Following the description of the autopsy findings, the district attorney played the videos for Dr. Lyon.

"Doctor, as we watch this," the attorney intoned, "based on your medical expertise and your training and your experience as a medical pathologist, if a young child is being swung around, or hit against the wall, or kicked while in that room, could that cause injuries that could have resulted in this child's death?

"Yes," was Dr. Lyon's brief but certainty-filled reply.

> What kind of state would this child be in after a short period of time after sustaining this much trauma and blood loss? Would he be alert, running around, playing like he normally does?
> We would not expect him to behave as a normal child.
> How would he behave?
> Well, he might be crying. He might be becoming unconscious. Might be dying. Might be dead.

Dr. Lyon observed the video recording of the child becoming limp while Deterryon tried to stand him up. Attorney Solomon continued:

> Does the victim appear to be trying to support himself?
> No.
> Does he kind of look limp?
> Yes.
> Is that indicative of an individual who is trying to sleep, or is that more indicative of an individual who has been injured and may be slipping into unconsciousness?
> The latter is my opinion.
> Slipping into unconsciousness?
> Yes.

The attorney showed Dr. Lyon the video of Deterryon throwing the child into the air.

"In a second, we will see him throwing the child through the air," Attorney Solomon continued. "It's a little washed out, but you can look at the shadow. You can see how he's flying all over the place in that shadow."

> Yes.
> Is that indicative of someone who's asleep?
> He looks unconscious, and maybe he's dead.

Your opinion at this point?
That's my opinion.
Thank you, Doctor. You can take a seat.

To sum it up so far, the doctor provided the scientific evidence for the theory developed by the attorneys and the police, and then confirmed that theory in front of a jury. All of this was arguing in a circle—basically with the doctor, prosecutors, and police concluding what they wanted to conclude with little regard for the observations of others outside that circle. They accepted only those observations that supported their theory, and ignored or rejected those that did not.

This, of course, was confirmation bias in full flower—the same problem plaguing all court cases in which a forensic doctor diagnoses past events like a medical Sherlock Holmes.

Notes

1. Parra E. Ex-chief medical examiner gets probation. *The News Journal (Wilmington, DE)*, October 2, 2015. http://www.delawareonline.com/story/news/crime/2015/10/02/ex-chief-medical-examiner-sentenced-probation/73199198/. Accessed on November 12, 2017.
2. Judd A. Outside work challenges medical examiner's credibility, judgment. *The Atlanta Journal-Constitution*, October 3, 2015. http://www.myajc.com/news/news/special-reports/outside-work-challenges-medical-examiners-credibil/nnr8D/. Accessed on November 11, 2017.
3. Judd A. "Embarrassed" medical examiner abruptly retires. *The Atlanta Journal-Constitution*, October 9, 2015. http://www.myajc.com/news/news/public-affairs/embarrassed-medical-examiner-abruptly-retires/nny2m/. Accessed on November 14, 2016.
4. Reporter's Record, The State of Texas vs. Deterryon Tyrell Kelly, Trial Court Cause No. 14-0275X, Court of Appeals No. 06-17-00001-CR. Volume 5.

Modern-Day Sherlocks 15

Journalists and others not involved in the court system have no problem spotting obviously flamboyant, Sherlock Holmes-style doctors.

Dr. Steven Hayne, a pathologist from Mississippi who performed 80% to 90% of criminal autopsies in that state from 1987 to 2008, claimed to have performed 1,500 autopsies per year—essentially more than four autopsies per day every day for 21 years. This would be one and a half times more cases than those claimed by Sir Bernard Spilsbury but over a shorter period of time (31,500 in 21 years vs. 20,000 in 40 years).

In the Cory Maye case, where Maye was alleged to have shot a police officer, Dr. Hayne's testimony was crucial for securing a conviction.[1] The Mississippi doctor could tell from the autopsy that Maye had to have been standing when he shot the officer and not lying on the floor as Maye had claimed.

In the Jimmie Duncan case, Dr. Hayne found bite marks in a body that no other medical professional had found, similar to the way he found bite marks in two previous cases.[2]

In the Tyler Edmonds case, Dr. Hayne concluded that two people had to have fired the same gun at the same time. He did this based on his examination of the gunshot wound in the victim.[3] As hard as it would be to imagine two people shooting the same gun at the same time, it apparently didn't seem that hard for the jury to believe at the time they rendered their verdict.

Flagrantly flamboyant doctors are easy to spot, but most people do not understand that Sherlock Holmes behavior is not confined to only a few odd doctors like Dr. Hayne. It is widespread. Respectable doctors behave like Sherlock Holmes every day, everywhere. You can find them in the news if you know what to look for.

Daily Mail, October 10, 2015: Doctor Whose Blunder Left Couple Accused of Abusing Their Baby Made the Same Mistake Six Years Ago[4]

> A doctor whose mistake led to a couple being wrongly accused of abusing their baby made a strikingly similar error six years ago.
>
> Radiologist Dr. Jo Fairhurst now faces a possible inquiry after lawyers for Karrissa Cox and Richard Carter said yesterday that they will make a formal complaint about her to the General Medical Council.

> Michael Turner QC said Dr. Fairhurst had been an expert witness in more than 1,000 cases of alleged child abuse.
>
> The Mail on Sunday can reveal that their case has strong parallels with that of Matthew Dean and his wife Katie, from Southampton.
>
> They had their baby, Louie, taken away for a year after they were wrongly accused of abuse in 2009. The case also rested on evidence from Dr. Fairhurst, who is based at University Hospital, Southampton.
>
> The Deans' ordeal started with a scan which found blood between Louie's brain and skull. Dr. Fairhurst also believed "there was a healing fracture" of a rib, "suggesting non-accidental injury."

We interrupt this news story for a few comments.

"Non-accidental injury" is a euphemism for child abuse. Child abuse involves a complex series of past events in which a parent or other caretaker during the passage of time decides to do something harmful to a child and performs a series of actions that leads to several injuries.

Dr. Fairhurst is not the only radiologist who "suggests" such diagnoses. These "suggestions" occur all the time in radiologist reports (radiologists are doctors who are specialists at looking at X-rays and other forms of imaging) on both sides of the Atlantic Ocean—in the United States and the United Kingdom—and in many other places. If radiologists fail to make such "suggestions," they may be accused later of failing to report a case in which a child was endangered.

When forensic doctors make comments about the possibility of non-accidental trauma (radiologists in these situations are forensic doctors because their work affects court proceedings), their comments are considered sacred and acted on by the authorities. When the comments later are found to be wrong, the doctors receive the full wrath of the authorities—at least in the United Kingdom.

Let's get back to the story:

> It was only after almost a year of misery that a judge ruled that the blood on Louie's brain was the result of an accident and the rib had never been broken at all. Dr. Fairhurst had misread the X-ray.
>
> Ms. Cox and Mr. Carter's nightmare began when the couple, from Guildford, Surrey, took their six-week-old infant to hospital after noticing bleeding in the mouth.
>
> Dr. Fairhurst saw bruises and what were thought to be fractures, and the child was taken into care.
>
> But experts later found the child suffers from a blood disorder which causes people to bruise easily. And the "healing fractures" were the result of vitamin deficiency.
>
> Dr. Fairhurst said yesterday: "Due to patient confidentiality, I am unable to comment regarding these cases."

We do not know from what we have read if the judge's ruling is correct. In spite of this, one thing is clear: the backward reasoning of Dr. Fairhurst is clearly evident, and we should know by now that backward reasoning is not reliable for getting correct answers.

The Gazette, September 24, 2015: Medical Examiner Testifies to Wounds That Killed Kerry O'Clair Jefferson[5]

> TOLEDO—Either of the two stab wounds to Kerry O'Clair Jefferson's neck could have been the injury that killed her, a medical examiner testified Thursday in the first-degree murder trial of her husband, Dustin Jefferson.
>
> Associate Iowa State Medical Examiner Jonathan Thompson said the autopsy showed two wounds on the left side of O'Clair Jefferson's neck, one that pierced the jugular and the other that went into the esophagus.
>
> The wounds were likely "applied in rapid succession," based on their proximity, he said.
>
> Dustin Jefferson's trial continues Friday in Tama County District Court, with the prosecution expected to wrap up and the defense to start. Jefferson, 38, is accused of aiding and abetting in the killing of his wife.

Notice how Dr. Thompson speculated about an activity that no witness ever observed: the wounds being applied in rapid succession. There are no published case reports or scientific studies that he can cite in which it can be shown that wounds close to each other were likely applied in rapid succession. Still, he was somehow able to testify about this issue because he is a doctor and he did the autopsy. This sounds like the Sherlock Holmes-like expert in Dr. Moritz's article who talks about the right-handed strangler.

The story continues:

> The medical examiner said O'Clair Jefferson also had blunt force injuries to her right eye, forehead and left temple and bruising on her upper chest, hands, wrist and fingers.
>
> Thompson said O'Clair Jefferson had no "classic" defensive wounds, which you might see when victims hold up their arms to block a knife. Dustin Jefferson lowered his eyes when the prosecutor showed the autopsy photos. He has not outwardly reacted during the trial, generally sitting still with his hands on his legs.
>
> Assistant Iowa Attorney General Laura Roan asked Thompson if a victim were physically restrained or unconscious, could that explain the lack of defensive wounds? Thompson agreed it could.
>
> On cross-examination, Tom Gaul, Jefferson's defense lawyer, asked if intoxication could be another reason for the lack of defensive wounds. Thompson said yes.
>
> A toxicology report showed O'Clair Jefferson's blood alcohol level was 0.203. She also tested positive for marijuana and hydrocodone, a painkiller. Thompson said there is no way to determine when O'Clair

> Jefferson last used marijuana because marijuana stays in the body for up to a month. The hydrocodone levels were within legal prescription usage, he said.

Dr. Thompson continued on, not about "defense wounds"—sharp force injuries in the hands of people who ward off a knife attack—but about the *lack* of defense wounds as somehow being meaningful. We might know why someone would have defense wounds, but do we know why someone would *not* have defense wounds? How would anyone know from observation why someone would *not* have something?

Furthermore, having a level of hydrocodone—a narcotic, pain-killing drug—"within legal prescription usage" implies that the victim would behave like someone who was using hydrocodone legally as a prescription drug. That behavior would not seem likely with the high level of alcohol in her system: a substance that would add to the effects of the hydrocodone. Even so, no one could learn how the victim would behave with these levels just from the levels. The levels could be reasonably compared to a witness account for consistency or inconsistency—whether or not what was witnessed is possible or not possible given the levels—but this was never done.

The medical testimony in this case was far from scientific. It was speculation untethered from any witness account.

Meanwhile, defendant Dustin Jefferson sat quietly in the courtroom, not outwardly reacting, sitting with his hands on his legs. The medical examiner was never asked to address Mr Jefferson's account of what happened. We never learn from the news report what the defendant saw or heard. In the end, it would not matter to the jury what the defendant saw or heard. The jury will believe Dr. Thompson before they will believe the defendant. There will be no consequences to Dr. Thompson, even if he gave the wrong answers. Dustin Jefferson, however, will suffer grave consequences even if he never did what he was accused of doing.

Great Falls Tribune, September 21, 2015: Jaraczeski Defense Shifts Blame[6]

> The defense continued calling witnesses in the deliberate homicide trial of Thomas Jaraczeski being held in Chouteau County on Monday.
>
> It aimed to shift blame onto another person and poke holes in the time of death of Geraldine veterinarian Dr. Bryan Rein in July 1996, which was established by the state.

How did they poke holes in the time of death?

> The defense also called its own forensic pathology expert, Dr. Carl Wigren, who provided further analysis regarding Rein's time of death. The doctor who

performed the autopsy on Rein did not include a time of death in his report. He testified there were too many variables to consider.

Wigren used the original autopsy report, notes and photos, along with photos from the crime scene to complete his analysis.

He provided detailed testimony about gastric emptying, the process of food leaving the stomach. The autopsy report showed that partially digested eggs, peppers and tomatoes were present in Rein's stomach when he died. There was no evidence of steak.

Wigren estimated that the steak dinner would have taken nine hours to completely leave the stomach, then he would have had to eat the egg meal after that and give it about two hours to digest to match what was found during the autopsy.

He testified that the level of rigor, or the stiffening of muscles after death, indicated Rein died around 36 hours prior to the autopsy. Wigren qualified that answer by explaining that number was an estimate and can vary from person to person.

The third factor in Wigren's analysis was the rate of decomposition, specifically discoloration caused by bacteria released into the bloodstream due to the gunshot wound to Rein's chest. The bullet damaged internal organs including the stomach.

Wigren compared photos of Rein at the crime scene to autopsy photos, showing the jurors the discoloration present in the autopsy photos. He called the decomposition that occurred in the 24-hour time frame between the photos rapid. Wigren attributed that to his theory that Rein was shot later than Friday, explaining that Rein's body wouldn't look as "freshly dead" in the crime scene photos if he'd been shot Friday night.

"My opinion is that it doesn't seem like a plausible time of death," Wigren said of the state's claim that Rein was shot Friday night.

Determining the time of death from examining a dead body did not originate from peer-reviewed scientific research. The notion that a doctor can determine the "time of death" by examining the body is instead a well-entrenched notion in detective fiction, the kind of backward reasoning that is so popular in these novels. It does not take much to see how complex Dr. Wigren's theory is and how much of a long shot it would be to get the correct answer by what he does.

Akron Beacon Journal, November 13, 2015: Evidence Shows Pregnant Woman was Strangled From Behind in 1985, Examiner Testifies in Scott Purk Trial[7]

Summit County's deputy medical examiner told a jury Friday that victims strangled from behind with a ligature typically have bruises in the lower back.

Dr. Dorothy E. Dean, a forensic pathologist for 16 years, then went a step further.

> Jurors were shown a close-up photo of a Summit County autopsy of a strangulation victim. The man had a bruise in the small of his back, circled with a marking pen, just above the waistline.
>
> That photo was displayed on a courtroom TV monitor to the right of a photo from the 2011 autopsy of Margaret Purk—taken some 26 years after her death was first ruled a suicide by hanging.
>
> "Mrs. Purk had a bruise," Dean told the jury, pumping her index finger in pointing to the photo of the male murder victim, "in the exact same spot."
>
> Dean's testimony appeared to support the central prosecution theory in the trial of Scott David Purk for his pregnant wife's 1985 death.
>
> Prosecutors opened the trial Monday by telling the jury that Purk, now 53, strangled his wife from behind with a belt, then set up the scene to make it look like she hung herself from a stairway railing at their Timber Trail apartment in Akron.
>
> In a detailed narration of her autopsy findings, Dean stood in front of the bench only a few feet from the jury box.
>
> Bruising to the lower back in strangulation cases is a vital clue to murder, because the assailant, Dean said, "needs something to brace himself from behind" when tightening a ligature around the throat.
>
> Dean told the jury that she saw something else in her findings after Margaret Purk's body was exhumed in September 2011.
>
> "This is very important," she said, pointing to a neck bone, the hyoid, which was removed during the second autopsy.
>
> Although the hyoid was not fractured or bent, it did have bruises to the ligaments on both sides of the horsehoe-shaped bone—typical injuries, Dean said, in strangulation cases.
>
> She did not pass over the prosecution claim that the ligature allegedly used was a belt.
>
> Narrating a photo of Margaret Purk's neck, Dean told the jury that she clearly noticed "pinpoint marks" on the front—marks "that are not consistent with a suicidal hanging," she said.
>
> Prosecutors said those marks were made by the belt stitchings.

Dr. Dorothy Dean examined a body that had been previously autopsied, handled by morgue staff, handled by funeral home directors, embalmed, casketed, and left underground to be altered and discolored by mold and other microorganisms for 26 years. From that exhumed body, she detected subtle clues: a bruise in the lower back that had to have been made by a strangler, and pinpoint marks consistent with having been made by stitches from the belt used to strangle the poor woman. She compared the bruise in the back from a previous strangulation case and used that evidence in a novel and strange way: because the bruise in the exhumed body of Margaret Purk was "in the exact same spot" as the other strangulation victim, she also had to have been strangled. All of this is like a far-fetched Sherlock Holmes story.

The prosecutor, however, was not content to let one backward-reasoning doctor tell the tale. He also used another doctor to confirm Dr. Dean:

> After Dean's testimony, prosecutors then presented an analysis of her findings by a second forensic pathologist, Dr. Dean Hawley, director of the pathology department at the Indiana School of Medicine in Indianapolis.
>
> Hawley said his conclusion from reviewing both sets of autopsy photos and reports was the same as Dean's. The cause of Margaret Purk's death was "ligature strangulation" and the manner of death was homicide, he said.

Inventing past-event scenarios from physical evidence is not reliable, no matter how many pathologists can be found who do it. If any of you were to attend a forensic-pathology meeting where autopsy and crime-scene findings of cases are presented, you would hear a wide variety of scenarios offered by multiple pathologists for the same evidence. Doctors who reason backward are not reliable, but there are plenty of them. All the prosecutor has to do is to find some willing expert with great academic credentials to agree with his theory. Experts like this are not hard to find. When one is found, the jurors think that this kind of confirmation is special and meaningful.

What about the pathologist who did the original autopsy in 1985?

> The original autopsy was done by a physician from the coroner's office, Dr. Roberto Ruiz, who was not trained in the science of forensic pathology.
>
> Hawley said the first autopsy was "tainted," because Ruiz only referred to the hyoid bone in his report, without actually examining it.
>
> Dean's conclusion about the bruising to the hyoid ligaments, Hawley said, is "definitive proof" of ligature strangulation.

Note the arrogance: as if to say, "My credentials are better than his credentials, so you should believe me and not him." Dr. Hawley uses words like "definitive proof" to be persuasive in a way that is beyond reasonable and scientific. He claimed to know how the autopsy pathologist in 1985 did not examine a neck bone, but Dr. Hawley was not present at that autopsy to witness what he claimed.

Finally, at the end of the news account, we learn a little more information, but very little.

> When Margaret Purk died, she was 24 and due to give birth to her first child within days. The baby was still born during a C-section, according to testimony, after she was transported to St. Thomas Hospital.
>
> She died a short time after that.

We know very little about the pregnant mother from this story. Was she depressed? Did she tell others that she wanted to kill herself? Had she ever attempted to kill herself? Was the hanging a complete surprise to those who were present at the time, or was this the almost anticipated outcome of someone who was profoundly depressed or disturbed? What did Dr. Ruiz know about the case at the time? We never find this out from the news account, nor do we ever find out much of anything that would tell us even what would likely happen.

Throughout all of this, no one seems to realize how difficult a task it is to strangle someone and then to make the death look like a suicidal hanging. It is difficult for one person to strangle another and then to prop up the body by himself to stage a hanging. When perpetrators do this, it is easy for investigators to spot and suspect from all the physical evidence left behind, including autopsy evidence; yet somehow, it took an exhumation autopsy 26-years later to disclose something that the ill-trained Dr. Ruiz and police investigators missed in 1985.

How much longer will it take before the public sees that this is silly science perpetrated by highly-credentialed but foolish forensic doctors? Maybe 26 more years?

The Wilson Times, November 6, 2017: State Rests Gregory Parks Murder Case on Pathologists' Testimony[8]

Not only can Sherlock-style forensic pathologists do what they do with dead bodies that have been underground for 26 years, but they can also determine what happened from bloodstains at the scene and no body.

> GREENVILLE—Experts in forensic pathology testified Monday that the state's evidence led them to a conclusion: Isabel "Chaveli" Palacios suffered a significant amount of blood loss.
>
> That blood loss, experts said, was enough to require medical attention.
>
> Dr. Mary Gilliland and Dr. Karen Kelly testified they were able to render that opinion based on years of medical experience, including crime scenes and autopsies, even without a body to examine in the case.
>
> "The victim would have required medical attention very quickly," Kelly told jurors.
>
> After two weeks of multiple witnesses, the state rested its case Monday in the murder trial of Gregory Parks, who prosecutors say kidnapped and killed Palacios. The 20-year-old was last seen at Parks' Wilson home on July 31, 2015. No one has seen nor heard from her since. Police have never recovered her body.
>
> Parks, 58, has told police Palacios walked away from his house that day. He has denied any involvement or knowledge in the young mother's disappearance.

One of the doctors described the bloodshed and claimed that the blood loss was "significant."

> Wilson County Assistant District Attorney Joel Stadiem questioned Gilliland as she explained her opinion to jurors Monday morning. Gilliland said certain small spots of blood on portions of the wall inside Parks' bedroom is what's known as "castoff." She said that means that something with blood on it was flicked on the surface, causing the pattern.
>
> She also testified that the blood on the candlestick had a "transference" pattern, meaning something bloody touched the candlestick.
>
> Gilliland described the stains on the hallway bathroom cabinets as blood drop and the shower door had a blood "smear."
>
> She said the blood found on the hamper, which was found inside Parks' half-bathroom in the master bedroom, could have also been a result of transference. But the bloodstains on the purple bathmat and carpet padding, which investigators found in an outside trashcan, represent a "significant amount of blood" loss.
>
> But could those medical experts measure the amount of blood?
>
> That was one of the questions Parks' defense attorney, Tom Sallenger, spent some time on during cross-examination. He argued that both doctors rendered their opinions based only on photographs and neither went to the scene of the home, nor did they physically examine the items police collected.
>
> He also argued that the pathologists couldn't determine how much blood loss there was from photographs.
>
> Gilliland said they can only estimate.
>
> "How can you measure if it's dried blood?" Sallenger asked.
>
> Gilliland said she couldn't, but she could compare the scene to her past experiences.
>
> "I've seen bloodshed," Gilliland snapped back.
>
> Sallenger said if they added up every (blood) "dot" on those photographs, the total would only amount to a thimble of blood.
>
> Gilliland said what made the biggest impression on her and her opinion was the "volume" of blood on the purple bath rug and carpet padding.
>
> Sallenger also asked Kelly how she knew Palacios didn't seek medical attention. She said there was no record of medical treatment from law enforcement.
>
> "The same people who have said she's deceased and they can't find a body?" Sallenger replied.

Dr. Gilliland used terms like "castoff" and "transference" in her testimony. These are terms forensic scientists use with bloodstain pattern analysis.[9] Bloodstain evidence from a crime or death scene can be effective, *if* it is compared to witness accounts for consistency or inconsistency. A doctor can listen to a witness account and tell if the bloodstains line up or do not line up with that account; however, bloodstain pattern analysis can be a disaster if doctors use it to develop past event theories, to "surmise past events from physical evidence." Terms like "castoff" and "transference" are categories, and those category names imply the behaviors that led to those stains; in other words, both doctors engaged in "categorical intuitive deduction" by surmising the past events that led to the bloodstain patterns. I have often compared witness accounts to bloodstain evidence in cases I have studied. What I have found is that bloodstain-evidence categories often oversimplify what witnesses actually describe.

Doctors Gilliland and Kelly may claim expertise on the basis of "years of medical experience" ("I've seen bloodshed," Gilliland snapped back), but they can't claim the experience of a witness who actually watches the bloodshed take place. Their "years of medical experience" simply amount to "categorical intuitive deduction" performed repeatedly.

Dror IE, June 8, 2020: Cognitive and Human Factors in Expert Decision Making: Six Fallacies and the Eight Sources of Bias[10]

This is not a news article; rather, it is an article by an eminent neuroscientist who studies the forensic sciences. Many like Dr. Itiel Dror believe that problems with forensic doctors and scientists boil down to bias.

Dr. Dror rightfully points out that bias—the tendency we all have to prefer one inference from evidence over another—affects all of us. Essentially, to be human is to be biased.

Forensic medicine and science involve more than testifying in court. More often, forensic scientists and doctors spend their time investigating cases. Bias, as Dr. Dror rightfully points out, can lead to misdirection in an investigation. Even a toxicologist—as objective as the science of toxicology may be—can still prefer the wrong choices for identifying a drug or poison because of bias.

Perhaps the problem with modern-day Sherlocks is bias: something we ultimately can't control for which there may be no easy solution.

I don't think so.

Regardless of our biases, surmising complex past events from physical evidence like Sherlock Holmes is doomed to fail. This is not what I think; this is a fact. Past events are exceedingly complex and variable, much more than the choices available to a toxicologist or any other forensic scientist following leads in an investigation. Why should any of us think we could correctly determine something as complicated as "what happened?"

On the other hand, comparing witness accounts to physical evidence in a forward fashion vastly reduces the potential for bias. There are two reasons I can think of: first, since witnesses supply the complex past events, we are not faced with innumerable choices. Secondly, the choice of "consistent" or "not consistent" is binary: it is either "yes" or "no."

Undoubtedly, we might prefer one binary choice over the other, but detailed accounts from more than one witness make it difficult to make the wrong choice. Selecting the wrong answer leads to contradictions: conclusions readily falsified by the rest of the evidence.

Maybe there is no easy solution to the innate problem of bias, but I believe there is an easy solution to what is valid, or invalid, for a declaration of certainty from the witness stand. That easy solution is the Inferential Test:

> One can be reasonably certain if witness accounts of the past are consistent or not consistent with physical evidence in the present, but one cannot reliably surmise past events from physical evidence unless there is only one plausible explanation for that evidence.

***

In the famous detective novel, *Murder on the Orient Express*, Dame Agatha Christie's retired Belgian detective and supersleuth, Hercule Poirot, uses his great powers of observation and his keen understanding of the human mind to solve the mystery of who stabbed to death his neighbor in the next berth on the train. Accompanying him in his investigation and eventually providing scientific confirmation for his theory is Greek physician, Dr. Constantine.

With any murder in which a body is discovered, a doctor must determine the time of death. In detective novels, the time of death is never disputed because it is scientific. A friend of Poirot's introduces him to the doctor[11]:

> There is worse to come. Dr. Constantine—I forgot, I have not introduced you. Dr. Constantine, M. Poirot.
>
> The little dark man bowed, and Poirot returned the bow.
>
> Dr. Constantine is of the opinion that death occurred at about 1 a.m.
>
> "It is difficult to speak exactly in these matters," said the doctor, "but I think I can say definitely that death occurred between midnight and two in the morning."

Further scientific confirmation for that opinion occurs later in the story.[12]

> From the breast pocket he brought out a gold watch. The case was dented savagely, and the hands pointed to a quarter past one.
>
> "You see?" cried Constantine eagerly. "This gives us the hour of the crime. It agrees with my calculations. Between midnight and two in the morning is what I said, and probably about one o'clock, though it is difficult to be exact in these matters. *Eh bien*, here is confirmation. A quarter past one. That was the hour of the crime."

On the third day of the Kelly trial, Dr. Justin Morris testified after Dr. Lyon. Dr. Morris was an emergency department physician for the Good Shepherd

Medical Center in Marshall at that time. He provided care to Ja'Keen on the morning of his death.

"Do you remember the state of that child when the kid came in?" inquired District Attorney Coke Solomon.[13]

"Yeah. He was not breathing, no spontaneous respirations. He did not have a pulse. I could not detect any vital signs. He did not respond to any kind of external stimulus," the doctor responded.

> Okay. So for all intents and purposes, in laymen's terms, what does that mean?
> That would be a dead child.
> So when the kid came into the ER, at that point, he was already deceased?
> In my opinion, yes.

Dr. Morris then described a critical observation of the dead body following Attorney Solomon's next question:

> Did y'all take the child's temperature?
> Yes.
> Do you recall what the temperature was?
> It was in the low 80s. I believe it was 80 degrees; 84 or 80 degrees were the two numbers I recall.

The attorney had the doctor consult the medical record, and the doctor confirmed a recorded temperature of 80.0°.

The attorney asked more questions: "What's the normal temperature of a child?"

> 98.6 is what we consider to be normal.
> Okay. So how many degrees below normal was the temperature of this kid?
> 16.
> Do you know how long it takes for a body temperature to drop to that?
> I believe it is, on average, about one degree per hour.
> Okay. So it could potentially be 16 hours…
> I'm not sure exactly…
> We're talking about in a vacuum?

In a vacuum?

"I'm sorry?" the doctor replied.

The attorney tried to explain: "In a vacuum, where it's just one degree an hour?"

> I'm not sure exactly about one degree an hour, but there is a steady decline in temperature after death, and that's been proven. That one degree drop per hour that I'm quoting may not be accurate, but it takes hours to get to a body temperature of 80 degrees.

> Are there any other external factors that could cause that to decline or speed up?

"That" refers to the change in body temperature over time.

> If someone was submerged in water in a cold environment, if someone is hypertensive, if there is blood loss, if a patient is in shock, then the core body temperature can drop quickly.

Mr. Solomon then made reference to the digital readout of a temperature from the air conditioner seen in the sex video:

> If you were told that the room temperature in the hotel was about 66 degrees and the kid was not covered by blankets, would that have caused the child's temperature to decrease a little faster?
> I wouldn't think so.
> "Young child, small, not stocky? Possible or not possible? You don't know?" continued Attorney Solomon.
> Yeah. Well…that's not something that we were trained in, so…
> You don't have any expertise in how fast or slow the body temperature could drop?
> Right.

The doctor's admitted lack of expertise did not prevent him from offering the opinions that follow. The attorney set up the question:

> Now, when you looked at the child and you looked at the temperature measurements and things of that nature, were you able to make a determination, based on the state of the child when he came in, as to how long that child may have been deceased?
> Not an accurate one.
> Well, based on your expert medical opinions, what would be a fair guesstimate?
> I would say well beyond several hours.

The doctor didn't stop with his inexpert expert opinions on body temperature. He also viewed the videos, just as Dr. Lyon had.

"Something had happened in that vending room. The child walked in on his own but was not able to walk out on his own," Dr. Morris opined.

Mr. Solomon: "Does it appear that the kid is able to support himself?"

> No.
> Does it appear that the kid's even conscious?
> No.

Did you see the part where he was throwing the kid up in the air, and he was doing the flips and all that kind of stuff?
Yes.
Could you make that out on the laptop?
Yes.
Based on your medical expertise and the fact that you've had kids and you've been a parent, does it surprise you that there's no reaction out of that kid?
Yes.
Do you believe that a kid that's just asleep, getting thrown up in the air like that, would he wake up or stay…
No. He would wake up. There would be a response.
Did it appear that this kid had some form of response after that happened?
Yeah. I did not see a response.
Thank you, Doctor.

Attorney Richard Hurlburt cross-examined the witness:

So, Doctor, you feel that his lethal injuries occurred in the vending room?
Yes.
You believe he was dead when he was thrown into the air?
I can't make that determination from the video.
But soon thereafter?
Well, by the time he arrived in my emergency room, yes, he was dead.
And you said—I think you said that he had been dead for several hours; is that correct?

The doctor responded affirmatively.

"Now," continued Attorney Hurlburt, "tell the ladies and gentlemen what rigor mortis is and what lividity is."

Rigor mortis is stiffening of the muscles. Lividity is a color change of the skin. Basically, these are laymen's terms for signs of death.
And you didn't see rigor mortis in this child, did you?
No.
Because you would have noted it if it were present, correct?
We would have.

Let me interrupt with this side note: please keep in mind that *rigor mortis*—a term in Latin for the stiffening of the muscles after death—and *livor mortis* or lividity—the settling of noncirculating blood with gravity—occur much quicker after death in a small child than in an adult. Also, the decline in body temperature after death—referred to in Latin as *algor mortis*—also occurs much quicker after death in a child than in an adult if…*if*…the child was dead.

"Now, what is PEA?" continued Mr. Hurlburt.

> Pulseless electrical activity.
> And tell the ladies and gentlemen of the jury what PEA is.

Dr. Morris went on to describe a situation where electrical activity in the heart continues but the heart muscle does not contract: "The heart can actually stop beating, but there's an electrical signature that we can pick up either with an EKG or the monitor in the room. The electrical activity makes it look like there is a heartbeat, but there's actually no work being done by the heart."

> So it's trying to work, but it's just not working, correct?
> Correct.
> And you said in your records there was PEA upon arrival to the emergency room, correct?

The doctor was caught off guard: "I would have to review that."

> "Well, go ahead," encouraged the attorney. Let me show you the record. May I approach, Judge?"

The judge gave his permission. Doctor Morris responded: "That actually says pre-hospital course."

"Okay," continued the attorney. "So he presented with PEA?"

"Uh-huh," replied the doctor affirmatively.

> What does that mean? He had PEA rhythm; is that correct?
> Yes.
> And PEA rhythm could not possibly be there after he had been dead for several hours. Would you agree with that?

Don't expect any forensic doctor to agree with anything on the witness stand that would show he made a serious mistake.

"Not necessarily," replied the doctor.

> You don't agree with that?
> No.
> You think someone could still have PEA activity after being dead for several hours?

Stop for a moment and consider this carefully: the child had no *rigor* or *livor mortis*, items that would be expected in a small child who has been dead for several hours. He also had complex electrical activity occurring in the heart: delicate proteins in cell membranes allowed the passage of electrically charged ions in and out of cells. With death, such delicate machinery would be wiped out with the chaos that occurs in cells after death. Although PEA can represent a desperate, near-death situation, it is still a vital sign—a sign of life.

The doctor responded to Mr. Hurlburt's question, indicating that PEA could have existed for several hours after death by replying:

> Not necessarily.

"You don't agree with that?" replied Attorney Hurlburt incredulously.

> No.
> You think someone could still have PEA activity after being dead for several hours?
> The heart…I've seen…you know…quite a while after someone is pronounced, still has electrical activity. Kind of like a static electricity discharge sort of idea.
> After being dead several hours?
> That's an—you know, an exception.

Dr. Morris then performed the kind of song-and-dance an expert performs when he has been caught.

> I have seen people with PEA, electrical activity in their heart, when we know that they—when we've pronounced them dead.
> Attorney Hurlburt persisted: "You've seen PEA after someone has been dead for several hours? Is that what you're telling this jury?"
> No. I said that it would be an exception to be several hours.
> Okay. So that wasn't something you would see, right?
> Not on—not on, you know, multiple patients.

Later, the doctor described intubating the child (placing a breathing tube inside the child's airway) and performing a chest X-ray—all on a child who was supposedly dead for several hours. Most emergency medical technicians (EMTs) do not have a problem identifying when a child has been dead for several hours, but Dr. Morris didn't seem to have that skill. He and his staff instead intubate such children and perform chest X-rays on them.

Dr. Morris continued his song and dance: "Like I stated earlier, that's not my training to determine time of death. Our training is to save lives."

Mr. Hurlburt replied: "Well, it's not your training to determine time of death, but you were determining time of death to this jury under oath."

> I was giving my opinion.
> Your opinion based on your training and experience. But you testify as a lay witness and not an expert witness if you haven't been trained. Do you agree with that?
> I'm not understanding the question.

If you have not been trained, then you're not suitable for offering opinions about the time of death to this jury. You haven't been trained in that. Don't you agree with that? That wouldn't be fair.

How so?

Well, it would be like me offering opinions about something I'm not trained in to the ladies and gentlemen of the jury. That would not be fair. Don't you agree with that?

Well, we have experience in treating folks that have been dead, like this case. You don't get to a core temperature of 80 degrees in ten minutes.

Okay.

I may not be the expert on exactly how long it takes for the core temperature to drop, but I have never seen someone ten minutes after they have passed…

Judge, I object. The witness is nonresponsive.

"Overruled," responded the judge.

And so on. The back-and-forth continued during re-direct and re-cross-examinations. At no point did Dr. Morris acknowledge the injustice of what he was doing, of choosing to testify as an expert in an area where he had no expertise, of trying to bluff his way through his testimony like some Sherlock Holmes wannabe. Dr. Morris would suffer no penalty for his failure to "first do no harm"—something for which medical doctors have taken an oath. He would not go to jail for any crime.

Unlike Deterryon Kelly.

Notes

1. Balko R. The Case of Cory Maye. Reason, October 2006. http://reason.com/archives/2006/10/01/the-case-of-cory-maye. Accessed on November 15, 2016.
2. Balko R. Manufacturing Guilt? Reason, February 19, 2009. http://reason.com/archives/2009/02/19/manufacturing-guilt. Accessed on November 12, 2017.
3. Adriano J. Pathologist's work raises questions. Anderson Cooper 360° August 21, 2009. http://ac360.blogs.cnn.com/2009/08/21/pathologists-work-raises-questions/. Accessed on November 12, 2017.
4. Gallagher I, Manning S. Doctor whose blunder left couple accused of abusing their baby made the same mistake six years ago. *Daily Mail*, October 10, 2015. http://www.dailymail.co.uk/news/article-3268007/Doctor-blunder-left-couple-accused-abusing-baby-mistake-six-years-ago.html. Accessed on November 12, 2017.
5. Mehaffey T. Medical examiner testifies to wounds that killed Kerry O'Clair Jefferson. *The Gazette*, September 24, 2015. http://www.thegazette.com/subject/news/public-safety/medical-examiner-testifies-to-wounds-that-killed-kerry-oclair-jefferson-20150924. Accessed January 6, 2016.
6. Fisher-Nitschke A. Jaraczeski defense shifts blame. *Great Falls Tribune*, September 21, 2015. http://www.greatfallstribune.com/story/news/crime/2015/09/21/second-motion-dismiss-jaraczeski-trial-denied/72577776/?from=global&sessionKey=&autologin=. Accessed on November 12, 2017.

7. Meyer E. Evidence shows pregnant woman was strangled from behind in 1985, examiner testifies in Scott Purk trial. *Akron Beacon Journal*, November 13, 2015. http://www.ohio.com/news/break-news/evidence-shows-pregnant-woman-was-strangled-from-behind-in-1985-examiner-testifies-in-scott-purk-trial-1.640245. Accessed on November 12, 2017.
8. Neeley O. State rests Gregory Parks murder case on pathologists' testimony. *The Wilson Times*, November 6, 2017. http://www.wilsontimes.com/stories/state-rests-murder-case-on-pathologists-testimony,102992. Accessed on November 14, 2017.
9. A Simplified Guide To Bloodstain Pattern Analysis. http://www.forensicsciencesimplified.org/blood/. Accessed on November 14, 2017.
10. Dror IE. Cognitive and Human Factors in Expert Decision Making: Six Fallacies and the Eight Sources of Bias. *Anal Chem* 2020;92(12):7998-8004. https://doi.org/10.1021/acs.analchem.0c00704. Publication Date: June 8, 2020. Accessed on November 21, 2020.
11. Christie A. *Chapter 5: The Crime. Murder on the Orient Express.* HarperCollins Publishers LLC, New York, NY, 1934.
12. Christie A. *Chapter 7: The Body. Murder on the Orient Express.* HarperCollins Publishers LLC, New York, NY, 1934.
13. Reporter's Record, The State of Texas vs. Deterryon Tyrell Kelly, Trial Court Cause No. 14-0275X, Court of Appeals No. 06-17-00001-CR. Volume 5.

The Battered Football Player Syndrome 16

American medicine and Hollywood credited a forensic doctor for a major scientific breakthrough. The American Medical Association honored forensic pathologist Bennet Omalu, MD with the Distinguished Service Award in 2016 for discovering chronic traumatic encephalopathy.[1] Hollywood actor Will Smith portrayed Dr. Omalu in the movie *Concussion* presented in theaters in December of 2015.

One Saturday morning in 2002, Dr. Omalu examined the dead body of former Pittsburgh Steeler football player Mike Webster while on duty at the Allegheny County Medical Examiner's Office in Pittsburgh, PA. Webster died in the hospital from what seemed to be natural disease, but Webster's treating physician listed "post-concussion syndrome" as a significant condition on the death certificate. Any mention of injury on a death certificate will trigger the involvement of the local coroner or medical examiner, so Dr. Omalu got to examine the embalmed body of the former professional football player.

Dr. Omalu described the morning of his encounter with Mike Webster in a PBS (Public Broadcasting System) Frontline interview.[2] It was Saturday morning. Dr. Omalu was single, living in a condo at the time. It was his habit to turn on the television news and find out what his workload would be for that day—who was dying and who was killing whom. The news that morning was filled with Mike Webster, a man Dr. Omalu had never heard of.

Dr. Omalu is from Nigeria, where American-style football is not played. He never had any reasonable encounter with football. He thought people who played the game looked and dressed like aliens from outer space. As a child, he wondered why football players had to dress strangely with all of those bulky pads.

The news talked about Webster, how he was once a football star but then deteriorated after retiring. Mike Webster lived as a vagabond and a drug addict. He even had to sell his Super Bowl rings to support his degraded lifestyle. Dr. Omalu wondered why the football player plunged from prominence to this kind of tragic obscurity.

The doctor continued to ponder as he prepared for work. He knew—based on the medical literature and not some kind of "voodoo"—that, more likely than not, Mike Webster deteriorated because of repeated blows to the head suffered by people who play the game of football. Dr. Omalu considered that professional athletes dressed like extraterrestrials who slam into each other constantly must suffer significant head trauma throughout their long, active careers. The repeated trauma justified the need for helmets.

Then, something occurred to Dr. Omalu. Could what happened to Webster be similar to dementia pugilistica?

Older medical literature described a condition called "dementia pugilistica": a problem with the brain noted in boxers. Another forensic pathologist first described this condition in 1928.[3] Boxers during those years were subjected to repeated head injuries without any protective gear. Several of those athletes had traumatic brain damage visible to the naked eye.

What did Webster's brain look like? Prior to the autopsy, Dr. Omalu thought that Mike Webster might have a shriveled up, ugly looking brain similar to a brain with Alzheimer's disease, similar to the brains seen from boxers in 1928; however, upon opening the skull, the doctor found a brain that looked normal. Dr. Omalu was crestfallen. "No, this is a joke," he thought.

There was commotion outside the autopsy suite from members of the media who were trying to get a scoop from Webster's autopsy. Deflated by the lack of findings up to this point, Dr. Omalu began a conversation with Webster's spirit. Omalu asked Mike to prove everyone wrong. Mike needed to show the world how he was a victim of football and how dangerous the sport could be. Mike, wherever he was at the time, needed to help Bennet Omalu.

In spite of the disappointment, "It ain't over till it's over"—like the late Yogi Berra said. Dr. Omalu had more work to do. He placed the brain in a solution called formalin. This hardens the brain and preserves it, allowing it to be examined in greater detail weeks later. While he was waiting for the brain to harden in the solution, he searched the medical literature for something that would help him establish that Webster's career ruined his brain.

Eventually, Dr. Omalu examined the brain and submitted the tissues so that a laboratory could prepare glass slides for examination under the microscope. Technicians in the laboratory cut thin slices of brain tissue, mounted them on glass slides, and stained them with special immunoperoxidase stains. Immunoperoxidase stains involve antibodies attached to enzymes that color abnormal protein collections. Dr. Omalu took the specially stained glass slides from the laboratory to examine under the microscope, but he left them on his desk without looking at them for a couple of months.

He was afraid to look at the slides. The interviewer asked the doctor what he was afraid of. "The unknown," Omalu replied. He didn't want to let Mike down. He was afraid he was going to fail.

His life changed on a fateful Friday night a couple of months later. He was single, so he stayed at work after seven in the evening. While in his office, he pulled out the slides and examined them under a microscope while eating an apple.

Whoa! He had to make sure that the slides belonged to Mike Webster. He saw changes that shouldn't be in the brain of a 50-year-old man, certainly not in a brain that looked normal to the naked eye! There were tangles of abnormal proteins in some of the special immunoperoxidase stains, but those tangles were different from those in Alzheimer's disease. He took the slides home because he knew he needed to spend more time with them.

After further studying the slides, Dr. Omalu was convinced that there was something significant here. His thoughts went into overdrive. What should he do with this?

He knew he had to name it.

This was something that should be published in the medical literature, he thought, but he didn't want to make the mistake of just describing the condition without making it memorable. While attending business school at Carnegie Mellon University, he learned about brand management: how to create brand equity, how to make information a commodity, how to add value to and market a concept. He needed to give the disease a name, something that people can remember, something with a good acronym.

Still, there was the possibility that he might be wrong about what he was seeing and why he was seeing it, so he wanted to choose a name that was general and had descriptive terms. How about this: "chronic" means long-term, "traumatic" means associated with trauma, "encephalopathy" means a bad brain?

CTE. Chronic traumatic encephalopathy. Amazing!

It is amazing that Dr. Omalu chose to be so frank about items like "branding" and turning human disease into a "commodity," but such is the thinking of a Nigerian Sherlock Holmes—someone who looks at clues through a microscope, then comes up with a simplistic explanation for exceedingly complex past events.

You may recall the story of the wannabe Texas Sharpshooter I presented previously. In this case with Mike Webster, do not think of the farmer painting targets around clusters of gunshot holes. Think instead of Dr. Omalu painting a target around a *single gunshot hole.*

Even a savvy promoter and marketer like Dr. Omalu realizes that it takes more than one case to make a disease, just as it takes more than one bullet hole to demonstrate that you can hit the target. He needed to confirm it. He already found a sentinel case to publish. Now, he and his peers needed to find a second case and a third case. With the third case, it becomes a case series that also can be published. He said he learned to do this from epidemiology courses he took in school.

Dr. Omalu took those next steps, and others over the years have been helping him to confirm CTE. Dr. Omalu presented the Webster case at first as a poster at professional meetings, and he eventually published the case in a medical journal in 2005.[4] Seven more cases of former NFL players followed the Webster case, according to a publication from the College of American Pathologists.[5] Other case reports involved a professional wrestler[6] and a 27-year-old Marine veteran from the Iraq war.[7]

Eventually, neuropathologist Ann McKee and her colleagues set up the Boston University Center for the Study of Traumatic Encephalopathy. Family members of football players, professional and nonprofessional, have sent brains retrieved at autopsy to this center for study, adding to a continually growing number of positive cases.

All of this makes for exciting copy in a newspaper or news broadcast. It certainly makes for a dramatic situation of a Nigerian doctor pitted against the powerful National Football League.

In spite of all the confirmation and the movie, Dr. Omalu's idea is still a hypothesis that is not ready for prime time.

How do I know this?

Remember what Dr. Moritz said back in 1956 about Sherlock Holmes-like experts who have a "happy faculty"?

> This Sherlock Holmes type of expert may see certain bruises in the skin of the neck and conclude without doubt that they were produced by the thumb and forefinger of the right hand of the stranger. ... He ignores the essential component for proof of the correctness of any such scientific deduction, namely, the nonoccurrence of such lesions or changes in control cases. Such a pathologist usually has the happy faculty of failing to remember the many similar bruises of necks that were known to have been produced by mechanisms other than pressure by the thumb and fingers.[8]

In the case of the right-handed strangler offered by Dr. Moritz, we could imagine and even wish that Moritz's Sherlock-Holmes-type of expert asked himself at some time before his court testimony, "Are 'certain bruises in the skin of the neck' *only* produced 'by the thumb and forefinger of the right hand of the stranger'? Could other situations have produced those bruises?" Asking those kinds of questions, however, might produce doubt about the expert's otherwise impressive and emphatic testimony: where he says, "without doubt."

What if Dr. Omalu asked himself a similar important question: Do the changes in Mike Webster occur in people with no head injury? We do not know the answer to that question because Dr. Omalu does not tell us. We do not know if he asked it. We do not know if he even looked or if he even thought about it.

Dr. Omalu described Mike Webster in the PBS Frontline interview as a vagabond and a drug addict. He was homeless. He suffered from severe depression. His relationships deteriorated. Sometimes he couldn't find his way home. Couldn't Dr. Omalu find cases involving people who had all of these conditions but no head trauma?

Neuropathologist Ann McKee, Dr. Omalu's source of confirmation mentioned above, does not report doing this. She mentions the brains of 165 football players, but she makes no mention of control cases *not* involving football players that may or may not have the same brain changes. One of her papers from 2009 where she and her colleagues detail findings from three professional athletes and review another 47 cases from the literature makes no mention of such control cases.[9] Control cases would be cases that have the same findings but no head injury.

What about studies where there are stated control cases? What do the results look like?

One study published in December of 2015 presents findings from a brain bank of neurodegenerative disorders at the Mayo Clinic.[10] They reviewed the medical records of 1,721 men for "evidence of past history of injury or participation in contact sports." They processed samples of the brain and performed tau protein immunohistochemistry—tau protein is the microscopic marker for CTE—not only on those cases with a history of sports exposure but also in age- and disease-matched men and women without exposure to sports. The study found problems not only with professional football players but also with people with a "history of injury or participation in contact sports." There didn't need to be any documented head injuries in this study—just a history of "participation in contact sports."

"Age- and disease-matched men and women without exposure" are control cases. The scientists found no cases of CTE pathology in the 198 individuals without exposure to contact sports, even though there were 33 of these cases that had a single-incident traumatic brain injury from "falls, motor vehicle accidents, domestic violence, or assaults."

Consider the following:

- Many of the people who submitted the brains of loved ones to the neurodegenerative brain bank had concerns about that loved one having a brain disorder from his involvement in sports.
- The doctors used immunoperoxidase-stained slides of brain tissue to detect tau protein—the abnormal protein associated with CTE.
- When the results were positive, it confirmed the sports-related issues related to the brain submission in the first place. Those issues were already mentioned in the medical record. If the results were positive in cases not originally thought to be sports-related, further inquiry would be made about sports involvement. A positive history for a positive stain would confirm CTE. It is interesting that "available medical records of 1,721 *men* were reviewed for evidence of past history of injury or participation in contact sports." There is no mention of women in the experimental group. Participation in contact sports among males in our society—particularly during adolescence—is ubiquitous, so positive histories for positive test results would be expected.

- On the other hand, the doctors would expect a negative result with control cases that had no initial documentation of contact sports involvement. No further inquiry would be made about sports involvement with a negative result, so no mention of sports involvement would be seen in those medical records. Sports involvement was not the reason for submitting those brains in the first place. Consequently, we would expect that there would not be a single mention of sports involvement in control cases.

If the condition tested for is already believed to be due to trauma from contact sports, then further testing in the fashion described in that article only confirms what is already believed. This is circular thinking, where what is concluded is already accepted as a premise. Such thinking does not allow the discovery of anything other than what is already believed.

Before an idea is ready for prime time and a Hollywood movie, a wide variety of scientists from many places need to perform numerous carefully designed studies that are published in peer-reviewed journals. Scientific discovery does not involve just one doctor; it also involves a community of peers who try to prove a doctor wrong, who are skeptical about the ideas. This does not mean that they presume negatively. On the contrary, it means they are willing to test the idea with many other cases, including *control cases with the pathologic findings but no previous head trauma*, to see if the idea holds up after much testing.

Most hypotheses in science do not hold up with the passage of time; most are demonstrated to be wrong. The human organism and past events are highly complex and not easily explained by simplistic, scientific-sounding notions.

But this does not stop Dr. Omalu. Where his data is lacking, his imagination fills in. He said the following during an interview for the local news where he lives[11]:

> Now, what do we know about CTE? In every human activity whereby you expose the human skull and brain to repeated blows, with or without helmets—helmets do not prevent this types of injuries—with or without symptoms, with or without reported concussions, or documented concussions. Over time this repeated blows of your head and brain would have an inherent significant risk of resulting in permanent brain damage—sometimes five, ten, twenty, thirty, up to forty years later. And the permanent brain damage is irreversible and could begin to manifest in a very subtle manner—subtle but progressive—with a constellation of symptoms that would include mood disorders, severe depressions, suicidal attempts, bipolar disorders, drug abuse, alcoholism, diminishing intelligence,

> and—much later in life—dementia. So as physicians and pathologists our role really—we are required to provide the accurate information to patients, to parents, to provide the scientific facts and to adequately educate parents and players about the risk of playing, so that when you make a decision whether to play or not to play, you are making an informed decision. …
>
> … We must let parents know that there may not be any symptoms, when a child may suffer injury on a microscopic level that may not manifest with symptoms—that may not manifest as a concussion. That over time, cumulatively, this repeated microscopic injuries that sometimes we call "subconcussions" can accumulate and result in permanent brain damage, so what we advise really, there is no cure—you cannot reverse this disease—there is no cure for a concussion. So the best cure actually is prevention.

Amazingly enough, since his discovery, Dr. Omalu is able to predict what will happen to a person "5, 10, 20, 30, up to 40 years later" even though this has not been observed or measured. Also, the "constellation of symptoms" like "mood disorders, severe depressions, suicidal attempts, bipolar disorders, drug abuse, alcoholism, diminishing intelligence and—much later in life—dementia" may occur without any head trauma. The "constellation of symptoms" are common even without trauma, and retired professional football players can be affected by them too.

Dr. Omalu's interview has a feeling of "deja vu all over again"—another famous saying of the late Yogi Berra. In describing what would later become the shaken baby syndrome, another forensic doctor, Dr. John Caffey, wrote about how subtle whiplash-shaking could be. It was something that repeatedly occurred every day in the United States. The incidence of the problem was unknown, of course, but it was undoubtedly substantial. Such whiplash-shakings might be concealed for years without even arousing the slightest suspicions of educated individuals or even well-trained pediatric doctors. There may be no signs outwardly to suggest a head injury, no trauma to the scalp, skull, or face. Dr. Caffey described whiplash-shaking as "precarious, pervasive, prevalent, and pernicious," occurring in the home, the street, nurseries, schools and preschools, orphanages, day-care centers, playgrounds, shopping centers, and even in the waiting rooms of doctor's offices. Parents who would never think to strike their children in the head might instead give their small children a good shaking. The effects of such jostlings might be cumulative, leading to consequences that might not be seen for many years. Such shakings might be more dangerous than single blows to the head, according to Dr. Caffey.[12]

As Dr. Omalu did, Dr. Caffey built up the number of his whiplash shaking-cases from a few to 27 and more, thanks to confirming cases offered by other doctors. Also as Dr. Omalu failed to do, Dr. Caffey did not use control cases. It took until the next millennium for doctors to realize that many other conditions and situations besides child abuse can produce multiple fractures, subdural hemorrhages, retinal hemorrhages, and brain damage in infants.

As Dr. Caffey did, Dr. Omalu believes that even subtle injuries to the brain of a mild-to-moderate nature may lead to horrible consequences down the road. Also as Dr. Caffey failed to do, Dr. Omalu presents no data to support his strong and self-assured statements. They are a product of his imagination, just as the pernicious, "p"-filled, purple prose of Dr. Caffey was a product of his imagination. Later on, Dr. Caffey was shown to be wrong about mild-to-moderate head injuries leading to horrible consequences like shaken-baby syndrome. The same thing will probably happen to Dr. Omalu with chronic traumatic encephalopathy.

Past events and the human body are both highly complex. A brain examination after death does not explain a lifetime of past events involving such an exceedingly complex and highly organized structure as the brain; still, many forensic doctors think that a brain examination can provide such explanations. After their pronouncements are made, the "science" offered by these forensic doctors is not self-correcting. Mistakes often do not become apparent until many years later, if they become apparent at all. Ideas offered by seemingly brilliant forensic doctors are simply accepted uncritically by the public, and nobody learns anything—especially the forensic doctors.

Before moving on from CTE, we note that Dr. Omalu has been in the news for other matters. One story involves a child-abuse trial.

The Davis Enterprise, October 19, 2016: Neuropathologist Says Davis Toddler Suffered Abuse-Related Trauma[13]

This news article reports on a court trial in which Dr. Omalu described traumatic brain injury in an infant to be like a balloon floating in a bottle: the shaking of the infant smashes the brain against the sides of the skull, just like a balloon striking the inside of a shaken bottle. The brain swelling and bleeding, the retinal hemorrhages, and the bruises in the inner scalp are all part of shaken-baby syndrome, according to Dr. Omalu. "It tells you it's an adult-induced nonaccidental trauma in a child," the doctor testified. According to the article, the shaken-bottle scenario he described appeared in the movie *Concussion*, the movie that sensationalized Dr. Omalu's discovery of CTE.

Another story involves the 2016 campaign for the United States presidency.

Fitsnews, September 13, 2016: Expert: Hillary Clinton Poisoned by Donald Trump, Vladimir Putin[14]

The authors of this article facetiously claim that Dr. Omalu will enter the history books as the originator of one of the most bizarre conspiracy theories of all time. Dr. Omalu took to Twitter to suggest that Hillary Clinton was being poisoned and that toxicologic testing of the presidential candidate should be performed. He tweeted following Ms Clinton's collapse at a 9/11 commemorative event in New York City.

Dr. Omalu, who, according to the article, billed himself as "the world's leading expert in forensic pathology and forensic neuropathology" placed the blame for the alleged poisoning on presidential candidate Donald Trump and Russian president Vladimir Putin. "With those two, all things are possible."

In all fairness, Dr. Omalu never tweeted that he was certain that the former first lady was being poisoned or even that it was probable. He claimed that it was "possible" and should be considered; nevertheless, Dr. Omalu and all forensic doctors need to understand that conspiracy and other conjured-up past event theories—including simplistic notions involving the complex human brain—are possibilities so unlikely that they are not even worth considering.

***

As the testimony phase of the trial continued, Deterryon became more and more agitated. He did not like the way the jurors looked at him. Investigator Reinhart was doing what he could to keep the defendant calm. While I sat between Deterryon and his attorney at the defense table, the defendant wrote me occasional notes, just as I wrote several notes to his attorney during the trial. I responded to Deterryon at one point with a short message: "Don't lose hope."

Deterryon, wherever you are right now, don't lose hope. Eventually, judges, attorneys, and the rest of society will figure all of this out. When they do, your freedom will be restored.

Following the testimony of Dr. Morris, attorney Kristin Kaye examined the lead detective in the case, Sergeant Daryl Griffin.[15] He provided the testimony about the surveillance videos, describing to the jury detailed descriptions of what each video showed. He also explained a DVD video of one of two police interviews of the defendant.

"Tell the jury a little bit about some of your interview techniques," Ms. Kaye requested, prior to playing the video.

> You just talk to him, try to get him to give you the facts. Most of the time, you let them tell you the story. The first time he talks, about 90 percent of it is not true. You catch him in a few lies. You correct those. He has to change, so you go

> over the story again. Each time, you get a little bit more of the truth. In doing so, I can tell him one thing that might not be true to get him to tell me the truth.
> Are you allowed to lie to suspects?
> Yes.
> Do you try to establish a rapport with the person that you're interviewing?

The sergeant continued: "It depends on the circumstances and the mood. Sometimes you have to be stern and get in his face. Sometimes you have to be a best friend."

Ms Kaye then referred to the second interview: "What interview techniques did you use when you conducted the interview of the defendant on May 7?"

> I tried to talk to him with respect and to try to get him to come forward with the truth. When I saw that he was telling some non-truth, then I told some non-truths to get him to come clean a little more. Then I did some checking on some of the statements that he made.

Following a short recess, Ms Kaye played the interview video from May 7: the second interview video.

Then, Mr Hurlburt cross-examined the witness.

> The interviews that were done of Deterryon Kelly and Jameshia Cooks were not taken to the pathologist, correct?

Sgt Griffin agreed, and Attorney Hurlburt continued:

> You talked earlier about getting all the information to the pathologist, correct?
> Yes, sir.
> And—to be fair to him—he did not receive all of the information; is that correct?
> He was told what the defendant's scenario was, where he found the baby.
> But y'all had an interview for almost an hour-and-a-half and then another one for about 30 minutes. Obviously, he wasn't able to see those videos. Would you agree with that?
> Yes, sir.

Mr. Hurlburt later made mention of the Jameshia Cooks interviews.

> You have no reason to believe she was being untruthful to you about anything, correct?
> I don't think so.
> Do you recall her telling you that the baby was tossing and turning after he had brought the baby back in the bed? Do you recall her telling you that…

Immediately, the questioning drew several objections of hearsay from the prosecutor. The judge overruled the objections.

"Do you recall her telling you that the baby was tossing and turning in the bed?" continued Attorney Hurlburt.

> No, sir, I don't.
> Do you recall her telling you that when she got…

More objections of hearsay. "Judge," explained the defense attorney, "It's not hearsay. I'm not offering it to prove the matter asserted. It's the information that he received."

The judge overruled the objection. Mr. Hurlburt continued.

> Do you recall her telling you that the baby was under the covers initially but when she got up to pee that night the baby was not under the covers?
> I recall her telling me that she got up and—yes, sir.
> She told you that at about 6 something in the morning, when she got up to pee again, that her son was not on the bed?
> Yes, sir.
> And that obviously wouldn't be possible if the baby was dead coming out of the vending room, correct?

Detective Griffin then began to sing and dance.

> No, sir.

I'm sorry?" replied the defense attorney.

> No, sir, I—I don't believe that.
> You don't believe that she was telling the truth?
> No. I think she's telling the truth that the baby wasn't on the bed when she woke up at 6:21 in the morning.
> Right, so if the baby was dead coming out of the vending room, the baby wouldn't have been off the bed when she got up at 6 something. Do you agree with that?
> No, sir.
> You think that somebody just got him up and put him on the floor?
> I sure do.
> You do? How do you believe that?
> I believe Mr Kelly, while she was asleep, picked the baby up and placed him on the floor so she would be the one to find him.
> Oh, okay. That's just something that you came up with on your own?

The detective looked uncomfortable. "No. It's just by—by my investigation."

> All right. Do you believe the first time she got up to pee, he took the child out from below the covers and laid him on the bed with the covers not on him?

> I don't know about that.
> If the baby's dead, somebody would have had to do that. Do you agree with that?
> Yes, sir.
> Do you think she did it, or do you think he did it?
> I don't—I don't know.
> Doesn't make sense if he's dead, does it?
> I don't know.
> Pass the witness, Judge.

Ms Kaye continued on redirect examination:

> When you interviewed the defendant, did he have a possible scenario for how the child could have passed away?

Sergeant Griffin responded: "All he would say was that the baby died; it was because he fell between the dresser and the bed."

> Is that possible?
> I don't see that baby falling between the dresser and the bed at all, period.

Ms Kaye followed up: "If the defendant put the baby on the floor, would that be consistent with the story that he gave to y'all with his scenario?"

> Yes.
> Pass the witness.

Richard Hurlburt re-cross-examined.

> Detective Griffin, you didn't put anything in your report about saying, 'I believe Deterryon Kelly put that dead baby on the floor in order for her to find the baby the next morning,' did you?
> No sir.
> That's just something you came up with today.
> No, sir.
> Pass the witness.

Following the testimony of Detective Griffin, the State of Texas rested, and the jury was dismissed. The defense would present their case the next morning to the jury, offering testimony from their sole witness, Dr. Thomas W. Young.

Before that happened, however, the prosecutors asked for a *Daubert* hearing that afternoon. A *Daubert* hearing allows the judge to assess the scientific validity of scientific expert testimony. If my testimony did not pass scientific muster, I would not be allowed to testify before the jury the next morning.

Before the judge, Mr Hurlburt asked me questions regarding my training, education, and experience—the same kinds of questions experts are asked prior to giving testimony. Regarding the Kelly case, I stated that I read and viewed police investigative reports, the videos, the medical records of the child, the autopsy report, autopsy and scene photographs, and the microscope slides from the autopsy.

"Would that be standard procedure for a forensic pathologist for determining cause of death?" asked the attorney.

"That's an important part of it, yes," I replied.

Just tell the Judge the techniques a forensic pathologist uses to determine cause of death.

I turned and spoke to the judge: "Essentially the same kinds of techniques described by Dr. Lyon earlier today. He obtained information about the case about the circumstances, what was seen and heard, about the scene of death—essentially information that would come from outside of the morgue. Also, the pathologist performs an autopsy and looks at various laboratory tests generated from the autopsy, including toxicology tests and a microscopic examination of glass slides. Then it is a matter of synthesizing the whole thing—putting it all together."

> Referring to the autopsy report, is that the kind of report you have seen in many cases in the past?

"Yes," I replied.

> It's very detailed?
> Yes, it is.
> Obviously you heard Dr. Lyon testify today, correct?
> Yes, sir.
> Was there information that he did not have that you had?
> I don't know if it is fair for me to characterize what he knew and what he didn't know. I can only go by what he described. He mentioned learning about the situation with the child being pinned between the nightstand and the bed. He did not describe anything about the resuscitative attempts made by the defendant.

Mr Hurlburt continued: "Detective Grifffin testified that the video statements from my client and Jameshia Cooks, the mother, were not provided to Dr. Lyon."

> That is correct.
> Is that very important to have?
> Any way that you can get as much information as you can is important. The one thing that medical examiners think in the back of their minds—or at

> least I certainly think in the back of my mind—is 'What is out there that I don't know?' This is because what I don't know could embarrass me or cause problems or cause me to get the wrong answer in the end.
> There could be so many variables involved with how something might have occurred. Would you agree with that?
> Certainly.
> So more facts about what people saw at the scene would be very important for your determination. Would you agree with that?
> I would agree.

Attorney Hurlburt continued, "In fact, the more information you have from people who were with the person that died, the better you are able to determine if what they are saying is feasible or not feasible, correct?"

> That is fair, yes.
> It doesn't mean you can determine exactly what happened with that information, but you can determine if what they said happened is plausible or not plausible, agree?
> I agree. The people who were there were the ones who knew what happened. Since I wasn't there, I don't know what happened, but I can read or listen to witnesses and tell if what they said is possible or not possible, consistent with the evidence or not consistent, feasible or not feasible.
> So really, there is no expert who can get up and say, 'What I am saying are the facts of what happened to this person,' correct? An expert can only give an opinion based on the facts he has been given. Would you agree with that?
> Exactly right, yes.
> Earlier, I think you said you used the same scientific techniques that Dr. Lyon testified about in trying to form an opinion from all the information you received regarding this case, correct?
> Correct.
> When I called you and asked you to look at this case, did I ever tell you, 'This is what I need you to say'?
> No. I viewed the items, and then I called you and gave you my opinions.
> Go ahead and tell the Judge this morning what your opinions are that you plan to testify about.

I turned to the judge: "What was described by the defendant in the video was that the child was still alive when he was put to bed at night. The defendant and the child's mother didn't see the child on the bed in the morning, but Mr Kelly found the child between the nightstand and the bed. He pulled the child out and performed CPR, first with the child on the bed and then on the floor. My opinion is if a child like this is between the nightstand and the bed, that child can develop what is called a 'mechanical asphyxia,' which basically means that the child is not able to move his chest wall to breathe. With this, the child cannot receive oxygen. Without oxygen, the child's heart gradually slows down, eventually leading it to stop."

> You had a disagreement earlier today with Dr. Morris about PEA. Tell the judge about that.
> If a child or anybody has a situation where he is deprived of oxygen, his body at first reacts with an adrenaline surge, making the heart pump quickly. If the oxygen remains low and as long as he is not breathing, then the heart pumps slower and weaker to preserve as much of the remaining oxygen as possible. When the oxygen level gets really low, then there is only enough energy to allow the cell membranes in the heart to depolarize in their usual pacemaker fashion but not enough energy to allow the heart muscle to contract. This ends up in a situation of pulseless electrical activity.

I continued: "It makes no sense for a child to have pulseless electrical activity after the child has been dead for several hours or even several minutes. With death, there is no electrical activity of the heart."

Attorney Hurlburt: "So when you heard the doctor testify that you could have PEA after three hours being dead, you find that impossible?"

> That is absurd. Impossible.

I described what a child is like after being dead for several hours, including the *rigor mortis*. Performing an intubation on a child in rigor is problematic because the jaw is stiff and doesn't readily open. On the other hand, if the body is limber and if emergency medical technicians detect PEA, they will perform a full-blown resuscitation, with hopes of reviving a dying but *still living* child. They will "scoop and run"—take the child to the emergency department of the nearest hospital as quickly as possible.

Attorney Hurlburt: "In your experience, when EMTs arrive at a scene and find a body that has been dead for several hours, what do they generally do?"

"They call the coroner or the JP." In Texas, JP means "justice of the peace"—essentially the Texas version of a coroner.

The attorney then addressed the gaping liver laceration: "You would agree that if that kind of liver laceration had occurred in the vending machine room, he would die as a result of it?"

> I think that's reasonable. With that kind of liver laceration, if the child had an actively beating heart, there would be very rapid bleeding. Such lacerations frequently lead to massive blood loss in several minutes.
> Not several hours?
> No.
> Do you feel that your testimony about your findings, after looking at all the information, which is actually more information than what Dr. Lyon had, would your testimony aid the jury in their ultimate decision regarding the cause of the death in this case?"
> I believe that to be the case.
> I'll pass the witness, Judge.

Mr Solomon replied, "Can we have one second, Judge?"

The judge agreed. "That one second" turned into several minutes as the two attorneys went outside of the courtroom to discuss what they would do. Upon returning, the district attorney said:

> Judge, I don't have any questions.
> All right then. Is Dr. Young going to be your first witness in the morning?

"Yes, Your Honor," Mr Hurlburt replied.

> All right then.
> Thank you, Judge.

Mr Solomon: "I mean, just for the record, I'm assuming you're, obviously, finding that he's an expert?"

The judge: "I'm finding he's an expert."

Notes

1. Rosin T. AMA presents distinguished service award to forensic pathologist who discovered CTE. *Becker's Hospital Review*, 14 November 2016. http://www.beckershospitalreview.com/hospital-physician-relationships/ama-presents-distinguished-service-award-to-forensic-pathologist-who-discovered-cte.html. Accessed on November 12, 2017.
2. The FRONTLINE Interviews: Dr. Bennet Omalu (interview by Michael Kirk on 25 March 2013). In: *League of Denial: The NFL's Concussion Crisis*. http://www.pbs.org/wgbh/pages/frontline/sports/league-of-denial/the-frontline-interview-dr-bennet-omalu/. Accessed on November 12, 2017.
3. Martland HS. Punch drunk. *Journal of the American Medical Association* 1928;91(15):1103–1107. doi:10.1001/jama.1928.02700150029009.
4. Omalu BI, DeKosky ST, Minster RL, Kamboh MI, Hamilton RL, Wecht CH. Chronic traumatic encephalopathy in a National Football League player. *Neurosurgery* 2005;57(1):128–134.
5. Put It on the Board: Neuropathologist Dr. Omalu in spotlight at CAP '15. *CAP Today*, 2015 October;29(10):94–93.
6. Omalu BI, Fitzsimmons RP, Hammers J, Bailes J. Chronic traumatic encephalopathy in a professional American wrestler. *Journal of Forensic Nursing* 2010;6(3):130–136.
7. Omalu B, Hammers JL, Bailes J, Hamilton RL, Kamboh MI, Webster G, Fitzsimmons RP. Chronic traumatic encephalopathy in an Iraqi war veteran with posttraumatic stress disorder who committed suicide. *Neurosurgery Focus* 2011 Nov;31(5):E3.
8. Moritz AR. Classical mistakes in forensic pathology. *The American Journal of Forensic Medicine and Pathology* 1981;2(4):299–308.

9. McKee AC, Cantu RC, Nowinski CJ, Hedley-Whyte ET, Gavett BE, Budson AE, Santini VE, Lee HS, Kubilus CA, Stern RA. Chronic traumatic encephalopathy in athletes: Progressive tauopathy following repetitive head injury. *Journal of Neuropathology and Experimental Neurology* 2009 July;68(7):709–735.
10. Bieniek KF, Ross OA, Cormier KA, Walton RL, Soto-Ortolaza A, Johnston AE, DeSaro P et al. Chronic traumatic encephalopathy pathology in a neurodegenerative disorders brain bank. *Acta Neuropathologica* 2015 Dec;130(6):877–889.
11. Interview: Tackling concussions with Dr. Bennet Omalu (transcription from video). *The Sacramento Bee*, October 5, 2015. http://www.sacbee.com/entertainment/ent-columns-blogs/video-break/article37843899.html. Accessed on November 12, 2017.
12. Caffey J. On the theory and practice of shaking infants. *American Journal of Diseases of Children* 1972;124:161–169.
13. Keene L. Neuropathologist says Davis toddler suffered abuse-related trauma. *The Davis Enterprise*, October 19, 2016. http://www.davisenterprise.com/local-news/crime-fire-courts/neuropathologist-says-davis-toddler-suffered-abuse-related-trauma/. Accessed on November 17, 2016.
14. FITS. Expert: Hillary Clinton Poisoned By Donald Trump, Vladimir Putin. Fitsnews, September 13, 2016. http://www.fitsnews.com/2016/09/13/expert-hillary-clinton-poisoned-by-donald-trump-vladimir-putin/. Accessed on November 17, 2016.
15. Reporter's Record, The State of Texas vs. Deterryon Tyrell Kelly, Trial Court Cause No. 14-0275X, Court of Appeals No. 06-17-00001-CR. Volume 5.

17 Tree People and Forest People

It seems that forensic science is up-to-date in Japan. The police in Tokyo, for example, are turning to private companies to help them detect substances to even as little as a quadrillionth of a gram.[1]

Scientists in the United States are also reaching new heights in detection by studying how trace evidence from cell phones can serve as a "fingerprint" for criminal investigations, according to another report.[2] Scientists can detect much chemical information from a cell phone, including molecules from skin creams, hair-loss treatments, medications, foods, and other various and sundry substances. A co-author of the reported study remarked that she could tell if a subject is probably female, uses expensive cosmetics, drinks coffee, dyes her hair, drinks beer or wine, prefers spicy foods, takes medication for depression, and uses insect repellant or sunscreen—indicating, of course, that she spends much time outdoors. Sherlock Holmes has indeed become cutting edge.

With new technologies, evidence detection is now reaching the molecular level. Scientists can measure more and more from less and less.

There is a quip often made about scientists with PhDs: These are doctors who learn "more and more about less and less until they know absolutely everything about nothing."

During my years of residency training in pathology—particularly surgical pathology where doctors examine tumors under a microscope—I often heard from my teachers that "high power microscopists make low power pathologists." A microscope has *objectives*—lenses that magnify what is on the glass slide sitting on the microscope stage. An objective with "high power" may magnify an image by 20 times (20×) or 40 times (40×). If a pathologist were to spend most of her examination time with these higher power objectives, she would miss the context that only an examination of the tissue under a 2× objective could give.

PhD scientists and pathologists may think they are learning more and more from less and less, but they may potentially miss the forest because of focusing intently on the trees. Of course, there may be professionals who wouldn't make those kinds of mistakes, right? Professionals like superior court judges and Supreme Court justices?

A few years ago, while sitting outside of a courtroom waiting to testify, I met a judge who just finished his last day of being a judge. He mused out loud to me. From his perspective in the courtroom—sitting in his chair high above everyone else—he mentioned that lawyers are "tree people" who get mired in the fine detail of a case while failing to see the big picture—the "forest." He said that jurors are "forest people" who want the big picture, but too often tree-obsessed attorneys are not able to provide that kind of big picture.

Although I did not say this to the judge, it seems to me that judges are also "tree people," particularly when it comes to matters of science in the courtroom. This is often reflected in judicial decisions for the use of science in legal cases—decisions like *Frye v. United States* and *Daubert v. Merrell Dow Pharmaceuticals.*

The 1923 *Frye* decision set up the "general acceptance" standard for the admission of scientific evidence: Before the judge allows a scientific expert to deduce from the witness stand.

> ...the thing from which the deduction is made must be sufficiently established to have gained general acceptance in the particular field in which it belongs.[3]

The "thing" often refers to a measurement, a scientific test. In *Frye*, it was the use of systolic blood pressure for the detection of deception. The systolic blood pressure is the higher of the two numbers in blood pressure measurements. James Alphonzo Frye's systolic blood pressure did not rise from fear of the detection of deception while under questioning by a scientist. Frye's attorney offered those measurements as scientific evidence in court that Frye was telling the truth. The judge did not accept blood pressure measurement as a test for deception, so the jury was never allowed to hear the evidence. The appellate court upheld the conviction, stating that the test was not a "thing" generally accepted by physiologists and psychologists.

For 70 or so years, the courts allowed scientists to dictate what was acceptable or not acceptable as evidence according to the general acceptance rule; unfortunately, the courts did not understand that scientists rarely "generally accept" anything. Scientists fight with each other over a wide variety of matters, including what is true and not true, what is reliable and unreliable.

The United States Congress in 1975 broadened the role of science in the courtroom by enacting Federal Rule of Evidence 702:

> If scientific, technical, or other specialized knowledge will assist the trier of fact to understand the evidence or to determine a fact in issue, a witness qualified as an expert by knowledge, skill, experience, training, or education, may testify thereto in the form of an opinion or otherwise.

Scientists even many years before 1975 made regular appearances in the courtroom as experts, educating the "trier of fact"—the jurors and sometimes the judge who assess the facts in a case—with the science needed to make crucial decisions about the case.

The case of *Daubert v. Merrell Dow Pharmaceuticals* in the early 1990s put Rule 702 into the spotlight. It was no longer simply enough for something to be generally accepted by a relevant scientific community: the testimony of an expert was expected to pass scientific muster. It was supposed to be demonstrably reliable scientifically.

The *Daubert case* involved two children born with birth defects. The parents sued the makers of Bendectin, an anti-nausea drug, alleging that the drug caused the birth defects. Both plaintiff and defense presented conflicting expert testimony and scientific studies arguing whether or not the drug was a "risk factor" for birth defects.

Attorneys appealed the case to the Supreme Court of the United States. One of many arguments offered was that, under Rule 702, the court was expected to "qualify" an expert and his evidence before allowing him to present opinions to a jury. The opinion offered by the Supreme Court included general acceptance by the relevant scientific community as a qualification, but much more was added. The scientific testimony offered by an expert had to be grounded in established scientific methods and procedures. The "knowledge" offered by the scientific expert had to be demonstrably factual. Also, the judge needed to determine if the scientific facts were relevant to the case. The decision called upon the trial judge to make many specific considerations:

> Many considerations will bear on the inquiry, including whether the theory or technique in question can be (and has been) tested, whether it has been subjected to peer review and publication, its known or potential error rate, and the existence and maintenance of standards controlling its operation, and whether it has attracted widespread acceptance within a relevant scientific community. The inquiry is a flexible one, and its focus must be solely on principles and methodology, not on the conclusions that they generate.[4]

Over the years, judges have lost focus on what needs to be done with science in a court case.

The focus in the *Frye* decision was on the "thing from which the deduction was made"—in that case, it was the test of using systolic blood pressure to measure deception. In the *Daubert* decision, the focus was "the theory or technique in question"—whether or not scientists who claimed that Bendectin can cause birth defects could make that claim from "animal studies, chemical structure analyses, and the unpublished 'reanalysis' of previously published human statistical studies." In both cases, the courts focused on the wrong "things"—failing to understand that they had become victims of backward reasoning and the Sherlock Effect. Ever since 1923, we have been traveling in the tall weeds, thanks to legal "tree people" and their scientific helpers—people who can now measure evidence to near molecular levels but who now—as back then—routinely miss the forest for the trees.

With *Frye*, judges focused on a scientific technique that was not relevant to the issue of the court. The relevant issue was what has always been the relevant issue in a court case: whether or not James Alphonzo Frye was, beyond reasonable doubt, guilty of the crime he was accused of. It is understandable that an appellate court would need to focus on the systolic blood pressure test because of allegations of reversible error ("reversible error" means an error or mistake made in a trial sufficient enough to warrant reversal of a judgment), but it is not reasonable to let a side issue become a general rule followed by all the courts. Whether or not a scientific test is "generally accepted" had nothing to do with the facts of that specific case. The test did not measure the content of what witnesses said Mr. Frye had done or even what Mr. Frye said; it only measured Mr. Frye's physiological and psychological reactions.

With *Daubert*, there is no way any eyewitness could perceive whether or not Bendectin caused the birth defects. Scientists doing animal studies, chemical structure analyses, or any reanalysis of previously published human statistical studies—or even scientists for the drug company doing their own population studies—cannot answer questions only eyewitnesses can answer. What may or may not happen in an epidemiologic study, where groups of people are studied and statistical calculations made, cannot address with certainty or even with probability whether or not Bendectin caused the birth defects in the two children. The answer for causation in this civil case or any other case is not knowable without eyewitnesses being able to perceive the cause as it happened; nevertheless, *Daubert* has distracted jurists and scientists in criminal cases in which there are eyewitnesses to what happened. *Daubert* impels jurists, attorneys, and scientists to focus on scientific theories and techniques instead of on the witness accounts.

Most scientific tests measure consequent physical evidence and not the train of events leading to the evidence. Scientists, attorneys, and jurists fail to understand that surmising a train of events from consequent physical evidence is doomed to fail, regardless of the sophistication, precision, or accuracy of the technology; nevertheless, much of what is written about forensic science now is preoccupied with *Daubert*. The preoccupation is with "…whether the theory or technique in question can be (and has been) tested, whether it has been subjected to peer review and publication, its known or potential error rate, and the existence and maintenance of standards controlling its operation, and whether it has attracted widespread acceptance within a relevant scientific community." Eyewitnesses are forgotten. Scientists, judges, and attorneys miss the forest for the trees, so they end up "barking up the wrong tree."

In 1985, the courts began using testing for deoxyribonucleic acid (DNA) as evidence. DNA is a complex molecule containing the genetic information in all our cells. If material from a person containing cells is left at a crime scene—blood, seminal fluid, hair, and even saliva—the police could identify potential perpetrators of the crime with DNA analysis. DNA evidence involving a serial rapist led to the first conviction in 1987.[5]

At nearly the same time, DNA evidence also became the means by which innocent prisoners were exonerated from crimes they could not have committed. According to the Web site of the Innocence Project,[6] a nonprofit legal organization founded in 1992 that uses DNA evidence for exonerating the innocent, the first DNA exoneration took place in 1989. Seventy percent of wrongful convictions "involved eyewitness misidentification," and 46% involved the "misapplication of forensic science." DNA evidence, according to the Innocence Project, has exonerated 347 people, and 20 of those have served time on death row.

DNA exonerations called into question other forensic science techniques responsible for the conviction of the innocent. The "misapplication of forensic science" was never perceived to be an inferential problem—one that could be understood through the Inferential Test. Scientists and attorneys believed the problem was from tests and testing, the "theories and techniques" as stated by the *Daubert* decision.

The Innocence Project, of course, supports DNA testing but it decries other forensic science methods: hair microscopy, bite mark comparisons, firearm and tool mark analyses, and shoe print comparisons.[7] Their Web site decries an absence of scientific standards, little to no scientific validation of methods other than DNA, inadequate assessments of method reliability, and improper scientific testimony offered by forensic practitioners that goes further than what science allows.

What are the solutions? Spend more tax dollars, of course. The Innocence Project supports a push for more research, more assessment of testing for validity and reliability, more quality assurance, and more accreditation and certification of laboratories and practitioners, all to be done at a national level.

Never is there mention of eyewitness accounts, except to blame them for 70% of wrongful convictions.

The federal government of the United States heeded the clarion call. In 2009, the National Academy of Sciences published a treatise calling for vast expenditures of funds to correct and reform the science in forensic science,[8] calling for standardization, enforcement of "best practices," mandatory accreditation of laboratories, certification for analysts, peer-reviewed research, the development and introduction of new forensic investigation technologies, and many other proposals. In 2014, the National Institute of Standards and Technology (NIST) during the Obama administration proposed and implemented the Organization of Scientific Area Committees (OSAC), and the Obama administration also set the President's Council of Advisors on Science and Technology (PCAST). The intent of both was to look at forensic testing. According to the PCAST, many of the forensic tests applied in the courtroom were not scientifically valid.

Fearing an avalanche of appeals for previous convictions from forensic testing, the Department of Justice and the Federal Bureau of Investigation refused to adopt the report's recommendations.[9] Also, the incoming Trump administration under the authority of a new attorney general disbanded the National Commission on Forensic Science, another Obama administration holdover.[10]

It is important to use reliable methods, no doubt about that; unfortunately, in stressing the methods as scientists often do, scientific do-gooders often miss the forest for the trees. While trying to discern what is "scientifically valid," scientists, forensic doctors, and many others are not aware of what is logically valid.

Logically valid means deductively valid. What is deductively valid for past events is to compare the accounts of eyewitnesses with the consequent physical evidence discovered through forensic scientific tests for consistency or inconsistency, as described in the first part of the Inferential Test:

> One can be reasonably certain if witness accounts of the past are consistent or not consistent with physical evidence in the present…

Inventing a past-event theory and attempting to see if forensic tests support or deny it is not deductively valid. It is simply forming a complex *hypothesis* about past events that can never be tested reliably by scientific tests. A hypothesis is not a deduction. Floating hypotheses for complex past events that no longer exist is neither useful nor reliable in court. Supreme Court justices demonstrated their lack of understanding of this concept in *Daubert* by writing in their opinion:

> Scientific methodology today is based on *generating hypotheses* and *testing them* to see if they can be falsified; indeed, this methodology is what distinguishes science from other fields of human inquiry.

Because past events no longer exist and scientists cannot observe them directly for testing (as would be needed in any scientific experiment or test), then testing for past events remains at the hypothesis stage, regardless of the result. The tree people miss the forest when they try to test past event theories with scientific tests. Doing this is neither scientifically nor logically valid (something has to be logically valid in order to be scientifically valid).

On the other hand, if scientists, physicians, police officers, and attorneys were to use forensic tests to test eyewitness accounts for consistency or inconsistency, and if judges as gatekeepers were able to recognize the simple logic behind doing just that in courtroom testimony, then that could change *everything*.

Consider, as an example, the 70% of exonerations that were due to "eyewitness misidentification."

In those cases, something like this happened: an eyewitness claimed that he saw the defendant commit a crime, but the defendant who was also an eyewitness claimed that he didn't commit the crime. In any "eyewitness misidentification" case, there is conflicting eyewitness testimony: a "he said…he said…" case. Police officers and prosecutors who are accustomed to inventing past-event theories simply agreed with the witness who agreed with their theory and disagreed with the defendant who didn't agree with their theory; however, the DNA testing that came along later showed that the defendant's DNA was not present but someone else's was. This made the defendant's account consistent and the other eyewitness account inconsistent with the physical evidence. Consequently, the defendant was exonerated and eyewitness misidentification—not faulty police and prosecutor theorizing—was blamed in 70% of the cases.

Consider bite-mark evidence as another example.

Bite-mark evidence, in which forensic dentists match the pattern of a bite to a perpetrator, has been in the target sight of tree people for several years now. The outrageous conduct from a forensic dentist in Mississippi, Michael West, DDS, a colleague of the controversial Steven Hayne, MD, put bite-mark evidence into question years ago. In one important case, bite marks mysteriously appeared in the dead body of 23-month-old Haley Oliveaux, a little girl who drowned in the bathtub. A video documented the appearing of the bite marks when the child's body was in the custody of Drs. Hayne and West: there was evidence of Dr. West repeatedly and methodically pressing and scraping a dental mold of the defendant's teeth into the dead girl's skin.[11]

The conduct of these doctors is shocking, of course, but there is something in this story that tree people overlook: the dental mold was from a person whom prosecutors and police believed or theorized as the person who committed a crime, not someone who was actually seen committing the crime. There are no eyewitness accounts mentioned anywhere in the story. We do not know if the alleged perpetrator claimed he bit the child or if someone saw him bite the child.

Bite-mark evidence is useful as long as it is compared to the accounts of eyewitnesses for consistency or inconsistency. Such a comparison is scientifically and logically valid. In fact, any one of a number of "feature-comparison" forensic tests works scientifically and logically *as long as the comparisons are based on the accounts of eyewitnesses and not some doctor- or police-invented theory.*

But this is never done. Instead, scientists study bias—particularly cognitive bias—hoping this will improve their theories.

Cognitive bias refers to the innate human tendency to prefer particular outcomes to other outcomes. We all have this bias regardless of best intentions. Perhaps if cognitive bias could be addressed and controlled, maybe fewer people would be wrongfully convicted—at least, that is what tree people think.

But this thinking is wrong, and this is easy to demonstrate.

Consider something that should already be familiar to you:

$$\_\_ + \_\_ = 4$$

Our cognitive bias might predispose us to select 2 + 2 over 1 + 3, but such bias is irrelevant. Surmising a complex antecedent with more than one variable—like surmising past events—is not likely to lead to the right choice, regardless of our bias.

Some tree people want to use statistical analyses to determine how *most cases* would *probably* turn out and use such calculations from the witness stand. Even if, in 95% of cases, two was thought to have been added to two, such calculations cannot apply to a unique, individual case that has never occurred exactly the same way before or since. Applying statistics like this to court testimony would be a moral outrage; nevertheless, tree people talk about it without recognizing the disaster that it would be.

The retiring judge I spoke to may think of himself as a forest person, but many of his colleagues and others involved in the court process may not be ready for the forest. That could all change, however, and it could change quickly. If judges were to learn and apply the very simple Inferential Test, they would be able to put both the forest and the trees into proper context. They would learn when a scientist has gotten it wrong, even without knowing all the detailed science that currently intimidates them.

***

Before continuing with my account of the Kelly trial, there may be questions, ladies and gentlemen, that may have entered your minds. For instance, you may wonder why I chose not to mention the Inferential Test or any of the concepts in this book during the *Daubert* hearing.

The answer to that is simple: if I were to have brought up the Inferential Test, the prosecutor would have shot me down with questions about my "novel technique"—questions like:

- Is your "novel technique" generally accepted by the scientific community? I would have to admit that it isn't.
- Has your "novel technique" been subjected to peer review and publication? I would have to admit that it hasn't.
- Does your "novel technique" have a known or potential error rate? I would have to explain that deductive inference technically has an error rate of "zero" but such items are not measurable in the usual scientific sense.
- Do standards controlling its operation presently exist and are they maintained? I would have to admit that no such items exist.
- Has your "novel technique" attracted widespread acceptance within your scientific community. I would have to admit that it hasn't.

If I were then to explain that the Inferential Test is not a "novel technique" but a *tautology* (a tautology is a statement that is always true or has to be true) or theorem of deductive logic, I would then have to answer further questions about my qualifications in logic: Do I have an advanced degree in philosophy or logic? How many logic courses have I taught? What classes in logic have I taken? What papers have I written about logic? What seminars in logic have I presented? All of this is part of the *Daubert* admissibility calculus.

After all of that questioning, I believe the judge would not have allowed me to testify. I would have failed the *Daubert* test.

Also, any discussion by me about the Inferential Test would have defeated the role I play as a scientific expert in a courtroom.

Conversations about logic pertain to argumentation and persuasion. It is not my role to argue or persuade in a courtroom. Attorneys are the ones who argue and persuade, not scientific experts. My role as a courtroom scientist is to apply and explain principles of peer-reviewed, evidence-based medicine and pathology to a jury and to apply those principles to issues brought out in a court case. My role is limited.

As I testified in the *Daubert* hearing, it is not my job to tell the jury "what happened" or even to persuade them that I am correct. "What happened" is not something I can know for certain because I was not present at the Best Western Inn on the night and morning in question to observe what happened. "What happened" in any case is an "ultimate issue" for the jury to decide: something they are supposed to conclude and not me. I may have my beliefs, but they get to decide. The only thing I am supposed to do is to address the facts in the case and explain my area of science in a way that will aid the jury.

Outside of the courtroom, I do my best to explain everything I know and believe about the Inferential Test to my attorney clients and to others, particularly if they are ready to hear about it. What they do with that information is up to them. Inside of the courtroom, I tell my attorney clients to expect only opinions about my area made to a reasonable degree of medical certainty.

> Mr. Hurlburt, you may call your first witness.[12]
> Yes, Your Honor. I call Dr. Thomas Young.
> Dr. Young was sworn yesterday. You may proceed.

Once more before the jury, I responded to the attorney's questions about my education, job experience, licensures, board certifications, publications, presentations, organizations, etc. Also, I explained the fee I was charging the State for my services, including my hourly rate. I described to the jury the items I read and viewed prior to my appearance in court. Also, we covered some of the same topics from yesterday's *Daubert* hearing.

"During the testimony of Dr. Lyon," Attorney Hurlburt continued, "he said that the information he received was from the law enforcement officers at the autopsy. He did not receive any videos or witness statements to review. Do you recall that?"

I responded that I had.

> When I sent you the file, did you receive a lot more information than Dr. Lyon was privy to?
> Yes.
> You remember what I talked about with Dr. Lyon, about how 'you don't know what you don't know.' Is that a fear of a forensic pathologist?
> That's right. It's that piece of information out there that you may not be aware of that could change everything, correct.
> Was there some important information that Dr. Lyon was not aware of that you were aware of based on the information you received?

"Based on Dr. Lyon's testimony," I replied, "one particular item he didn't mention or seem to be aware of was the very, very aggressive cardiopulmonary resuscitation or CPR performed by the defendant."

Attorney Hurlburt went on to point out the video statements of witnesses that Dr. Lyon did not view, including the two interviews of Deterryon Kelly and the interview of Jameshia Cooks.

"We'll come back to that," the attorney said after discussing the video interviews. "Now, Judge, I'm going to need some assistance from the State with regards to their machinery and pulling –"

"You want me to pull something up?" asked the district attorney.

Yeah, if you don't mind. I want to pull up the first video when they first come out of the room.

Mr. Hurlburt invited me to stand near the television monitor. The jury sat to my left side as I explained my opinions—opinions I have already covered in an earlier chapter. When the image of Deterryon swinging his arm toward the child appeared, I heard an audible gasp from a juror.

I remember thinking, "This is not good." Still, I had to keep going.

> In looking at something like this, it is important to determine what I can actually see and what I can't see. I think that would be an important issue for anyone. What I can see is an adult coming out with a small child and both are walking. Furthermore, I can also see at some point the adult moving his hand quickly. What I can't see is if the child was hit. The child's shadow is obscured by the adult's right leg. We see the motion of the hand, but we don't see any motion of the child.

Mr. Hurlburt followed up: "Very important question here. You heard testimony that what law enforcement saw was him slapping the child on the side of his head, correct?"

> That's what I heard.
> Now, you saw the autopsy report. It was very thorough, wouldn't you agree?
> He did a very thorough autopsy, yes.
> Were there any injuries in the left side of the child's face where law enforcement said he struck the child?
> There were no injuries anywhere on the face at autopsy.
> Was there anything in the head that you would consider serious bodily injury?
> No.

The courts in Texas define "serious bodily injury" as something that would cause death or a protracted loss of use of an organ.

Later when asked about the manipulating of the child like a "sack of potatoes," I replied, "The motions are remarkably gymnastic, but those particular motions would not be consistent with any kind of injury."

I commented about the activity in the vending machine room: "We can't be sure what is going on by looking at this. You shouldn't fill in the blanks with your imagination, and that is what struck me about the detective's testimony. He's filling in with a lot of imaginary information. The video also jumps around because it takes images every several seconds. We just see shadows and we see some motion here, but we can't really see much more than that."

I testified about the nature of the abdominal injury noted at autopsy: "If the child received that kind of tear in the liver from a very, very severe blow, that child would be in incredible distress. It would be called an 'acute abdomen'. That basically means a surgical emergency. A child like that would be in exquisite pain. He would not even want to move. He would be yelling out. His abdomen would be rigid. It would be obvious. This kind of a situation where there is that severe of a blow to the abdomen, it's obvious."

Attorney Hurlburt: "Now, you also heard Detective Griffin say he was dead when he came out of the room. Also, Dr. Lyon said he could very well be dead, correct?"

> I heard that, yes.
> The reason Dr. Lyon would say maybe he was dead was because the massive tear in the liver would bleed so fast that the child would bleed out in minutes.

"Yes," I responded, "It would take several minutes with that kind of tear to bleed out." I admitted that a liver laceration of the type found at autopsy would be "serious bodily injury" if it had been inflicted from a severe blow. "The liver gets a lot of blood supply, and damage to the liver like that would cause profuse bleeding into the abdomen."

Mr. Hurburt: "Otherwise, it would make no sense for Dr. Lyon and Detective Griffin saying that the child was dead coming out of there, correct?"

"Correct."

We moved on to the next topic. Attorney Hurlburt asked, "Do you recall in Deterryon Kelly's statement to the police about the child being sleepy and cranky?"

> Yes, I do.
> Why is it important for you to have statements from witnesses who were with the deceased person before he passed away?

I replied, "They're the only ones who have the real answers. Deterryon Kelly knows better than anyone else what happened. Other people who were also there also know what happened, including the child's mother. So it's very important to listen carefully to what they say because the rest of us who weren't there can only guess. The only thing we can do is to listen to them and see if what they say makes any kind of sense."

> If you have a suspect who tells you everything that happened and your forensics tell you something different, what would that indicate to you?
> That the person is perhaps not being entirely truthful about what they are saying.
> If a person's statement to you about what happened fits the forensics, what does that mean to you?
> It means that there is no reason not to believe him. If what he says matches the evidence found in an autopsy or any kind of investigative scientific procedure, you basically affirm what he said. There is no reason not to believe him, especially if he was the one who was there to see what happened. The evidence supports what he said.

The defense attorney referred to the testimony of Wilma Laywell: "If the child sitting on his own appeared sleepy like her grandson and not in any distress, is that significant?"

> Yes. That is not a description of someone with a life-threatening injury who is internally bleeding. That is not the kind of behavior any child or even adult would have under that circumstance.
> Based on that injury, only minutes from death?
> Yes.

What about throwing the child up and down in the air? My reply: "That's not the sort of thing you can do with a child who has an acute abdomen. This child would not even allow anybody to touch him, let alone be thrown up in the air like that."

The testimony eventually came to Jameshia Cooks and her video interview. Attorney Hurlburt continued, "She told the police that she saw the child look sleepy, but Deterryon tucked the child in the bed. She saw he was tossing and turning. You heard that, correct?"

I did.
Is it even reasonable, with your extensive knowledge of forensic pathology, for a liver to be lacerated like that at 11:00 and for the child to be tossing and turning in the bed 30 minutes later?
It's not consistent. It doesn't make sense.
Would it make sense, if the child put in bed was dead, that mom would look in the room and come back out and sit on the stairway steps as if the child was still awake?
It doesn't make sense.
Would it make sense that the mother would say that whenever they would make too much noise, the child would look like he was being disturbed, so they had to be more quiet so he wouldn't be disturbed?
No, it doesn't make sense.

None of this made sense with the kind of liver laceration at autopsy being caused at 11 p.m.

Mr. Hurlburt then talked about when Jameshia got up to urinate, when she saw the child first under the covers and then out from under the covers. "Could a dead baby do that?"

No, sir.

Eventually, we addressed the child entrapment described by Deterryon Kelly. The attorney showed me photographs of the motel room.

"That's the bed and the nightstand where Deterryon Kelly said the child was?" asked the attorney, referring to one of the photographs.

Correct.
They are saying with only 3 inches there that it is impossible for the child to get down into that space. Do you think it would be impossible for a child to get down into that space?
I think it's possible.
Why do you think it's possible?
It is true that the surface part of the nightstand and the mattress are 3 inches apart, but what is not mentioned is that the rest of the nightstand is recessed in from the top ledge of the nightstand. Also, a mattress can be compressed. If you lie on the edge of a mattress, you are going to push the mattress down at the edge. As a child gets to the edge of the mattress, it is possible for him to push the edge of that mattress down and for him to slip underneath the ledge of the nightstand tabletop, even with a gap of 3 inches.

Mr. Hurlburt: "Dr. Lyon also noted the amount of blood loss in the body, correct?"

He did.

"Now, he says 50 milliliters, 150 milliliters, 25 milliters," pointing to different volumes of blood loss in the report. "That adds up to 225 milliliters."

"Yes," I replied. "He says 150 milliliters in the peritoneal cavity, another 50 milliliters in surrounding tissues, and when he makes an opening incision into the abdomen, he estimated that about 25 milliliters came out."

The attorney brings out a short water bottle.

> Can you describe what we're trying to show here with Defense Exhibit No. 10?

I described what I saw: "Defendant's Exhibit No. 10 is an Ozarka spring water bottle containing 237 milliliters, so 225 milliliters is a little less than the 237 milliliters marked on the container for total volume. This is what a 225-milliliter blood loss would look like."

I further described what doctors do with calculating blood loss: "One of the things done in a clinical setting in a child who is bleeding is to calculate or estimate his total blood volume. That means how much blood does the child have in his arteries and veins. The way to estimate that is to take the weight of the child's body in kilograms and then figure 80 milliliters of blood for every kilogram of body weight. If you do the math, you basically come up with an estimated blood volume in milliliters."

I continued: "The amount of blood loss seen by Dr. Lyon is 225 milliliters. The total estimated blood volume is 830 milliliters. The blood loss would be about 27% of his estimated blood volume. A child may have signs of shock with a 27% loss in blood volume, but it requires over 50% blood loss typically for the child to die from blood loss. If there are gaping liver lacerations but only a low amount of blood in the abdomen, that means that something else is going on other than death from blood loss."

> When I see this kind of a situation at autopsy, I wonder if the child had a heartbeat when he had the liver laceration. In cases where there was no heartbeat, when CPR is associated with the liver tear, I usually see around 5 to 10 percent blood loss. That little amount is squeezed into the abdominal cavity with the action from CPR. The 27 percent here is between the 5% to 10% and the 50%.

Unexpected levels of blood loss at autopsy prompt me to find out more of what witnesses observed at the scene.

Attorney Hurlburt asked if it was significant to me when the defendant said, "I did CPR; I hope I didn't do it too hard."

> Several injuries can occur in adults and children with aggressive CPR. You can break ribs. You can tear the heart. And commonly, you can tear the liver. Liver tears are commonly seen in adults and have been described in children where there has been repeated compressions that have been very aggressive.

I described to the jury—as I described previously in this book—how pushing a liver against the spine repeatedly and rapidly can form gaping liver tears.

"If the child has a very thready pulse or no pulse, you would expect less blood loss than if the child had an active heartbeat."

I further explained how a slow heart beat from a mechanical asphyxia, such as that described by Deterryon Kelly, could lead to more blood loss than no heart beat but less of a blood loss than with an active heartbeat.

I also talked about pulseless electrical activity and other complicated topics. I figured that the jury did not understand much of this, even as I tried to explain it all as simply as I could. Still, if jurors had a hard time understanding, how could someone like Deterryon Kelly invent a lie that explains complex physiology and the autopsy findings so well?

Following the direct examination came the cross-examination. The cross-examination was lengthy, too lengthy to describe in this chapter. There were some special moments, such as this one below having to do with the child at the emergency department or ER ("Q" means question from the district attorney and "A" is my answer):

Q: So you're going to agree that, obviously, the child was 18 degrees below normal when he came in?
A: I have no problem with that.

Q: Still, in the ER doctor's opinion, which he testified to, was that even though the kid was dead when he came into the ER, they still went ahead, hooked him up to the machines, and did all the lifesaving measures, correct?
A: That's what they did.

Q: That's what they did. That's—that's what I am asking. And when asked why he did that, he specifically said, "Because it's a child, and we always have hope that we can do something to save them." Isn't that what he testified to?
A: Certainly.

Q: All right. You disagree with that?
A: No.

Q: So to say that it doesn't make any sense that he would have done that if the kid would have been dead for a couple of hours is incorrect, isn't it?
A: You're mischaracterizing my testimony.

Q: I'm—I'm basically saying exactly what you said which is –
A: No, you're not saying exactly what I said.

Q: Well –
A: You're mischaracterizing my testimony.

Q: Doctor, I'm not trying to fight with you, okay? Let me make sure. Let me rephrase this then so that I make sure I'm characterizing it correctly, okay? You said that it made no sense for them to do work on somebody if they had been dead for two hours.
A: That's not what I said.

Q: Okay. What did you say?
A: I said having pulseless electrical activity in a body that is two hours dead makes no sense. I'm not making any comment about what the emergency room doctor did. The emergency room doctor did what he was supposed to do. I have no problem with that. He's doing his job, okay? But claiming that pulseless electrical activity can occur in a body that is two hours dead makes no sense. He doesn't know what he's saying.

Q: Pulseless electrical activity, what are the six H's?
A: I'm sorry?

Q: The six H's and the six T's, what are those?
A: The six H's?

Q: The six H's and the six T's regarding pulseless electrical activity.
A: I don't know what that means.

Q: Let me see if I can pull that out. I tried to learn a little bit more about pulseless electrical activity. Now, granted, the internet's the internet, all right? And I don't have access to your medical journals and books, but there's quite a bit of information out there about pulseless electrical activity, and it says that it can be caused by multiple factors.
A: That's correct.

Q: And it indicates the common practice in the medical field—or it's common terms are referred to as the six H's and the six T's. I honestly cannot say any of those words. Have you ever heard of that?
A: No, I haven't.

Q: Okay. So it could be caused by multiple things more than just the heart, can't it?
A: That's fair.

Q: It's possible that those readings could have come from something other than just the heart?
A: What do you mean by "just the heart"?

Q: Well, your testimony has been that it's—and maybe I misunderstood your testimony, that's why we're trying to go through this, so I can make sure I understand. Are you saying that the pulseless—I'm going to call it PEA, okay, because I don't want to mess it up. So the PEA, which is pulseless electrical activity, is not being caused by the heart in this kid, or it is?
A: Okay. The pulseless electrical activity means electrical activity in the body, okay?

Q: Okay.
A: If you've got a body that is two hours dead, there's not going to be any of that kind of electrical activity in the body.

Another special moment involved a baby doll and marker board. First, the district attorney had me come down from the witness stand and stand before the board.

Q: I'm going to put a line right here. Will you point to where 3 inches is so that I mark it right where you want it marked.
A: Right there (indicating).

Q: Am I putting it in the right spot?
A: Sure.

He then had me return to my seat. Then he drew parallel lines three inches apart.

Q: Now, Doctor, would you agree with me that the width from here to here is approximately 3 inches?
He pointed to the upper portion of the parallel lines.
A: Yes.

Q: And wouldn't you agree with me that the width from here to here is approximately 3 inches?
He pointed to the lower portion of the parallel lines.
A: Yes.

Q: Okay. This is a fair representation of the distance between the bed and the nightstand?
A: It is not a fair representation.

Q: Okay. Of the top of the nightstand, then, and the bed?
A: Yes.

Q: I understand that the nightstand kind of concaves in a bit so maybe it's about 4 inches. Is that about right?
A: I don't know.

Q: But in order to get to the bottom you've got to get through the top, right?
A: Not necessarily.

Q: Not necessarily?
A: No.

Q: So the other way to get to the bottom is, I guess, crawl in from the bottom?
A: I can explain it if you would like for me to explain it.

If I were to explain without being asked to explain, I would have drawn an objection: "Your Honor, the witness is non-responsive." The judge would have sustained the objection.

Q: I—I think you already have, and we're going to talk about that in a second. Yes or no: Could you crawl in from the bottom?
A: I suppose somebody could crawl in from the bottom. We don't know what the bottom is here. What is represented here is the top.

Q: Right. And that's all we're talking about. But you just testified that the bottom was different from the top, so I'm just trying to clarify to the jury that—when I asked, how did he get to the bottom through the top, and you said not necessarily. So I'm just trying to get some understanding of what are the necessary ways that you could get to the bottom.
A: Well, you're oversimplifying a great deal.

Q: Sometimes we need to simplify. How do you get to the bottom?
A: You can oversimplify, and that makes it inaccurate.

I was talking about the attorney's attempt to use a two-dimensional line drawing to characterize a three-dimensional, complex reality.

Q: I'm not trying to be difficult here, Doctor. I'm just asking you, how do you get to the bottom if you're not going through the top?

A: I don't understand your question.
Q: Okay. That's fine.

Mr. Solomon then brought out the doll.

Q: This is a baby doll. Do you agree with me on that?
A:. Sure.

Q: And if I were to measure this doll—actually, I'm going to do it up here so you see it.

He placed a ruler next to the doll.

Q: About how tall is this doll?
A: 23 inches.

Q: Okay. How tall is the victim in this case? 86 centimeters or something in that range?
A: 84.5 centimeters.

Q: Okay. Are you able to convert that to inches in your head?
A: Not very well. There are 2.54 centimeters in an inch, so if somebody wants to pull out a calculator and do the calculation…

Q: How about this? I've got my phone. iPhones are the greatest things in the world.

He sounded a lot like Peter Falk in a rerun of *Columbo.*

Q: Let's see, so we've got 84 point what centimeters?
A: 84.5.

Q: Multiplied by how many centimeters per inch—or how many inches in a centimeter? I guess they're divided by…
A: 1 inch is 2.54 centimeters.

Q: Okay. So if I took 84.5 and divided it by 2.54 centimeters to convert to inches is that the correct way to do that?
A: Yes.

Q: Okay. About how many inches tall was the child?
A: 33.

Q: It's about 10 inches taller than this baby doll.
A: Sure.

Q: Okay. So this baby doll is not to scale.
A: Correct.

Q: Okay. So this baby doll, you would agree with me, is smaller, honestly, because I couldn't find a 33-inch tall doll.
A: Sure.

Q: Okay. So you didn't—you've never actually seen the victim physically, have you?
A: Correct.

Q: But you have children. You've been a pathologist for a long time. You ever done autopsies on children?
A: Many.

Q: Would a 21-month-old child be larger than this?
A: Most 21-month-old children would be larger than that.

Q: Okay. Obviously, most. I mean, there could be an exception, obviously, right?
A: Certainly.

Q: All right. So would its head be bigger?
A: I think the head would tend to be bigger, yes.

Q: Okay. Body would be bigger?
A: Yes.

Q: Arms and everything would be bigger, longer?
A: Would tend to in most children at 21 months of age.

Q: They're growing, right.
A: Sure.

The attorney than placed the doll over the parallel lines on the marker board.

Q: Can you see the lines now, Doctor?
A: Pardon me?

Q: Can you see the lines underneath this child—this—this baby doll?
A: No.

Q: Why?
A: Because the body is blocking it.

Q: So this line is substantially—this area right here is substantially smaller than this baby doll?
A: The way you have set it up, yes.

Q: Okay. And your explanation to the jury as to how the baby passes through this area was that the bed compressed due to his weight, and he slipped through it? Is that your—that's what you told the jury earlier; is that correct?
A: Sure.

Q: Okay. So a child—a child substantially larger than this would have easily been able to compress the bed, slip through this tiny place that this little bitty doll is completely covering to fall down between the bed and the dresser. That's what you testified to earlier, correct?
A: In general, sure.

Q: Okay. I'm just making sure we understand. Again, it's that compression that caused the death of this child, not the defendant.
A: Right.

Imagine what it must have been like for the jury to make any sense out of this. Maybe by this point, they didn't even care to try.

Notes

1. Sato A, Kuroda B. Forensic science is reaching new heights with the latest technologies. *Nikkei Asian Review*, November 3, 2016. http://asia.nikkei.com/magazine/20161103-Small-catch-big-conflicts/Tech-Science/Forensic-science-is-reaching-new-heights-with-the-latest-technologies. Accessed on November 12, 2017.
2. Traces of grime on your phone reveal your life story: study. *AFP Relax News*, November 15, 2016. https://www.yahoo.com/tech/traces-grime-phone-reveal-life-story-study-085257687.html. Accessed on November 12, 2017.
3. *Frye v. United States*. 293 F. 1013 (D.C.. Cir 1923).
4. *Daubert v. Merrell Dow Pharmaceuticals* (92-102), 509 U.S. 579 (1993).
5. Prieto B. Rapist who was first DNA conviction in U.S. may go free soon. *Orlando Sentinel*, August 3, 2012. http://articles.orlandosentinel.com/2012-08-03/news/os-dna-tommie-lee-andrews-release-20120803_1_serial-rapist-tommie-lee-andrews-dna-evidence. Accessed on November 12, 2017.

6. DNA Exonerations in the United States. Innocenceproject.org. http://www.innocenceproject.org/dna-exonerations-in-the-united-states/. Accessed on November 12, 2017.
7. Misapplication of Forensic Science. Innocenceproject.org. http://www.innocenceproject.org/causes/unvalidated-or-improper-forensic-science/. Accessed on November 12, 2017.
8. National Research Council. *Strengthening Forensic Science in the United States: A Path Forward.* Washington, DC: The National Academies Press, 2009.
9. Templeton G. Here come the appeals: White House report attacks modern forensic science. Extremetech.com, September 22, 2016. http://www.extremetech.com/extreme/236040-here-come-the-appeals-white-house-report-attacks-modern-forensic-science. Accessed on November 12, 2017.
10. Hsu SS. Sessions orders Justice Dept. to end forensic science commission, suspend review policy. The Washington Post, April 10, 2017. https://www.washingtonpost.com/local/public-safety/sessions-orders-justice-dept-to-end-forensic-science-commission-suspend-review-policy/2017/04/10/2dada0ca-1c96-11e7-9887-1a5314b56a08_story.html?tid=a_inl&utm_term=.0b831b0f5676. Accessed on November 17, 2017.
11. Balko R. Manufacturing Guilt? Experts say this exclusive video shows a dental examiner creating the bite marks that put a man on death row. *Reason*, February 19, 2009. http://reason.com/archives/2009/02/19/manufacturing-guilt. Accessed on November 17, 2017.
12. Reporter's Record, The State of Texas vs. Deterryon Tyrell Kelly, Trial Court Cause No. 14-0275X, Court of Appeals No. 06-17-00001-CR. Volume 6.

The Perils of Pediatric Forensic Pathology 18

Double dipping is not the only way a seasoned, backward-reasoning, Sherlock-Holmes-style forensic pathologist can find himself in trouble. Forensic pathologists can have their careers suddenly destroyed by child-abuse cases.

Why does this happen? What makes these cases so risky for forensic pathologists?

Most violent deaths in which autopsies are performed have a lot of witnesses and a lot of physical evidence at a crime scene and elsewhere. Violent deaths are typically information rich: the more information that can be learned from witnesses or the more that can be observed by scientists, the more likely the doctor will draw correct conclusions.

In contrast, typical child-abuse cases are information poor. There are few witnesses, and the ones who witnessed what happened are typically not believed. Also, the "crime scene"—often the home or apartment where the child is taken care of—has very little physical evidence pointing to a violent death. The main evidence in these cases comes from the assertions of forensic doctors who reason backward from autopsy or clinical findings to the violent crime. These doctors do not work from information: they work from imagination!

Deaths involving children are filled with emotion, not only at the time the death happens but also in the courtroom. Jurors are swept up in that emotion, and they want the bad person who is responsible locked up.

Years after the trials have taken place and the sad and angry emotions pass, problems may appear. The media report the problems, and politicians are then forced to address them. When under media pressure, politicians typically look for and find someone to blame.

That someone to blame is not hard to find.

Even though child abuse pediatricians and other doctors chime in with their opinions during a court case, the person who is held the most responsible is the one who has the final decision about what happened. The forensic pathologist becomes a lightning rod for the tremendous rage directed at him from aggrieved families and an angry public. The bureaucrats and politicians find this doctor to be an easy target and a means of relief from a tricky situation. Also, other forensic physicians who are just as much Sherlock Holmes as the one being criticized are more than happy to offer their opinions about what a poor job the now-disgraced pathologist did.

One such disgraced forensic doctor was Dr. Charles Smith, former pediatric forensic pathologist. Dr. Smith was a Canadian doctor with impressive credentials. He was the head pathologist at the Hospital for Sick Children, a major center for the treatment of children with complex medical problems, in Toronto, Ontario. For over two decades, ending in the early 2000s, Dr. Smith performed autopsies on many children. Nobody questioned his abilities until several cases came to public attention. These led to judicial hearings presided by Justice Stephen Goudge.

The Star, October 1, 2008: Payout Urged in Smith Probe[1]

> People unjustly convicted through the work of disgraced pathologist Dr. Charles Smith deserve compensation, the final report of the Public Inquiry into Pediatric Forensic Pathology in Ontario concludes.
>
> The four-volume report released today by Justice Stephen Goudge also calls on the province to review additional cases of child deaths that may have resulted in wrongful convictions.
>
> Within hours of the report's release, the Ontario government said it would work toward compensation for the victims.
>
> The report lists 169 recommendations to restore the public confidence in a system that saw innocent family members and caregivers wrongly convicted, charged or suspected in the deaths of children.
>
> "My recommendations are the steps that I have concluded must be taken to restore and enhance public confidence in pediatric forensic pathology in Ontario, and its future use in the criminal justice system," Goudge said.
>
> "If acted upon, they represent the best way to protect the administration of justice from flawed pathology, to leave behind the dark times of the recent past, and to create the forensic pathology service that the criminal justice system needs and the people of Ontario deserve."

Justice Goudge placed great hope in those 169 recommendations, such as to "think truth" rather than "think dirty," to have better oversight in the performance of pediatric autopsies, to have more adequate training, to have more trained pathologists, to think objectively using an evidence-based approach, to have more adequate compensation for pathologists, and so on. As good as such recommendations sound, they only trim the weeds rather than attacking the root.

These recommendations do not point out the problems with Sherlock Holmes and backward reasoning. Justice Goudge would do well to have the Inferential Test printed on the wall of his courtroom.

The ugly truth is that Dr. Smith performed the same way as many hundreds of forensic pathologists perform all the time, every day, but Dr. Smith was the one who got caught. Many pathologists could be held responsible for the same sins as Dr. Smith, but only Dr. Smith received the punishment.

In the interest of public safety, one of these forensic doctors, the chief forensic pathologist of Ontario, suggested reviewing old cases to look for problems.

Toronto Star, October 7, 2008: Baby Death Review "Daunting"[2]

> Ontario's chief forensic pathologist, who was the first to suggest a review of old "shaken-baby" deaths, says the province has a "daunting" task ahead as it looks at 220 cases to determine if anyone was wrongfully convicted.
>
> The review will be a massive undertaking, not just because of the number of cases dating back as far as 20 years, but also because shaken-baby syndrome is being hotly debated in medical and scientific circles, Dr. Michael Pollanen says.
>
> "It's a daunting task. It's a considerable amount of work. Resources will need to be dedicated to it," he says, noting the review will involve poring over almost five times as many cases as were examined in the lead-up to a public inquiry that probed the mistakes of disgraced pathologist Dr. Charles Smith.

The task sounds "daunting," but is it really all that daunting? Why not figure that any case where a pathologist claims that someone abused a child is incorrect?

But that is not understood by anybody now, let alone at that time. Instead, one solution was to criticize the shaken-baby syndrome.

> "However daunting the task … it would be unsafe to rest a judgment" on an old scientific theory that is now in question, [Attorney General Chris] Bentley says.
>
> "We want to make sure that nobody was convicted or nobody was subject to other legal proceedings … based on science that would no longer be acceptable today because of the evolution of that science," Bentley explains.

What Attorney General Bentley does not explain is why shaken baby all of the sudden is "an old scientific theory that is now in question." Many doctors currently do not share his belief: they do not question the shaken-baby syndrome. There is no explanation from this attorney or from anyone what makes a particular theory true or not true. With this kind of confusion, how is it possible to conduct any meaningful review?

Front and center for this daunting task is Ontario's chief forensic pathologist.

> Pollanen called for a review of shaken-baby deaths while testifying at the inquiry last December. The Smith fiasco prompted him to look back at cases involving infants. In that preliminary review alone, Pollanen found 142 deaths between 1986 and 2006 that had been attributed to shaken-baby syndrome.

> A further review of old files by the chief coroner's office found 78 more cases. It has not yet been established how many of the 220 cases in question included trials, criminal convictions or child-protection involvement, but it's expected that a number did.

Dr. Pollanen was made to look heroic in all of this, but what he did was not heroic. He was simply protecting himself and others like him. One might think that Dr. Smith performed all of these cases personally, but the news report and Dr. Pollanen do not claim that these were only Dr. Smith cases. It is not reasonable to think that Dr. Smith was the only doctor in the large province of Ontario performing autopsies on children. Weren't there also other pathologists who also believed in shaken-baby syndrome? Maybe Dr. Pollanen himself performed several of these autopsies, but this was not reported. Also, the review was limited to the two decades where Dr. Smith was active, giving the impression that the mistakes were all due to Dr. Smith and not to anyone else. Why stop at two decades? Why not continue reviewing cases from before? Or after? Maybe performing a review on cases that came before or after Dr. Smith would have drawn attention to others besides Dr. Smith.

Yet Dr. Smith became the convenient scapegoat. Stamp out Dr. Smith—remove his license and his ability to practice medicine—and the problem is solved! Right?

Well…temporarily.

Years later, Ontario's chief forensic pathologist appeared in the news again. Beneath a large photograph of Dr. Pollanen, a caption reads:

> Dr. Michael Pollanen, Ontario's chief forensic pathologist, allowed his personal belief that a 2-year-old's death was a case of abuse to cloud his duty to provide objective, even-handed scientific evidence to the court, a judge ruled.[3]

The article further explains the findings of Superior Court Justice Anne Molloy and makes reference to Dr. Charles Smith:

> Pollanen fell into several major pitfalls laid out by the landmark Goudge inquiry sparked by Smith's work, Molloy found.
>
> Among them was confirmation bias—reaching a conclusion and working backward to find evidence to support it, and professional credibility bias—being unwilling to change an opinion once stated.

Dr. Pollanen, you could be the next Dr. Charles Smith. Hang on to your medical license for dear life!

The news also reports another forensic pathologist who has fallen from grace. This one is from Montana.

Montana is a state composed mostly of county coroners, but there is an appointed state medical examiner and a few other forensic helpers. In 2015, the state medical examiner and another important helper reportedly resigned from their positions because of their inability to prevent a third pathologist from performing child autopsies. Multiple attorneys general over many years kept the third pathologist around because he was great help to them in the prosecution of many of their child-abuse cases. Out of frustration after years of trying, the state medical examiner and his replacement resigned, leaving the current state attorney general in a quandary.

Missoulian, July 11, 2015: Forensic Pathologist Will No Longer Do Work for Montana County Coroners[4]

A forensic pathologist with a problematic record will no longer conduct autopsies for county coroners as an associate medical examiner, according to the Montana Attorney General's Office.

Thomas Bennett served as associate medical examiner in Montana since 1998, and appears to be a factor in the resignations of the state's chief medical examiners. Gary Dale resigned in April; Walter Kemp left on July 1, and mentioned Bennett's "un-appointment" in his letter of resignation.

Court records show Dale, as head medical examiner, repeatedly asked Bennett to stop conducting autopsies on children. Bennett had left Iowa as chief medical examiner after numerous authorities called into question his conclusions that infant deaths were caused by shaken baby syndrome.

Bennett conducted autopsies for coroners in eastern Montana through his private practice in Billings, Forensic Medicine and Pathology.

In recent correspondence, officials in the Attorney General's Office notified Bennett that his appointment would come to a close July 1. The State Medical Examiner's Office will hire a state employee to do autopsies in eastern Montana, and counties will no longer pay a fee for service to a pathologist appointed as an associate.

Last week, chief of staff Mike Milburn said the medical examiners' concerns about Bennett's work on children came to a head last September. After a lengthy evaluation, the Attorney General's Office decided to restructure the State Medical Examiner's Office.

Now, forensic pathologists who do autopsies for coroners will be under direct supervision by the state medical examiner, Milburn said. The change means Bennett's practice will no longer perform autopsies for county coroners.

The departure appears to address one of Dale's major concerns. But it was a long time in coming.

The former medical examiner had requested Bennett refrain from doing autopsies on children more than a decade ago, when Bennett first began working in Montana, records show.

Bennett apparently refused to comply with the head examiner, who is appointed by the attorney general. The Billings doctor continued to do child autopsies through the administrations of four attorneys general.

Dale declined to answer questions for this story. Kemp was in the middle of a move last week and unavailable for an interview.

However, correspondence that is part of a court record shows that Dale repeatedly demanded Bennett refrain from doing autopsies on children. In a letter from 2000, Dale said he had reviewed three deaths Bennett "opined were … due to 'shaken-slammed baby syndrome.'"

"It is my opinion that your continuing to conduct postmortem examinations of unexplained deaths of infants unnecessarily risks both wrongful prosecution of a caretaker and jeopardizes prosecution of the perpetrator if you are to encounter a truly injured child," Dale said in the letter.

In a 2005 letter, Dale informed county coroners and attorneys that any examinations of children by Bennett "are done so outside his appointment as an associate state medical examiner."

"Prior to coming to Montana in 1998, Dr. Bennett rendered problematic opinions regarding alleged non-accidental traumatic infant deaths in Iowa," Dale said. "Despite verbal and three written … instructions by me to "refrain from conducting Montana coroner-requested autopsies on children," Dr. Bennett has continued to perform these examinations."

In September 2014, the issue came to a head at the Attorney General's Office.

Last week, Attorney General Tim Fox said the department spent the better part of a year sorting through complicated and long-standing issues in the State Medical Examiner's Office.

"It's been something that we're still in some respects trying to get our arms around," Fox said.

However, he also said his team is putting into place a different model for autopsies conducted by the medical examiner, a structure designed to fix the previous lack of accountability, communication and peer review.

In the past, the head medical examiner designated an associate, but the associate worked, as needed, for county coroners. Going forward, the forensic pathologists who do autopsies for coroners will be state employees and report to the head medical examiner.

"Then, you have a very clear power to hire and to fire," Fox said. "You have a chief state medical examiner who has very clear supervisory responsibilities over deputy medical examiners."

The latter part of the article elaborates on Dr. Thomas Bennett and the four attorneys general.

Bennett did not speak with the Missoulian last week. His phone number returned a call, but the line quickly disconnected; subsequently, no one answered Bennett's phone number.

Fox said he did not believe any of Bennett's work on children would result in wrongful convictions because Dale and Kemp would have alerted the Attorney General's Office of any such cases.

The office did review some cases; officials declined to discuss any findings in detail due to legal constraints.

In Iowa, a couple was released from prison and exonerated of felony charges in 1998 after a judge found "false or misleading forensic evidence," according to the National Registry of Exonerations, a project of the University of Michigan School of Law. Bennett had declared the death a homicide.

Other child cases Bennett deemed homicides also came under fire. At least two court orders call his actions into question, including a Montana Supreme Court order in a felony assault conviction that cited his "problematic history." (The court was addressing controversy around Bennett as a possible expert witness.)

Former Attorney General Joe Mazurek is now deceased. Gov. Steve Bullock did not address the reason Bennett was allowed to conduct infant autopsies during his tenure as attorney general.

"As Attorney General, Steve Bullock agreed with the policy put in place by the state medical examiner, which precluded the state medical examiner's appointee, Dr. Bennett, from working on certain cases involving infants and young children," said spokesman Dave Parker in a statement.

Chief Justice Mike McGrath, who also previously was attorney general, declined to comment through his assistant in the Montana Supreme Court.

"I spoke with the chief, and he has no comment," said judicial assistant Lorrie Cole. "It wouldn't be ethical for him to comment."

In a deposition, however, Bennett admitted he had continued to do autopsies on children because he had run the matter past his "friend" McGrath. McGrath told him he did not work for the state medical examiner, Bennett said.

A lawyer in Georgia took the deposition last August and provided it to the Missoulian.

As a forensic pathologist, Bennett testifies as an expert witness in wrongful death cases on behalf of automobile manufacturers. James Butler of Butler, Wooten, Cheeley and Peak took the deposition after hearing Bennett testify multiple times.

"He hires out to the automobile companies all the time. He comes up with this bogus theory about how somebody who got killed didn't suffer at all," Butler said.

Other medical professionals discredit him, and the literature contradicts his theories, Butler said. The lawyer said he had grown tired of the sham.

"I just got to the point where what Bennett does was offensive, you know?" Butler said.

In summary, here is what happens:

- On the basis of an autopsy and without any reference to witness accounts, impressive and emphatic forensic pathologists declare "child abuse," "shaken-baby syndrome," or some other past event theory from the witness stand in one case after another.
- The public and the justice system are happy because a doctor with impressive credentials has spoken and they trust him.

- After years have gone by and problems become apparent, an impressive and emphatic forensic pathologist is made to look like a villain.
- At no time is there any understanding of why he was so impressive back then and why he is not so impressive now. Why was he so right back then and so wrong now? What changed?

Nothing changed. Nothing ever changes. Year after year, the same mistakes are made and nothing is learned. How can anyone learn anything when everyone is confused? How can anything be corrected when no one understands?

***

Prosecuting attorney Kristin Kaye was the first to offer her closing argument.[5] I summarize what she said happened in the list below:

1. While in the motel room with the defendant and his mother, Ja'Keen "peed on the defendant while he was changing the diaper."
2. The defendant became angry.
3. He "hit Ja'Keen to punish him for it."
4. Jameshia scolded Deterryon for spanking the child.
5. This made the defendant upset.
6. Without asking for Jameshia's permission, the defendant took the child outside of the motel room.
7. The defendant waited for the door of the motel room to close.
8. Then he hit the child outside of the room ("Watching the video, he waits for the door to the hotel room to shut before he hits the kid. Now why do you think he does that? So she won't hear him crying. You smack a toddler like that, and I guarantee you, he is going to cry.")
9. The "baby starts to cry."
10. This made him nervous ("So then after the baby starts to cry, I think it was loud enough that he got nervous").
11. The defendant "snatches the kid up."
12. The defendant "flings him around."
13. The defendant "slams the baby over his shoulder."
14. The defendant "carries him off quick to get him away from the door so that momma won't hear him crying."
15. The defendant "sets the baby down."
16. "You see the baby walk."
17. "They go into the vending machine room."
18. He intended to take "the baby somewhere where there's no obvious security cameras" because "he said in his interview that he knows there's cameras, right?"

19. "The baby won't stop crying."
20. He "picks the baby up."
21. And "puts him on the washing machine or the dryer."
22. He says, "Stop crying. Stop crying. You're not a baby. You're a big boy. You're a big boy. Ain't no babies here."
23. The defendant hits the child because the "baby won't stop crying."
24. The defendant "slams the baby into the wall" ("Where am I getting that from? I'm not making that up. Remember, the pathologist said that he had those scrapes on his back, and those scrapes didn't get explained. I think they're from slamming the baby up against the wall, and that's how he got those bruises.")
25. Then he "steps back" while "the baby's sitting on the floor."
26. "He's telling him, stop crying, stop crying. I'll give you something to cry about."
27. The defendant "picks him up…"
28. "…gets in his face…"
29. "…hits him again."
30. "They go back and forth like that until he realizes the baby's not moving. I've gone too far."
31. "He really starts to panic when Ms Laywell comes out to the vending room and says, what is going on out here? Is everything okay?"
32. The defendant says, "Oh, we're just trying to get a snack. Do you have any fruit? Do you have anything?"
33. "She goes back into the hotel to get the snack."
34. "He takes the baby outside, and he's going like, you're okay, you're okay, it's okay, you're okay, stand up, walk it off, walk it off."
35. "No. The baby's not standing. He's not going to walk that off. He's done. He's done. He is limp on the ground."
36. He threw the child in the air because "he wants y'all to believe that there is nothing wrong with this kid at this point."
37. The defendant took the child into the motel lobby because "Is he going to take him back to the room where the mom is a hypervigilant mom? No way."
38. He got on the computer and did something on it.
39. People "keep coming in there and bugging him about this kid. Is the baby okay? Is that baby okay? Is there something wrong with that baby?"
40. He's "getting increasingly nervous."
41. He "takes the banana and leaves."
42. He waited with the child outside the motel room because he didn't want to disturb Jameshia from her bath. ("He says, well, we're waiting for Jameshia to be done with her bath. Why? What is it about her being in the bathtub that prevents you from taking the kid and putting him to bed? That doesn't make any sense.")

43. He tried to feed the child the banana. ("I don't know why you're trying to wake your sleeping toddler up to feed him a banana.")
44. The "baby has no head control. He's floppy like this. He flops around."
45. "He takes the baby inside of the hotel room."
46. "He immediately gets Jameshia to come outside and sit on the stairs with him."
47. "And after that, everything that he does is designed to keep the mom away from the baby. You watch in the video. He's the one that's in charge of going back to check on the baby."
48. "She goes back one time to look in on the baby."
49. "He follows her, brings her back right away."
50. "Turned off all the lights in the room so now it's dark."
51. "Then they go to bed."
52. "He keeps her distracted and away from the baby. He's the one who tucks the baby in and everything."
53. "Sometime in that night, he gets up to check the baby…Remember that cell phone video where he went and videoed the baby, checking on him?"
54. "He starts trying to think of a story. How am I going to explain this? What am I going to do? What am I going to say?"
55. "So he takes the baby and puts the baby on the floor…"
56. "…comes up with this story about how the baby must have fallen, hit his head, or suffocated or whatever in the night. And it's just a mistake. It's all just a terrible accident."

I counted 56 events in her lengthy scenario.

Attorney Kaye had more to say, particularly about "yours truly." Among some of what she said was the following:

> I think it's interesting that his expert spent a lot of time looking at that video and discounting it. He's like the Wizard of Oz over here. Pay no attention to the man behind the curtain. We don't want to talk about the videos for our case. We only want to talk about what the defendant says because that's the only thing that the expert thinks is important. Why is that? Why is that? It's like he can't determine anything unless it's something that the defendant said, and then suddenly it's golden. That's a problem for them because the expert based his opinion on the defendant's statements. So you cannot believe their expert's opinion unless you believe the defendant's statements to the police. You cannot believe his statements to the police. You only have to listen to those statements and compare them to the evidence to see that they're not true.

Richard Hurlburt followed with his closing argument. In most court cases, the prosecutor gets both the first and final word. Because of the disadvantage of being the second of three arguments, Attorney Hurlburt had to make his count. Here is some of what he said:

> Ladies and gentlemen of the jury, this is an unbelievably tragic case in more ways than one. A child died in this case. And the State of Texas wants to take another life, to lock him up for the rest of his life for a crime he did not commit.
>
> They have to prove to you beyond a reasonable doubt that my client killed this child. They didn't come close. They told you their theory. Their theory doesn't fit the forensics. It doesn't fit. And it's clear that it doesn't fit.
>
> Defense attorneys have a huge job. Think of representing an individual charged with capital murder. It's on my shoulders to make sure an innocent person doesn't go to prison. Think of the responsibility. It's unbelievable. I would not ever want anybody who is innocent to spend the rest of his life behind bars.
>
> So beyond a reasonable doubt is important in every criminal case, especially a capital murder. What does "beyond a reasonable doubt" mean? It means that when you leave here you don't even think about whether or not you did the right thing. There's no question in your mind that you did the right thing on a capital murder case. But in this case there's plenty of reasonable doubt.

Mr. Hurlburt then went through the evidence brought by the state. He replayed several videos. He pointed out how Dr. Lyon did not have enough information but only a theory from detectives. He pointed out the grainy surveillance videos and talked about the allegedly dead child that the hypervigilant mother failed to notice (in spite of the "tossing and turning" she did notice). He talked about the absurdity of taking a dead child into a motel lobby, figuring that no one would notice the death. He recited all the evidence that supported the account of Deterryon Kelly:

> What do we have from the statements of Deterryon Kelly? What he says fits the forensics. Only that fits the forensics...The State's theory is impossible. Deterryon Kelly's story fits the forensics. Do you think Deterryon Kelly is clever enough to make things up that he's going to know later on will fit the forensics? Does that make sense? That he's going to think, well, I need to say that he was stuck between this bed and this dresser. You know, lo and behold, it fits the forensics.
>
> What the State says does not fit. If the child had not been stuck between something and could breathe and if the child had a lacerated liver, he would have bled out over 50% of his blood, and he would have done it very, very, very quickly. It could not have happened at 11 o'clock in the vending machine room. We know from the forensics that that is impossible.
>
> I can't imagine a jury going back there and saying, I believe beyond a reasonable doubt he's guilty of capital murder after you've heard what you've heard. I just can't imagine it.

Soon, the jury would do the unimaginable.

Notes

1. Boyle T, Tyler T. Payout urged in Smith probe. thestar.com, October 1, 2008. http://www.thestar.com/news/ontario/2008/10/01/payout_urged_in_smith_probe.html. Accessed on November 12, 2017.
2. Boyle T. Baby death review "daunting." *The Toronto Star*, October 7, 2008. http://www.canadiancrc.com/newspaper_articles/Toronto_Star_220_Shaken_Baby_Syndrome_Deaths_under_review_07OCCT08.aspx. Accessed on November 12, 2017.
3. Hasham A. Ontario chief pathologist slammed by judge for offering "incorrect" opinions in court. *The Toronto Star*, April 13, 2017. https://www.thestar.com/news/crime/2017/04/13/ontario-chief-pathologist-slammed-for-offering-incorrect-opinions-in-court.html. Accessed on November 12, 2017.
4. Szpaller K. Forensic pathologist will no longer do work for Montana county coroners. *Missoulian*, July 11, 2015. http://missoulian.com/news/local/forensic-pathologist-will-no-longer-do-work-for-montana-county/article_ca1fd980-d64d-5926-ab14-1de64a62be4d.html. Accessed on November 12, 2017.
5. Reporter's Record, The State of Texas vs. Deterryon Tyrell Kelly, Trial Court Cause No. 14-0275X, Court of Appeals No. 06-17-00001-CR. Volume 6.

Kayakers, Spider Bites, Jack the Ripper, and Speaking for the Dead 19

The next four news articles are strange but instructive.

The New York Times, September 10, 2015: Autopsy Cites "Intentionally Removed" Plug in Ruling Kayaker's Death a Homicide[1]

The medical examiner's conclusion is clear: Vincent Viafore, who the police say was killed by his fiancée during a kayaking trip on the Hudson River this past spring, was a victim of homicide caused by a "kayak drain plug intentionally removed by other."

But the lawyer for the fiancée, Angelika Graswald, said the medical examiner's office had overstepped its bounds with that determination. He said it was based on police speculation, not an examination of Mr Viafore's body.

"Clearly, the Orange County medical examiner failed to conduct any meaningful investigation of her own and relied on false information provided by the New York State Police," the lawyer, Richard A. Portale, said on Thursday, referring to Jennifer L. Roman, who performed the autopsy for the medical examiner's office in Orange County, N.Y.

"She ruled this a homicide without a scintilla of medical evidence," Mr. Portale added.

He argued that the reference to the kayak plug in the autopsy report could prejudice a jury.

Since May, when Mr. Viafore's body was pulled from the Hudson, prosecutors have declined to identify a cause of death or release the autopsy.

A copy of the report was obtained by *The New York Times*. It was unsurprising in some of its conclusions. It lists the cause of death as drowning (Mr Viafore, 46, who was not wearing a life jacket, capsized in 46-degree water, cold enough to quickly cause hypothermia). The toxicology results attached gave his blood alcohol concentration as 0.066%, close to the legal limit of 0.08 and consistent with Ms Graswald's account that the couple, who shared an apartment in Poughkeepsie, paddled to Bannerman Island on April 19, where Mr Viafore had a few beers.

The autopsy offers a grim, methodical accounting of Mr Viafore's body, which was recovered from the middle of the river on May 23. His face and abdomen were bloated, the report says, and marked by a mottled red and green discoloration.

Besides evidence of drowning, the only injuries noted in the report are a two-inch abrasion on the left torso and bruises on the lower chest and arm, also on the left side. The police have made no reference to a possible struggle between Mr Viafore and Ms Graswald, 35, while they were in their kayaks, though they have said Ms Graswald moved his paddle out of his reach after he went in the water.

Some legal experts agreed with Mr Portale's contention that the medical examiner's conclusions had gone too far. Jeanine Pirro, a former district attorney in Westchester County who now hosts "Justice With Judge Jeanine" on Fox News Channel, said medical examiners typically gave the manner of death, whether accident, suicide, homicide or undetermined, without elaborating.

"That is a very unusual way of describing manner of death," Ms. Pirro said in a phone interview. "It's rare that you get something next to the manner of death that is so outside the analysis of the body."

"Let's assume that the drain plug was removed," she added. "It doesn't mean it's a homicide. It could mean that it was removed by accident. What does that have to do with the drowning? If that's what the medical examiner thinks, she's going to have to back that up on the stand."

The medical examiner's office referred questions about the report to the Orange County executive's office.

The county executive's office defended the medical examiner's actions. Justin Rodriguez, a spokesman for the county executive, Steven M. Neuhaus, said a medical examiner could use facts outside of the autopsy, citing a state law that addresses determinations about cause and manner of death.

"Obviously this statute envisions that the autopsy is only one aspect of the medical examiner's examination into the cause of death," he said. "If medical examiners were limited to basing their conclusions solely on a physical examination of the body, there would be no coroner inquests. The coroners and medical examiners have been doing this for over 100 years."

The case has captivated residents of the Hudson Valley and beyond, for both its puzzling circumstances and the defendant's behavior. For more than a week after Mr Viafore's drowning, the police described it as an accident. Ms Graswald, meanwhile, was posting numerous photographs and videos to Facebook that showed her smiling broadly, doing cartwheels and kayaking.

After Ms Graswald was charged on April 30, the police said she had implicated herself in the killing. At a bail hearing later, they quoted her as having said, among other things, that it "felt good knowing he was going to die."

Mr Portale, her lawyer, said his client's statements to the police had been coerced.

Complicating matters is the assertion by Mr Portale that the kayak's drain plug had been missing for some time. Kayaking experts have said that a missing plug would not necessarily cause a boat to sink because the hole it closes, at the top of the vessel, is so small. (Mr Viafore's kayak did not sink to the bottom of the river, and was later found near shore.)

Such plugs, kayaking instructors say, are designed to make it easy to rid the kayak of excess water by flipping it over on dry land. In very choppy conditions,

> water can splash directly into the cockpit, causing the kayak to ride low in the water and making it unstable.
>
> Lawrence Kobilinsky, a forensics expert and chairman of the department of sciences at John Jay College of Criminal Justice in Manhattan, also found the reference to the kayak plug troubling, particularly the description that it was "intentionally removed by other."
>
> Calling the reference a "red herring," Dr. Kobilinsky said that medical examiners can and do consider police reports and other information besides the physical examination in arriving at a manner of death. However, he said, the leap from ruling a death a homicide to suggesting it was murder is not one a medical examiner should make.
>
> "That's not something the medical examiner should be writing down," he said of the reference to the plug's intentional removal. "It already presumes it's a murder. Homicide can be justified or not justified, or it can be an accident. It simply means that one person causes the death of another."
>
> "The way it was written," he added, "sounds like the medical examiner was saying it's clearly a murder based on pulling the plug. But that's a big hop, skip and a jump, and in a courtroom, all of this stuff will get dissected to the finest detail."

Or Dr. Kobilinsky hopes that "all of this stuff will get dissected to the finest detail." That frequently does not happen in court. Everyone is confused—including the doctor—and no one has the ability to understand what really happened.

The manner of death as a homicide is simply the opinion of the doctor. That opinion is supposed to be based on something factual rather than something imagined.

Judge Jeanine Pirro and the fiancée's attorney may sound reasonable with what they say, but there is something they are missing: a doctor cannot look at a body at the time of autopsy and figure that she knows everything she needs to know about the death. In fact, if witnesses do not tell what happened, then neither she nor anyone else can know what happened. Drownings all tend to look similar to each other at autopsy, and an autopsy by itself will not tell anyone if someone pulled a plug or did something else.

In this story, we never learn in detail what the only witness, the fiancée, ever saw or heard. We just hear a strange account from the police who quoted her as saying how it "felt good knowing he was going to die." That is a weird thing for anyone to say in these kinds of circumstances and not entirely believable. Was this a freely-offered account of what happened? Or was this the kind of forced "confession" often given by suspects to police officers when they find themselves in a "no-win" situation? We do not know from the news account.

But there is something we all should know that often happens with the medical examiner. Police officers show up at autopsies and give the forensic doctor the kind of "witness" account that they hope will convince the doctor to call this a homicide. Once the doctor goes along with their theory, it makes it easier to shove this case through court and get a conviction.

In a case like this, what the forensic doctor should do is (1) ignore opinions offered by police officers who attend the autopsy, (2) find out what the initial, detailed, freely-offered account of the witness was at the outset of the police investigation, and (3) compare that account to all of the physical evidence "clues"—not just the autopsy but everything else too. If the initial account does not square up with the other evidence, then ask witnesses many careful, non-leading questions that are not intended to accuse but instead to find out what really happened.

If detailed, freely-offered witness accounts square with all of the evidence and there are no items that do not square up, then those detailed accounts are highly likely to be what happened. Facts from witnesses and physical evidence clues are what both medical examiners and law-enforcement officers should try to learn in any investigation.

Daily Mail.com, September 16, 2015: EXCLUSIVE: Was Killer Professor Driven Mad by a Spider Bite? Delta State Academic Who Murdered Girlfriend and Colleague Was in Despair Over His Swollen Face[2]

Here is another complicated theory to ponder:

> The rage that led gunman Shannon Lamb to kill his girlfriend and a fellow university professor is thought to have been sparked by a spider bite, Daily Mail Online can reveal.
>
> Dr. Lamb had become increasingly upset after a spider bite became infected and caused his face to swell, triggering a spate of mental health problems.
>
> He became conscious of his bloated cheek, withdrew from work earlier this summer and failed to attend scheduled classes at Delta State University. He was allowed to reduce his hours at the college to seek medical treatment, but became increasingly 'disillusioned' and went into isolation.
>
> Senior police sources said he was 'tormented and full of anxieties' when he wreaked havoc, shooting his girlfriend dead and then hunting down professor Ethan Schmidt.
>
> Detectives are working on the theory that the two killings were not linked by motive and that Lamb, 45, may have been jealous of his college colleagues and wrongly felt his standing had been affected in his absence.
>
> Daily Mail Online can reveal that in several telephone calls he made to his elderly mother and other relatives, the gunman said he had shot his partner Amy Prentiss, 41, by accident.

> He claimed he had been trying to shoot himself when she attempted to stop him and the gun went off accidentally, blasting her in the head once.
>
> The call was made before he headed to Delta State University in Cleveland and targeted Professor Schmidt, who was a father-of-three.
>
> But another possibility being looked at by police is that Lamb and Prentiss may have entered into a suicide pact, with him blasting her to death with a 0.380 gun and then deciding he could not turn the weapon onto himself.

The story goes on like this, adding more possibilities and speculations; however, the main question is…

Did the spider make him do it?

WNEM.com, September 16, 2015: Coroner Disputes Delta State Professor "Spider Bite" Theory[3]

A local news agency in Mississippi followed up on the exclusive from the UK press agency. They wondered where the spider bite theory came from. The Daily Mail was the only news organization making this claim, according to WNEM News. They contacted someone from the Daily Mail staff, but the representative refused to reveal the source of the information or any details.

A news conference earlier in the week with the university president disclosed that the professor had cut back his hours due to a medical issue. They didn't know what the medical problem was.

Coroner Methel Johnson ordered an autopsy on Dr. Lamb. Lamb appeared to have shot himself in the woods after running from the police. The coroner said the gunshot left the decedent with bruises and lacerations in his head and face, but there wasn't anything that looked like a spider bite. He wasn't buying the spider bite theory.

Mississippi Department of Health Communications Director Liz Sharlot was not aware of any reports of spider bites causing mental problems. The health department does not track spider bites.

Perhaps toxicology tests from the autopsy might reveal additional information, mused Mississippi Department of Public Safety spokesman Warren Strain.

The Daily Mail reporter clearly does not identify any particular source for the spider bite idea. There is no one to verify if the professor who shot his wife (or girlfriend) was even bit by a spider and if any strange behavior was seen following a spider bite. It appears to be a speculation, and such speculations are often imagined from incomplete evidence. The probability of floating a theory like this and having it be true is very, very close to zero. Think of flipping the coin…

The news story from Mississippi, however, presents something more reliable than a theory from the UK. During a press conference, investigators revealed an important telephone call from the home shared by Lamb and Prentiss:

Lamb: Um. You need to send some units over to 2320 Santa Cruz.
Dispatcher: What's going on there?
Lamb: I shot my wife last night.
Dispatcher: You said its 2320 Santa Cruz?
Lamb: Yes. There's a dog in the house. He's a sweet dog and he won't bother anybody but I'm sure he's upset.
Dispatcher: What is your name?
Lamb: Um. That's all I feel like saying right now. Just go and take care of her. You'll find all of her family phone numbers in her phone. You can contact them.
Dispatcher: What is her name?
Lamb: Amy Prentiss.

Speculations aside, there is one thing we can know for certain: if Professor Lamb's freely-offered statement to a 911 operator matches what was found at the house and there is nothing inconsistent, then his statement to that operator is highly likely to be true. Police, prosecutors, forensic doctors, and news reporters cannot invent past-event theories that fit all available physical evidence without inconsistency, yet eyewitnesses often make statements that fit *all* available physical evidence without inconsistency. Because of the complexities of past events and physical evidence, such statements are highly likely to be true when they fit.

Here is another story about speculations piled upon speculations.

CBS News, October 25, 2015: The Undying Fascination Over Jack the Ripper[4]

Shortly before Halloween in 2015, CBS News treated their viewers and readers with something fitting for the holiday.

The author of the story tells of a successful business in London's East End: a tour that leads avid tourists down the very same streets traveled by London's famous villain from Victorian England, Jack the Ripper.

Mick Priestly is the tour guide. He stays busy every night, treating his curious customers to details from this enduring mystery. He brings the fog, the top hats, the capes, the gaslights, and the cobblestones of long-ago Victorian London back to life again.

Jack the Ripper, a nineteenth century serial killer of supposed education and nobility brutally preyed on the poor and the prostitutes, on people living desperate lives in the slums. Priestly tells about the killer's first victim, Mary Ann Nichols. The Ripper cut her throat deeply: a nine-inch cut from one direction met another six-inch cut from another direction. Priestly also describes other murders as the tour visits scenes of savage brutality.

All of this fascinates his customers. Why? Because, according to Mick Priestly—unlike Sherlock Holmes, Dr. Jekyll, and Mr. Hyde—Jack the Ripper was real.

Really?

Much has been said and written about Jack the Ripper. Dr. Joseph Bell, the famous pattern for Sherlock Holmes, dabbled in this case, and many have dabbled ever since. A search of news accounts on the internet shows a steady stream of Jack the Ripper articles appearing constantly, even up to the present. Much has been said and there have been a lot of data collected, but there is one important missing item:

Where are the witnesses?

No witness ever came forth to provide any detailed account of any of the murders. Without witnesses, we do not know anything for certain most of the time. We can only guess.

We do not know if there even was such a person as Jack the Ripper. We do not know if many different perpetrators murdered the prostitutes. There is no physical evidence linking one case to another in a way that would indicate one perpetrator.

Prostitution is a dangerous business, and the people prostitutes deal with may be dangerous. Those who seek the services of prostitutes often want to remain anonymous, so it is understandable that witnesses may not surface. Without witness accounts, we cannot know what happened. All we can do is pile speculation upon speculation, creating a monster called Jack the Ripper.

Still, who needs witnesses when we have modern DNA technology?

Back in 2002, according to the article, crime novelist Patricia Cornwell got into the Ripper game, claiming to have solved the crime, something several have claimed for many years. She found DNA from one of the supposed letters from Jack the Ripper that matched artist, Walter Sickert. Sickert was also fascinated with the Ripper, even painting a picture entitled "Jack the Ripper's Bedroom." Someone fascinated with the Ripper might have handled one of the artifacts of the case, leaving traces of his DNA, but that doesn't mean he was Jack.

The latest to use DNA evidence to solve the crime was Russell Edwards, a self-described "armchair detective." Russell claims that the murderer was a barber from Poland: Aaron Kosminski. Russell claims to be "100% certain" that Kosminski was the man. He found the DNA on a silk shawl that he bought at an auction in 2007: a shawl supposedly recovered from the crime scene of victim Catherine Eddowes who was killed in 1888.

Russell hired a molecular biologist from Liverpool John Moores University to do a DNA analysis. Some of the DNA from bloodstains could be traced back to relatives of Catherine Eddowes and some to relatives of Kosminski.

At one point in the Ripper investigation, the police considered Aaron Kosminski as a suspect, but he was never charged. He later died in an asylum.

According to Russell Edwards, the case is now proven. All of the evidence fits like a jigsaw puzzle.

Unfortunately, the shawl has chain of custody issues: no one knows through whose hands the shawl has passed after all these years. Many could have contaminated the shawl with their DNA well after the murder or even before it.

Jack the Ripper is still at large. Do not expect this intriguing mystery to be solved anytime soon.

Dateline NBC, August 20, 2007: Dead Men Talking: Inside a Medical Examiner's Office[5] and *Eden Prairie News*, November 2, 2017: Speakers for the Dead[6]

These stories are only two examples of many like them: stories that claim that forensic doctors "speak for the dead." "Dead men tell no tales," is what Long John Silver, the murderous pirate in Robert Louis Stevenson's classic tale, *Treasure Island*, both menacingly observed and threatened, but thanks to forensic doctors who behave and think like another fictional character, Sherlock Holmes, dead people are now able to tell us what happened. "My job is to let the victim tell me what they can tell me through the physical evidence," according to the former chief medical examiner featured in the *Dateline NBC* story. "We're the people who can speak for the dead," claims the chief medical examiner in the Eden Prairie News story.

They are not the only people who make this kind of claim. A simple internet search using the words, "I speak for the dead," discloses a memoir written by another former chief medical examiner[7] and a television series featuring a coroner from Pennsylvania.[8]

Claiming to "speak for the dead" is egregiously arrogant—even godlike. The public buys it because they like and respect the arrogant Sherlock Holmes. The public does not realize the serial injustice brought about by this strange but self-aggrandizing way of thinking. Doctors who think like this do not realize how limited they are. The only activity that forensic doctors can do that is reliable is to explain the science behind what someone else saw and heard—someone who is living. They can't reliably conjure up some story of what happened from a person who is no longer living. Even if they do that, they might believe the story they imagine, but they don't know how truthful and factual it is.

Long John Silver was right: Dead men tell no tales. Only living and breathing eyewitnesses tell the kinds of tales worth considering in a court of law.

***

District Attorney Coke Solomon offered the final closing argument for the Deterryon Kelly case[9]:

> Mr. Hurlburt has said that he doesn't know how he's going to live with himself if an innocent man goes to prison. He'll be fine because the defendant is not an innocent man. When Mr. Hurlburt finds one, then he'll have to suffer that. But we know this man isn't innocent.
>
> How would I feel if I thought I was sending an innocent man to prison? Do you think I want to stand up here and make an argument when somebody I believe is innocent committed a crime? Absolutely not. None of us would. In fact, every lawyer in this room took an oath not to do that.
>
> Mr. Hurlburt says he believes this man is innocent. I'm telling you right now, I believe this is one of the most guilty people I have ever seen.
>
> Mr. Hurlburt wants us to think his client is a hero. He tried to save this child. This man should be given a medal. I should stand up and dismiss this case. His client is the victim here, not this little kid.
>
> What is Mr. Hurlburt hanging his entire hat on? His entire case is based off of a hired gun, a man, a forensic pathologist, who specializes in testifying in trials.
>
> You heard him say he is in private practice, and this is what he does for a living. They asked, "Why didn't Dr. Lyon sit here to listen to their doctor's testimony? Because he had to go back to work. Because he had bodies piling up. Because his office does pathology for four or five counties.
>
> He's not a hired gun who can sit here and listen to everything. We don't have the luxury to have someone who can sit here 24 hours or a couple of days to watch everything and pick it apart. Hindsight is 20/20.
>
> Well, their expert says the forensics match his client's story and not Dr. Lyon's determination based on his pathology findings. Well, of course his expert says that. That's what he's paid to do.
>
> How do we know that's what he's doing? How do we know that the forensics match his client's story? Because his expert makes it match his client's story. His entire testimony is focused on fitting his client's story like he tried to fit the kid through that space.
>
> You heard the defense expert say how this isn't even a good representation of how big the kid would have been. The kid's actually bigger, taller, wider, longer. Fit all that through this space!
>
> Let's talk about why what his expert is saying is the most garbage thing we've ever heard in our life. In order for this kid to get through here (Attorney Solomon points to his drawing), we have to think of his 33-inch tall, 24-pound body—the whole thing. Not just his head. Not just his waist. Not just his chest.
>
> This 24-pound kid put enough pressure on this bed so that he could slip through this 3-inch space to wedge himself between the nightstand and the

bed. That is the dumbest thing I have ever heard in my life! That's unbelievable! That is unbelievable and absurd!

Pay me $300 an hour, I guarantee you I'll tell you that. That's what I'd do for a living. That's exactly what this man just did, and it's appalling! He should be held accountable for coming in and talking garbage like that!

He says, "I have all of the evidence and Dr. Lyon didn't have anywhere near as much," so that's why he wasn't able to come up with this cockamamie theory of the kid who weighed enough to allow him to slip between the bed and the nightstand in this 3-inch section.

Come on, folks. You can use common sense. When did common sense not come into a courtroom? When does common sense get checked at the door? Never. Does that make any sense? Can you think of any area in the world where that makes sense?

Certainly, I'm almost speechless! I don't even know what to say about that, it's so absurd!

The only reason that the parents obviously didn't know he was there was because he slipped into this space at the speed of light. Stuck. Can't scream. Can't do anything. Just like somebody stuck between glass doors. Really?

That caused the kid to slowly die. So the adults wake up and momma says, "Where is my kid?" What did momma tell you from this witness stand? They don't want you to remember that.

There is so much that they don't want you to think about. There is so much that this expert can't let you think about in order for his story to work. Momma said, "I saw the kid on the floor." Not between the nightstand and the bed. You heard her testify to that.

This is garbage! This is a really convenient explanation for the defendant to come up with to get out of being busted because he got pissed off and killed this kid. That's what we've got.

This is the thing you've got to remember. When you go back into this room for deliberations, you're going to be thinking about all of this evidence. How does the evidence match? How does this evidence fit to the crime that we're charging him with, which is capital murder? We're asking you to convict this man of capital murder. He intentionally and knowingly killed this kid because he was pissed off at this kid. The kid was under the age of 10. Capital murder. Simple.

So when you go back into that jury room, you need to consider that the only way you can believe anything their expert says, you have to believe the defendant.

You have to believe everything he says before you can even begin to believe their expert. Because their expert believes the defendant. The expert takes every fact he can find, every piece of forensic evidence, and makes this work. This is impossible. It's impossible.

I'm not showing you all the graphic photographs. Take those back there. I'm telling you, please suffer through those. They're as important as this video, which I'm going to ask you to watch on a laptop. You've got to watch it a couple of times. Do it. Because no matter what this guy says, even though

> he tries to tell you that the image is not better on the laptop, you know better than that, folks. Watch it on the laptop. You can see it a little better than this TV.

Mr. Solomon continued with discussing specific evidence. One item he mentioned was the sex video.

> The phone video. Look at that video. The defendant even knows that he was recording. Watch him. He goes over, and holds that phone above that child.
>
> Well, if somebody is sleeping and you want to know if they're alive, do you look to see if the chest is moving? Watch that video, folks. That kid's chest never moves. It is stone silent. Not moving.

He mentioned the *rigor mortis.*

> They want you to believe not only is this (the entrapment) is what led to the kid's death, but this kid was alive when he got to the hospital. Had to have been because there is no other way this electrical pulse could have been there.
>
> Rigor mortis? No way it would not have been there. It takes two to six hours for rigor mortis to set in, depending on the temperature that the victim's body is in. They say 66 degrees when it fits them, but they don't say that when it does not. The temperature of that room could have slowed down the speed at which rigor mortis set in on that kid.
>
> The ER doctor, does he have any reason to lie? He was willing to testify. I thank him for that because doctors are hard to get in the courtroom. He didn't try to come up with some cockamamie story of how it happened. He said the kid was dead when he came to their ER. This kid was dead. It was cold. It was 80 degrees.
>
> They want you to believe that as you sit here right now in this frigid courtroom, your body is 80 degrees because you're just climatizing. Really? That is the dumbest thing I ever heard. That's an absurd argument. It's the only way to make this expert's ridiculous story fit. It's impossible, ladies and gentlemen.
>
> Dr. Morris has nothing to gain from coming in here and testifying. He missed out on half a day of work. I'm sure he probably makes more than $300 an hour.

Mr. Solomon wrapped up his argument to the jury:

> Guys, if you believe otherwise, this doesn't work. The only way this works is you have to believe that man over there (points to the defendant) and everything he told law enforcement. You're not going to do that because you can use your common sense.
>
> The best evidence in the world is the evidence that you can see. Watch that video. Tell me that kid is okay when he comes out of the room.

I will ask you to find this man guilty of capital murder, because when you look at that video, you're going to know that the kid is not okay when he comes out of the vending machine room. The only person who was with the child in that room was the defendant, regardless of what their expert said, that there may have been some other person in there.

Thank you.

Notes

1. Foderaro LW. Autopsy cites "intentionally removed" plug in ruling Kayaker's death a homicide. *The New York Times*, September 10, 2015. http://www.nytimes.com/2015/09/11/nyregion/in-autopsy-report-medical-examiner-says-kayaker-was-victim-of-homicide.html?_r=0. Accessed on November 12, 2017.
2. Bhatia S. EXCLUSIVE: Was killer professor driven mad by a spider bite? Delta State academic who murdered girlfriend and colleague was in despair over his swollen face. Daily Mail.com, September 16, 2015. http://www.dailymail.co.uk/news/article-3236958/Delta-State-professor-Shannon-Lamb-murdered-girlfriend-colleague-spider-bite-left-face-swollen-descened-despair-claimed-partner-s-death-accident.html. Accessed on November 10, 2017.
3. Conaway B. Coroner disputes Delta State professor "spider bite" theory. WNEM.com, September 16, 2015. http://www.wnem.com/story/30046004/article-claims-delta-state-professor-driven-mad-by-spider-bite. Accessed on November 12, 2017.
4. Cowan L. The undying fascination over Jack the Ripper. *CBS News*, October 25, 2015. http://www.cbsnews.com/news/the-undying-fascination-over-jack-the-ripper/. Accessed on November 12, 2017.
5. Corderi V. Dead men talking: Inside a medical examiner's office. *Dateline NBC*, August 20, 2007. http://www.nbcnews.com/id/20364031/ns/dateline_nbc/t/dead-men-talking-inside-medical-examiners-office/?hasFlash=true&#.WDxfB3fMyem. Accessed on November 12, 2017.
6. Jones H. Speakers for the dead. *Eden Prairie News*, November 2, 2017. http://www.swnewsmedia.com/eden_prairie_news/news/speakers-for-the-dead/article_e8ab5f6a-fdba-5586-8660-2aad7176c48c.html. Accessed on November 10, 2017.
7. Amazon.com. https://www.amazon.com/Speak-Dead-Joye-M-Carter/dp/097037223X. Accessed on November 12, 2017.
8. The coroner: I speak for the dead. *Investigation Discovery*, 2016. https://www.investigationdiscoverygo.com/the-coroner-i-speak-for-the-dead/. Accessed on November 12, 2017.
9. Reporter's Record, The State of Texas vs. Deterryon Tyrell Kelly, Trial Court Cause No. 14-0275X, Court of Appeals No. 06-17-00001-CR. Volume 6.

CSI, Adam Ruins Forensic Science, Forensic Tree Teams, Divinity School, and a Bridge in Melbourne

20

Here are more strange but instructive stories:

Variety, September 17, 2015: "CSI" Farewell Panel Talks How DNA, Hair Fibers & Plushies Changed TV & Society[1]

This is a report of the celebration for the end of a long-standing hit television series:

> Actors, writers, producers and creators of CBS hit show "CSI: Crime Scene Investigation" gathered Wednesday night for a panel to mark its series finale at the Paley Center for Media in Beverly Hills. The Q&A concluded the 2015 PaleyFest Fall TV Previews.
>
> Devoted fan and *Entertainment Weekly* writer Lynette Rice moderated the event and began with a question directed to creator Anthony E. Zuiker. Rice asked how he thought to redefine the television crime genre, singing the iconic theme song, "Who were you, who who who who?"
>
> "I was watching a show called 'The New Detectives' on the Discovery Channel and saw a forensic docudrama… about a cheerleader who was killed and they pulled a long blonde hair out of the headrest," Zuiker started.
>
> After a voice-over explained the cause of death from studying the strand, Zuiker said, "That's when I learned that the body really is the perfect specimen and it was quite the tweak I needed to reinvent the cop drama."
>
> Zuiker was a tram driver in Las Vegas when he hit the jackpot on his first script ever, "CSI." Zuiker shared that in his last pitch attempt to CBS—after other networks declined—the network immediately bought the series as its last addition to the 2000 fall lineup. And the rest is history.
>
> The show's cinematic style and focus on coroners, instead of police officers, set it apart. William Petersen shared his experience at a pathology convention when coroners thanked him for highlighting their profession.
>
> "They said, 'We are finally out of the closet now. We get invited to parties, I can talk to girls and they call me back because they think it's cool that I'm a coroner'," Petersen remembered.

The U.S. courts system also changed with the public's new understanding of forensic science. Exec producer Jonathan Littman revealed that there is a federal jury instruction, called the "CSI" instruction, where prosecutors ask jurors if they can separate real life and TV.

"They were losing too many cases because the jurors were expecting to have fingerprints and hair fibers and DNA... they expected Billy Petersen," Littman explained.

The show's ripped-from-the-headlines plot also educated the public on some unbelievably shocking stories that were society truths—including the Plushie and Furry fetish communities.

"One of the weirdest storylines I ever experienced was Ted Danson's first episode," actress Elisabeth Harnois recounted. "It was about a shooting on a transit train and an octopus is found with a gunshot wound; it turns out the octopus was the sexual partner of a woman. This is based on a true story. Not the shooting part, but this kinky sort of world."

10-year "CSI" veteran John Wellner told *Variety* that "CSI" inspired a number of television programs that brought heroism to the sciences.

"So many other shows that you see now, 'NCIS,' 'Criminal Minds,' 'Cold Case,' all of those shows I feel like came from what 'CSI' created," Wellner said while adding that the show provided him with the expertise to consult on the upcoming Fox drama "Rosewood."

Other panelists that bid farewell to the show were original stars Marg Helgenberger, Jorja Fox, Eric Szmanda, Robert David Hall, Paul Guilfoyle, David Berman along with Wallace Langham, exec producer Jerry Bruckheimer, co-creators and exec producers Carol Mendelsohn and Ann Donahue as well as Danson, who will continue within the franchise on "CSI: Cyber." CBS' Leslie Moonves was also on hand to support the cast and crew.

The two-hour series finale of "CSI" airs at 9 p.m. Sept. 27 on CBS.

Forensic doctors, judges, and prosecutors routinely hate CSI. It has caused them to talk about the *CSI effect*, where juries supposedly do not want to convict anyone without the kind of science seen on their favorite television program.

For my part, I am thankful for programs like CSI and many others. It has helped get the attention of the public for what goes on with science in the courtroom. Without CSI and other forensic science fiction, it is possible that few people would have enough interest to purchase the book you are now reading.

I do not believe that forensic science fiction is a problem with *jurors*—at least from all that I have seen. I believe the problem with forensic science fiction has to do with *police officers, judges, prosecutors, and forensic doctors*—people who believe that forensic doctors can think like Sherlock Holmes and get reliable answers. Frankly, all of these professionals are the suckers who have been conned by Sherlock Holmes, and it is a shame that they manage to pass on such foolishness to jurors.

Also from the little I have seen, much of the drama in CSI does not take place in a courtroom but out at the scene of the death or in the laboratory. When a case is being investigated, there is nothing wrong with floating theories as a means of generating leads. The problem comes when forensic doctors, police officers, and prosecutors fail to tell the difference between facts—items that can be seen or heard—and beliefs—items that are imagined. Beliefs about what happened should be hypotheses to be tested with other evidence, and beliefs should spur investigators to keep looking for more facts and for ways to test the facts with other factual information. Once a case goes to court, all the theorizing should stop.

truTVEps, October 21, 2015: "Adam Ruins Forensic Science"[2]

A friend of mine brought to my attention this 21 minute episode on YouTube and truTV—a part of a series entitled, "Adam Ruins Everything." This series features Adam Conover, an irritating, know-it-all character with a pompadour and black-rimmed glasses who debunks nearly everything held near and dear by nearly everyone. One of the episodes exposes what is wrong with forensic science.

The video is entertaining, so you should consider watching it.

The story starts out with Adam arrested by police officers after he is found loitering around a crime scene. Adam can't stop talking, even though he is reminded of his "right to remain silent," even though they wish he would remain silent.

Prior to receiving a polygraph—a "lie detector" test which measures his physiologic responses to questions asked—Adam points out to the interrogating female cop that polygraphs don't work. Convicted serial killers who are relaxed and in control of their heart rate and blood pressure can defeat the testing, but truthful people who are nervous can fail them.

Later, after one of the officers points out that Adam was spotted at the crime scene, Adam responds by calling eyewitness testimony completely unreliable. Our memories can't be trusted. Our minds add and alter details over time, and witnesses are easily influenced by interrogating police officers, according to Adam. Elizabeth Loftus, a professor at the University of California at Irvine, suddenly appears as a character. She describes her pioneering research in the field of false memories, telling how she and her colleagues were able to alter the memories of test subjects through leading questions. Our memories work like a Wikipedia page that others and we can edit. Police officers can contaminate the memories of the witnesses they interview.

What about fingerprints? Adam argues that there is no proof scientifically that fingerprints are unique. There is also a large potential for error and bias, especially with smudged and partial prints. The details of a case can alter an examiner's interpretation of fingerprint evidence. University of California at Irvine criminologist, Simon Cole, then appears, stating that fingerprinting has not met the requirements of scientific reliability in the *Daubert* decision.

Adam goes on to blast hair comparison analysis, bite mark analysis, and the analysis of pouring patterns in arson investigations. Adam claims that forensic methods like these are great for sending people to jail but they are terrible for figuring out what actually happened. That means that the wrong person gets sent to prison and even executed.

Adam debunks nearly everything about forensic science. Now it is time for me, in part, to debunk Adam.

What is seen in this episode reflects the views of scientists who advised President Obama and the Innocence Project. These people think that eyewitnesses and forensic science are the reasons for why innocent people are wrongly accused and sent to jail.

Regarding eyewitnesses, much of what Adam presents is accurate, but it is misleading. Memories do degrade and they can be influenced profoundly, but even if the memories are faulty, the faults can be disclosed after a comparison to physical evidence for consistency or inconsistency. Much of what is said about faulty memory also does not apply when police officers question witnesses immediately or shortly after an event or when the event is described in a 911 telephone call. What happened immediately or even shortly before in an emergent situation is remembered in stunning detail, before there is even time to make any calculations about what to say or not to say, before there is even time to be biased for a particular outcome.

Eyewitness accounts may not be perfect, but they work much better than scientists speculating about complicated past events like Sherlock Holmes (which does not work at all).

Regarding forensic scientific tests, the techniques may not be perfect (nothing human is perfect), but they are typically not a problem *if the results are compared to eyewitness accounts for consistency or inconsistency.* They become a problem *if they are used to support past event theories*, like too many scientists, doctors, attorneys, and police officers are accustomed to doing. "What actually happened" comes from eyewitnesses and not from physical evidence. The physical evidence, including fingerprints, bite marks, and hair comparisons can affirm witness accounts as possible or deny them as not possible—nothing more, really, and nothing less. (Note: a polygraph is not really physical evidence of "what happened," so that test doesn't apply here.)

If a subject stated he held an object, then finding fingerprints on the object consistent with his would affirm that statement. If a subject says he bit someone, then finding a bite mark on the person he bit consistent with the subject's dentition would affirm that statement. Such comparisons of witness accounts to physical evidence disclosed by forensic tests are deductive, like affirming that two plus two equals four and denying that two plus three equals four. If there are a lot of data to compare on both sides of the equal sign, then such comparisons are highly likely to be true.

One technique that uses a lot of data in a comparison is DNA testing.

The cops release Adam near the end of the story after they reluctantly agree with him, but before he walks out the door, the female cop asks him if there is a forensic test that does work. Innocence Project attorney M. Chris Fabricant suddenly appears. He states that DNA evidence freed 330 wrongfully convicted people, half of whom were put in jail by old, outdated forensic techniques.

In other words...DNA good...all other, outdated forensic techniques bad. This is because DNA testing was actually developed in laboratories by scientists rather than by police officers who pretend to be scientists. DNA is backed up by "real" research, unlike the older pseudoscientific forensic techniques.

Real science with real research, right? Maybe...but so what?

The only thing that DNA evidence did in those 330 wrongful convictions is affirm the accounts of the eyewitness defendants ("I told you I didn't do it!") and deny the invented theories of doctors, scientists, and law enforcement officers. Unfortunately, the Innocence Project and members of the former Forensic Science Commission do not understand this. If they did, they would be quick to condemn the theorizing and not the eyewitness accounts.

What is not disclosed in "Adam Ruins Forensic Science" is that DNA evidence—as powerful and as full of data as it is—can also lead to wrongful convictions if used to support past event theories. Past event theories invented by scientists, doctors, attorneys, and police officers are not going to be correct, so using DNA evidence to support that theory—whatever it is—is also not going to be correct. One day, Adam will have to come along and ruin that use of DNA evidence too.

Hannibal Courier-Post, September 24, 2015: "Forensic" Team to Look at South Main Tree Death[3]

Here is news, hot off the presses from Mark Twain's hometown of Hannibal, Missouri.

In 2015, Hannibal had problems with the trees located downtown on South Main Street next to B & B Theaters Main Street Cinema 8: the trees kept dying, and no one knew why. The city's Tree Board elected during the city's September meeting to put together something like a "forensic pathology" team to investigate the cause of death.

There were many factors to consider for why five Skyline Locust trees planted in the sidewalk cutout areas next to the theater were dying. Did the trunks still have wire girdles on them? Was there rubble where the trees were planted? What about root disease?

What appeared to be called for was a tree "autopsy" of sorts. Personnel from the Street Department would extract one of the trees for examination.

Brian Chaplin, the Public Works superintendent, was nervous. Who knew if they would encounter root ball? Who knew if the job would require popping up sidewalk? He dreaded the process, but he knew it had to be done.

The trees by the B & B theaters might not have been the only trees needing attention. A representative from the Mark Twain Hotel Apartments across Church Street from B & B also consulted the Tree Board about replacing a pair of their Skyline Locust trees. Those trees were also in poor condition and needed to be investigated.

I suppose the reporter went after the "cute" angle, writing about a "forensic pathology" team, making it look like he was reporting on *CSI: Midwest*, but there is nothing forensic going on in this story. There is no crime. No one is arrested and taken to court. No one is arguing a case involving what happened to a tree. No one is being punished.

It is not so much what "happened" to the trees; what is "happening" to the trees is what is important. It is a present situation that needs to be treated and not a past event that is no longer going on. There is a substantial amount of money involved in planting trees, and that investment needs to be protected. Depending on what the tree doctors find, their diagnoses will be tested by planting new trees and seeing if they survive.

On the other hand, what forensic doctors say in court will not be tested. The people declared guilty will not be treated but punished. Forensic doctors will forget these people as they move on to the next case.

WBUR, November 1, 2017: Opioid Epidemic Inspires New Hampshire Medical Examiner to Enter Ministry[4]

Prior to his interview by this public radio station, former chief medical examiner of New Hampshire, Dr. Thomas Andrew, saw his office swamped by a tsunami of drug overdose deaths. Drug deaths per year increased more than 17-fold during his tenure since he started the job in 1997.

Dr. Andrews eventually became tired of counting and cataloguing the overdose deaths in his state, so he decided to do something perhaps a little more meaningful: he decided to leave his job and enroll in divinity school so that he could minister to people with drug problems.

I admit that very little of what he said in the article has to do with the Sherlock Effect, but I saw something in the news report that caught my eye: I am intrigued by his description of the life of a medical examiner and the nature of the work.

He described "seasons" in the life of a forensic pathologist. Early on, one finds out if he or she is "hardwired" for doing the job for the next 30 years.

Many decide that they can't do it after a short while. Those who continue develop an attitude and a "fair amount of swag." The seasoned ME, according to Dr. Andrew, has seen and done everything: nothing bothers him anymore. Dr. Andrew claims that this is dangerous because it makes us fail to see the humanity in front of us on the autopsy table.

What is it like to have seen and done everything? What is it like to know most everything like Sherlock Holmes?

Experience can be a tricky thing, and long experience can be even trickier. Professor Moritz pointed out that "categorical intuitive deduction" is "prevalent among experienced forensic pathologists."[5] Experience in "categorical intuitive deduction" however is not useful experience. It is a mirage, a disappointment, and a tragedy. It is making the same mistake over and over and thinking that you are learning more and more as you make that same mistake.

I don't feel the same as Dr. Andrew about what we do as forensic pathologists and medical examiners. Instead, I find myself more and more realizing how little I understand about a vast number of things. I realize how humbling it is to be taught by eyewitnesses who have no training and experience in my field, who utter things I never considered before. Over time, my "swag" is not developing—it is shrinking and close to disappearing.

The Guardian, October 30, 2015: Murder of Girl Thrown From Bridge by Father "Could Not Have Been Predicted"[6]

Here is a report from "down under."

> Six years after a little girl was thrown from a Melbourne bridge during peak-hour traffic, a coroner has found no one could have predicted her father was going to murder her.
>
> Victorian Coroner Ian Gray released his findings on Friday into the death in 2009 of Darcey Iris, who was thrown from the West Gate Bridge by her father Arthur Freeman.
>
> Darcey died in hospital on 29 January, hours after Freeman stopped the car carrying her and her siblings, picked the four-year-old up and threw her from the bridge. Darcey was en route to her first day at school.
>
> Minutes earlier, Freemen had told his former wife to "say goodbye to her children" and that she would never see them again.
>
> Several motorists witnessed the peak-hour incident before Freeman got back into his car and drove to the federal court complex in the city centre, where he was arrested in a distressed state.
>
> He stopped once briefly when Darcey's brother repeatedly asked his father to go back to get Darcey because she could not swim.

> Freeman was found guilty of his daughter's murder by a jury in 2011 after they rejected his defence of mental impairment. The father denied remembering what he had done but accepted he had caused his daughter's death.
>
> He was sentenced to life in prison with a minimum period of 32 years.

I added this final story to address those of you who by now wrongfully conclude that I do not believe child abuse exists.

How absurd of you to think that! Over many years as a medical examiner, I have investigated child homicides that were unspeakably cruel—more cruel than I would dare write about in a book like this. You can't even imagine what I have seen during those investigations!

This case from Melbourne, Victoria, Australia involves a tragic murder of a small child. This is child abuse, no doubt about it.

There is something about this case, however, that differs from the other cases I have been writing about in this book. The difference in this case is that there were multiple eyewitnesses to the cruel event. The murder occurred at rush hour, and several motorists witnessed what happened. Darcey's brother witnessed what happened. Even Arthur Freeman's wife heard about what would happen shortly before the murder. I am certain that the evidence at the bottom of the bridge affirmed those witness accounts. Freeman's acknowledgement of the crime was not needed to know what happened in this case. His non-confession based on a faulty memory did not change anything.

Notice that no forensic doctor diagnosed child abuse in this case. When cases are well witnessed like this, it doesn't take a Sherlock-Holmes-style forensic doctor to make a diagnosis. No surmising about unwitnessed past events was required.

This story, however, is about forensic doctors. We learn about this as the story continues:

> The coroner found no one could have predicted Freeman was going to throw his daughter 58 metres to her death that day.
>
> "The evidence before me leads me to conclude that Freeman's actions, and Darcey's death, were unable to have been predicted with any great certainty," Gray wrote.
>
> It is important to place the responsibility for her death where it properly lies—solely on her father—the coroner says.
>
> Darcey was murdered the day after a court made final orders in a long-running custody battle between Freeman and his former wife, Peta Barnes.
>
> As part of that battle, Freeman and his history of family violence had been assessed by a psychologist.
>
> Barnes told the inquest she had expressed concerns to her GP [general medical practitioner] that her estranged husband might be vengeful enough to kill the couple's children to "get back at her."

> The GP told the inquest they did not recall having concerns about the children or witnessing any worrying behaviour from Freeman.
>
> Two other GPs who treated Barnes, Freeman and Darcey also said they did not see anything to suggest Darcey and her siblings were at harm. "At no time was I concerned that he was in any way a violent character with regard to his children," one said.
>
> The coroner made no adverse findings against the GPs or other professionals who saw Darcey and her father but said there was scope generally for better training about the risk of family violence.

What would that better training be? Would it be to inform doctors that there is a risk of family violence, that family members can be violent with other family members? Don't they already know this? Would it involve making judgments about people doctors may see briefly in their medical clinics and hospitals—people who are often on their best behavior, who don't behave there like they behave at home? Should doctors be asked to accuse those people of something they haven't done yet?

Here is the truth of the matter: No doctor can predict from observing a patient what that patient might or might not do, no matter how well trained the doctor is in medicine. Human behavior is complex and easily misunderstood, and doctors are not in a position to witness how someone behaves outside of the clinic.

But there is something doctors can do—if they knew to do it. This also involves eyewitnesses.

Family members know other family members better than anyone else. If a family member observes erratic and dangerous behavior in another family member, this could mean that something deadly might take place. Doctors need to be aware of such possibilities. Doctors need to listen carefully to witnesses with an open mind. Then doctors need to alert authorities who can evaluate and carefully investigate possible problems.

This did not happen, according to the ex-wife:

> Barnes told the inquest she had expressed concerns to her GP [general medical practitioner] that her estranged husband *might be vengeful enough to kill the couple's children to "get back at her."*

The doctors did not observe anything amiss:

> The GP told the inquest they did not recall having concerns about the children or *witnessing any worrying behaviour from Freeman.*
>
> Two other GPs who treated Barnes, Freeman and Darcey also said *they did not see anything to suggest Darcey and her siblings were at harm.* "At no time was I concerned that he was in any way a violent character with regard to his children," one said.

What doctors personally observe in this kind of a situation is not nearly as important as what eyewitnesses observe. Doctors see potential offenders for a short time, but family eyewitnesses may see that potential offender day after day, month after month, year after year. Doctors who fail to listen to witnesses but instead rely on their own judgments and observations often make mistakes.

Let me repeat: *Doctors who fail to listen to witnesses but instead rely on their own judgments and observations often make mistakes.* This is not only true with what could happen in the future; this is especially true with what definitely happened in the past.

The coroner in Victoria was merciful to the doctors for failing to pick up what could have happened (and what eventually did happen). I agree with the coroner. To fail to pick up something that might or might not happen in the future is understandable.

But will coroners, judges, and other leaders be merciful to forensic doctors when one day these officials finally understand how badly forensic doctors have failed them in past event cases?

***

Now I offer my closing argument for *State of Texas v. Deterryon Tyrell Kelly.* It is an argument I can't imagine any attorney would be willing to offer. It involves a little bit of mathematics (and attorneys often seem confused by mathematics).

The jurors in this case, as in every criminal case, were instructed that the burden of proof belongs to the prosecution. The prosecution had to prove "beyond a reasonable doubt" that Deterryon Kelly was guilty of the crime he was accused of committing.

You may recall the 56-point scenario summarized by Ms. Kaye in her closing argument.

You may also recall what I wrote about what happens with past events. One event leads to the next, and the next event will not occur without the prior event having occurred. The third event cannot occur without the second event having occurred prior to it, and the second event cannot occur without the first event having occurred. The final event—the pronouncement of Ja'Keen's death—cannot have occurred until all the 56 prior events listed in the 56-point summary occurred prior to it in the exact sequence listed. Any deviation would alter subsequent events. For example, Deterryon could not have assaulted Ja'Keen in the vending machine room unless Deterryon and Ja'Keen walked to the vending machine room prior to the alleged assault. The subsequent events would have changed drastically if Deterryon and Ja'Keen had decided walk somewhere else.

Do you remember the coin-flipping example from the "Brides in the Bath" case where pathologist Sir Bernard Spilsbury offered a theory of how a man killed multiple wives in bathtubs? Do you also recall the famous shaken-baby syndrome paper where "the most common scenario may be a child who is shaken, then thrown into or against a crib or other surface, striking the back of the head and thus undergoing a large, brief deceleration"?[7]

We are going to apply similar calculations to Ms. Kaye's 56-point scenario. Let's say that there is equal likelihood for any event listed in the scenario of occurring or not occurring. With the succession of each event dependent on the previous events, inventing a scenario like hers and expecting each event to be correct would be like flipping a coin and expecting to get "heads" every time. The probability that she got "heads" every time with her scenario is 0.5 multiplied by itself 56 times:

$$(0.5)^{56} = 0.00000000000000001388$$

...or 1.388×10^{-17} in scientific notation (1,388 with 16 zeroes and a decimal point to the left of it).

This means the probability that her scenario is wrong is infinitesimally close to 100% certain. No one would ever expect to flip a coin and get heads 56 times in a row, but this is something like what prosecutors do every time they invent scenarios with numerous past events: they are doomed to fail the very moment they try to do it.

But it is even worse than this.

I assumed equal odds for each event occurring or not occurring. The truth is that the event having occurred is not equal in likelihood to not occurring. For example, Deterryon supposedly got mad at Ja'Keen after Ja'Keen urinated on him, supposedly causing Deterryon to hit the child savagely outside the motel room, but the number of possible ways Deterryon could have reacted other than savagely hitting the child are numerous—actually too numerous to count.

Instead of flipping a coin, we will now use the example of the English QWERTY keyboard that comes with each of our computers. A computer password requires the entry of a variety of symbols—upper and lower case letters in the alphabet, numbers, and special characters—in an exact succession. Someone has counted 95 characters available for a computer password.[8] The probability for selecting the correct symbol would be 1 divided by 95, or 0.0105. Assuming that Deterryon could have acted 94 ways other than what the prosecutor claimed for each of the 56 events, the probability of selecting the correct choices for all 56 scenario items is:

$$(0.0105)^{56} = \mathit{Error}$$

My calculator cannot calculate something so infinitesimally close to zero, so it says, "Error." This would be like entering the correct succession of letters, numbers and symbols in a 56-character password without having been told the password first.

"Wait a second!" I can almost hear you say. "Isn't there actual video data with Deterryon and Ja'Keen for much of what Ms Kaye said? Doesn't factual, witness information incorporated into a theory make it more likely to be true?"

I suppose you could argue that. Take a look at Ms Kaye's 56 events. Even if we were to be fair to her and accept that she invented only half of the items in her complex scenario (and witnessed the other half in some video), the probability that she is correct is still:

$$(0.0105)^{28} = 3.92 \times 10^{-56}$$

The number 392 with 55 zeroes to the left of it and a decimal point. My calculator can still calculate it, but it still means 100% wrong.

But it is even worse than this.

The first prosecutor had 56 items in her sequence of events, but in truth, what actually happened is not limited to 56 items.

Both the prosecution and the defense accept as factual that Deterryon, Jameshia, and Ja'Keen checked into the motel in Marshall on the evening of May 5, 2014, "shortly before" 7 p.m. and that Ja'Keen was pronounced dead about 12 hours later (May 6, 2014, at 6:55 a.m.). Those 12 hours comprise 720 minutes or 43,200 seconds. Because events can unfold even in split seconds, we can further divide that into tenths of a second as an approximation, leading to a number of 432,000. Expanding the 56 events to a possible 432,000 events, we have:

$$(0.0105)^{432{,}000} = \textit{Error}$$

Even if we were to reduce the exponent to account for all the time there was a video recording, the probability would still be so infinitesimally close to zero (i.e., false) that my calculator would still not be able to calculate it.

In other words, the probability that the police and prosecution got the right scenario in the Deterryon Kelly case is not much different than the probability of their making a successful bicycle trip to the moon. What is "beyond a reasonable doubt" is that the police and the prosecutor got the wrong answer. Absolutely no way can prosecutors reasonably claim that Deterryon Kelly is guilty.

I could stop right now, but I won't. I have more to say.

Being a forensic pathologist is not easy. In many cases, it is a no-win situation—where doctors are "damned if they do and damned if they don't."

Years ago, the forensic pathologist who supervised me during my residency training warned me not to go into forensic pathology. All too often, forensic pathologists are overworked and underfunded, expected to do more and more with less and less.[9] Dr. Irving Root, my supervisor during that forensic pathology elective, told me that politicians prefer not to allocate funds for death investigation because politicians often do not believe that dead people are that important. They certainly don't vote. Still, when mistakes from overwork and underfunding are made, the beleaguered forensic pathologist is made to accept the full brunt of the blame.

Ladies and gentlemen, reasoning like Sherlock Holmes is not one of those kinds of mistakes.

Regardless of the workload, there is no excusing this mistake. There are no politicians who should be blamed for this. Forensic pathologists, scientists, and doctors who do this kind of nonsense should accept full responsibility.

I don't know how busy Dr. Lyon was when he autopsied Ja'Keen Sanders, but it really doesn't matter. He would have made this mistake even if he had hardly anything to do.

Dr. Lyon didn't stop with his autopsy report and the death certificate. He testified in court to a "reasonable degree of medical certainty" that the prosecutors' farfetched theory was true. He joined the police and prosecutors in their crazy way of accusing. He not only put them on their dangerous path but he also offered his stamp of approval—his confirmation—to what they did.

That certitude and that testimony put a spring in the prosecutors' step. Forensic doctors give prosecutors the moral authority to accuse people of crimes no one ever saw committed. Dr. Lyon gave the prosecutors in the Deterryon Kelly case the confidence to play games—adding an imaginative story to indistinct surveillance video images, stoking the prejudices of jurors and witnesses, pushing a plastic doll into a two-dimensional drawing, and inventing a scurrilous story about a defense expert from out of town. That confidence comes from a belief that they are on the side of God and holy angels as they use any means necessary to put someone away for life.

At least that is what I hope is the case. It would be horrible if the prosecutors knew they were doing wrong but kept doing it.

Anyway, regardless of prosecutorial motivation, forensic doctors provide prosecutors with cover. A forensic doctor allows prosecutors to claim "plausible deniability."[10] They do not have to accept responsibility for any wrongdoing when an expert like Sherlock Holmes supports what they believe, when there is no convincing evidence that the expert is wrong.

But that has now changed, hasn't it? Prosecutors everywhere: as of now, your plausible deniability is gone.

I do not believe you are stupid. I mentioned initially that the basic point of this book is so simple that even a 12-year old can understand it. Twelve-year olds understand that ___ + ___ = 4 is not solvable. If they can understand it, then someone like you with all your education can understand it too.

So if you are smart enough to understand, then you must stop inventing complex past-event scenarios; you must test witness accounts instead with evidence and evidence-based science. Police investigators will then follow your lead if you allow them too: they will provide you the kind of data you need to make accurate and logical decisions.

As for judges, I do not believe you are stupid either. No amount of legal precedent can substitute for simple logic. Why not stop experts and attorneys from building scenarios in your courtrooms and from using scientists to confirm those invented stories?

Also, I believe it is time, judges, for you to pull out the master key. Rather than spending a lot of money and many hours retrying old cases, why not simply unlock the prison door of anyone convicted of a doctor-invented theory?

Notes

1. Holmes M. "CSI' farewell panel talks how DNA, hair fibers & plushies changed TV & society. *Variety*, September 17, 2015. http://variety.com/2015/scene/vpage/csi-crime-scene-investigation-farewell-finale-paley-center-1201595644/. Accessed on November 12, 2017.
2. truTVEps. Adam Ruins Forensic Science, October 20, 2015. https://cartoonhd.in/show/adam-ruins-everything/season/1/episode/4. Accessed on November 12, 2017.
3. Henley D. 'Forensic' team to look at South Main tree death. *Hannibal Courier-Post*, September 24, 2015. http://www.hannibal.net/article/20150924/NEWS/150929326. Accessed on November 12, 2017.
4. WBUR. Opioid Epidemic Inspires New Hampshire Medical Examiner To Enter Ministry. http://www.wbur.org/hereandnow/2017/11/01/opioids-new-hampshire-medical-examiner. Accessed on November 10, 2017.
5. Moritz AR. Classical mistakes in forensic pathology. *The American Journal of Forensic Medicine and Pathology* 1981;2(4):299–308.
6. Australian Associated Press. Murder of girl thrown from bridge by father 'could not have been predicted.' *The Guardian*, October 30, 2015. http://www.theguardian.com/australia-news/2015/oct/31/of-girl-thrown-from-bridge-by-father-could-not-have-been-predicted. Accessed on November 12, 2017.
7. Duhaime A-C, Gennarelli TA, Thibault LE, Bruce DA, Margulies SS, Wiser R. The shaken baby syndrome: a clinical, pathological, and biomechanical study. *Journal of Neurosurgery* 1987;66:409–415.
8. Fazio D. How many characters are represented on a US English QWERTY keyboard? Quora.com, February 24, 2016. https://www.quora.com/How-many-characters-are-represented-on-a-US-English-QWERTY-keyboard. Accessed on December 28, 2016.
9. Root I. Forensic Pathology—Catch 22. A No-Win Situation (?). *The American Journal of Forensic Medicine and Pathology* 1986;7(3):237–240.
10. Plausible Deniability Law and Legal Definition. USLegal.com. https://definitions.uslegal.com/p/plausable-deniability/. Accessed on November 12, 2017.

21 Confessions of a Former Chief Medical Examiner

On June 3, 2014, several officers of the Marshall Police Department converged on the Marshall City Park. Deterryon Tyrell Kelly had an outstanding warrant for his arrest for Capital Murder. One detective previously noted Mr Kelly to be on Pope Street on the north side of the park, standing by a parked car near the volleyball court, wearing a black shirt and white shorts.

One of two officers who encountered Mr Kelly that day ordered him to place his hands on the vehicle. Deterryon did not do this; instead, he asked what he did wrong. After another order to place his hands on the vehicle, Mr Kelly turned away from the policemen. One police officer, a sergeant, grabbed Deterryon's arm to restrain him, but Deterryon broke away and ran to the east on Pope toward South Washington Street. During the foot pursuit, the sergeant successfully deployed his X26 Taser. Deterryon fell to the ground after being struck in the back by the two barbs and receiving an electric jolt. He resisted while being handcuffed, so the other police officer deployed barbs from his Taser X26 into Deterryon's right buttock and left thigh. After that, there was no further resistance. The policemen transported and booked Mr Kelly into the Harrison County Jail without further difficulty.

Nearly two and a half years later, the local newspaper announced his court verdict to the world:

The Marshall News Messenger, October 7, 2016: Kelly Found Guilty, Gets Life With No Parole in Marshall Baby Death[1]

> Deterryon Tyrell Kelly, 29, was found guilty of capital murder Friday after almost two hours of deliberation by a Harrison County jury.
>
> The sentence comes with an automatic life sentence with no eligibility of parole.
>
> Kelly was accused of killing 21-month-old Ja'Keen Naevon Sanders, his former girlfriend's son, while the three lodged at Best Western Inn in Marshall on May 5, 2014.
>
> The toddler was found unresponsive at the Best Western on May 6, and later died at Good Shepherd Medical Center-Marshall. Kelly, who was the boyfriend of the victim's mother, at the time, was arrested nearly a month later following the results of the autopsy and further investigation.

Kelly contended the boy had become stuck between a bed and a night stand. Testimony revealed a surveillance video from the hotel appears to show him striking the child the night before he was found dead.

Jurors rejected several lesser offenses included in their instructions. The verdict form, presented to the jury by 71st District Judge Brad Morin, charged jurors to either find the defendant guilty beyond a reasonable doubt of capital murder or find him guilty of a choice of the five lesser included offenses, which were: murder, manslaughter, intentionally or knowingly causing injury to a child, recklessly causing injury to a child, or causing injury to a child with criminal negligence. If they weren't sure beyond a reasonable doubt of either choice, the charge instructs the jury to find him not guilty.

The madding crowd offered reactions in the comments section of the website posting. Here were some of them:

Praise the lord! Justice has been served for Ja'Keen.

A Champion of Righteousness answers many fevered prayers!

Too bad we don't have courthouse lawn public hangings anymore. This animal is a prime candidate for public execution.

Why should we the tax payers have to feed and clothe him for the rest of his life? A person that would do something that horrific, deserves the electric chair!!!

May this baby rest in peace and his family find peace and comfort in knowing this will never happen to another child or family again. Prayers for all the jurors, prosecutors, law enforcement and citizens involved in this, glad they were able to see to it this baby and family received justice.

It is strange that the comments I made regarding Deterryon last night have been deleted. Odd?

Thank God for surveillance cameras. If a person is caught red handed, they don't deserve to live. The jails are too full of people like this, getting a life sentence. Death should be mandantory. Also, Women should be very careful who they date.

One more thing~~~take his face off the internet~~makes me sick just to look at him, and I don't like to be sick!!!

He will be killed in prison. There is a zero-tolerance a month prisoners when it comes to child or baby abuse. I hope they make it very hard on him before they kill him.

Life without parole is less than what he deserves!

***

Dear Imprisoned Victim of Injustice,

This is an open letter to you. Others may read this letter, but consider this to be between you and me.

First of all, how are you holding up?

I know that sounds like a ridiculous question. I know I have no right to ask it. If you were to answer me, I could say, "I understand," or "I feel your pain," but in truth, I do not understand and I do not feel your pain. There is no way I could, unless I was to go through what you are going through.

You may have lost a child. Something happened suddenly and unexpectedly, and now you are deprived of your precious baby. I have been told that pain never goes away, that it goes with you for the rest of your life, but I would not know that. My children are all adults now, having children of their own.

And I would not know what it is like, after having gone through such a tragedy, to be accused of murdering that precious loved one. To endure accusations from health care providers, social workers, and police officers. To be interrogated about this tragedy in a seemingly endless way. To watch attorneys bargain for my punishment. To sit in a prison cell day after day, enduring the indignities and dangers that come with that life. To sit through a trial, listening to a prosecutor and multiple witnesses accuse me of being a monster. To watch a judge or a jury point their fingers at me and declare that I am guilty as charged. To sit in prison year after year for crimes I never committed. To lose loved ones who have lost faith in me. To have my life, livelihood, and reputation destroyed.

I also would not know what it is like to listen to some learned pinhead—some forensic doctor—speak from the witness stand about how science shows I have committed a crime that I know I never committed. I would not know what it is like to look at jurors as they struggle to understand the kind the gobbledygook they are supposed to understand as they make decisions about my freedom and life. I would not know what it is like to endure the testimony of some learned pinhead like me.

Even if you had not lost a child but instead had been accused of some other crime based on some police, prosecutor or forensic doctor theory, I still could not possibly know how you feel.

One of the things I get to do as a forensic doctor is respond to letters, telephone calls, and emails from high school and college students who are considering doing what I do for a living. One of the questions they ask is, "What is the thing you enjoy most about your job?"

I often smugly reply that the thing I enjoy most is figuring out something about a violent or mysterious death or injury that others have yet to figure out. You know...kind of like Sherlock Holmes.

But since leaving full-time employment as a chief medical examiner, I have had an opportunity to look at many cases as a defense expert where a forensic doctor has claimed "child abuse," "strangulation," "homicide," or many, many other kinds of criminal behaviors. When I look at cases, I examine many kinds of documents and listen to many kinds of recordings: 911 telephone calls, police reports, ambulance trip sheets, medical records, interview/interrogation recordings and transcripts, court transcripts, and a variety of legal documents. I listen and read in recordings and documents how you describe what you saw, heard, and understood. I also get to read and listen to the accounts of many other eyewitnesses. Amazingly enough, I have found that most of the time your observations and the observations of others fit all the available evidence much, much better than forensic doctor, police, and prosecutor theories.

I also was amazed when I realized that if you were lying about what you saw and heard, you would have had to be a lying genius—a person even smarter than Einstein. How can a liar during a frantic 911 call describe so accurately what can happen to a person and have an outcome any scientist could predict?

All of this has caused me to reflect during my final years as a chief medical examiner and during my several years as an expert who is independent of the "system." I realized more and more that no person could invent a train of never-seen events and expect it to be true, just as I have described in this book. I also realized that you could not have possibly invented a story and have exactly the results that could be predicted from that story. You had to be telling the truth.

You had to be telling the truth! But now, look at you…

I guess you could say I figured out something that many other forensic doctors have yet to figure out, but I cannot say that it has brought me any pleasure. It has not made this job enjoyable. It has done the opposite. I am horrified at what I have found, and I can hardly stand it anymore.

That is why I asked at the beginning of this letter how you are holding up. Others by now may have long forgotten you, but I have not forgotten you. In fact, I think about you all the time. I really do wonder how you are holding up.

Regarding what is going on outside of your prison cell, I have some bad news for you.

I wish I could say that other forensic doctors understand what you have learned in this book, but the truth is that most do not understand. They do not want to understand. And in truth, a person cannot teach something to somebody if that somebody does not want to understand.

Doctors do not want to understand how their learning has failed them. They do not want to face the consequences of their repeated behavior and the injustice brought about by it. They want to be happy just as we all want to be happy. They want to live free and contented lives, figuring that many people are benefiting from what they, as forensic doctors, do.

So when I bring bad news, they do not want to hear it. They want to go on with their lives and pretend that victims like you do not exist.

I have tried many times and in many ways to get their attention. I have written articles for publication in professional journals and submitted abstracts for presentation at professional meetings, only to have them turned down. I chaired a committee for a few days to study this topic, only to have few members join and the committee disbanded. Forensic doctors are not interested in what I have to say and have repeatedly blocked any presentation. It is easier, perhaps, to write me off as some kind of "nut" than to have to confront what I have to say. I would not hold out any hope for most of these professionals to change their minds anytime soon.

I would also not hold out hope for the judicial system to change anytime soon either.

The courts have learned to rely on forensic doctors. They are intimidated by the gobbledygook that forensic doctors deliver—they do not understand much of it. They only figure that if a forensic doctor said it, then it must be true. The courts have profound respect for learned people like me who can speak with authority about matters that people in the courtroom do not understand. Unless the forensic doctors change, do not hope for the courts to change. Instead, figure that the courts, with all their legal machinery and their ways of doing things, will continue to chew you up and spit you out.

I have been working on this problem since 2007. After several years of testifying in court on behalf of criminal defendants—of trying to do the best I can with the system as it is—I can tell you not to hold out much hope for the courts to change anytime soon.

Still, as much as you resent the police, the prosecutor, the judges, and the jurors, please do not figure that they are mostly to blame. If it weren't for forensic doctors like me, none of this would have started. If it weren't for forensic doctors, none of the other people—police, prosecutors, judges, and jurors—would be doing what they are doing, grinding people up in the way that they do.

As I see it now, the only hope that you might have comes from a book like this. Perhaps if the public were to realize what is going on, then the system might have some chance of changing.

But frankly, I would not hold out much hope for this working either. I hate to sound like a pessimist, but I have seen too much, and I know how things usually happen.

The public is often fickle and unpredictable. Events splash on the headlines, but they are soon forgotten as something else draws the attention of the people.

Most people also continue to have great faith in scientists and doctors. If most doctors line up and call me a kook, the public will believe them no matter how carefully I point out the failings.

And most people also want to continue living their lives and being happy. It is much easier for them to forget that you exist, how much you are hurting, how much you have been wronged. It is much easier to march on and pretend that nothing is wrong.

But I will not pretend.

There is something I need to do—something that is long overdue.

It seems I have been harsh on forensic doctors in general and even on a few particular individuals, but to be truthful, I am as guilty as they are. I have done the very activities that have put several of you in prison. I know who some of you are, and there are some of you whom I have not identified.

Thankfully, I did not do this often. Even though I did not know years ago what I know today, I sensed that reasoning backward was not a good idea. My mentors even taught me not to invent past-event scenarios from autopsy findings.

Still, even if it happened a few times, it was a few times too many. I recall one case in the mid 1990s in which I diagnosed shaken-baby syndrome from the witness stand, thinking that it was the only explanation for what I found at the autopsy. That was not a good moment.

I could make excuses. I could say at the time I testified, scientists had not yet learned the science that would eventually show that I was wrong. I could say I was doing the best I could with what I knew at the time—that I would have had to be some kind of genie with a crystal ball to know several years ago what I know today.

Those excuses sound every bit as empty to me as I am sure they seem to you. The fact is I destroyed lives.

I find no pleasure in having done that, regardless of any excuse. I did not become a forensic doctor to harm innocent people and destroy their lives. Realizing that I have done what I have done has horrified me.

So after all of this, there is only one thing left for me to do. I will do this now.

Dear Sir or Madam—you who are a victim of my activity as a forensic doctor—please accept my sincere apology for all the wrong I have caused you. I am so, so sorry for what I have done, and I hope you will somehow find it in your heart to forgive me.

I figure I will not hear your response to my apology. Still, regardless of whether or not you forgive me, I want you to be sure of one thing.

I will continue to fight for you.

Not as an attorney or some other kind of advocate. I will continue to fight for you as a scientist, presenting fact-based science from the witness stand that allows your version of events to be compared to the physical evidence clues found by scientists. I will do this for those who have not entered the prison system yet and for those of you who are already in it. I assure you that I will do everything I can in that way, believing that in the end the truth will set you free.

I will speak up about you and the problems with forensic doctor testimony to all who will listen.

And I will not stop. I will continue to fight for you until it is not possible for me to fight anymore.

In the meantime, I hope you can hang in there. Please hold on for another day.

Sincerely and respectfully,
Thomas W. Young, MD

Note

1. Kelly found guilty, gets life with no parole in Marshall baby death. *The Marshall News Messenger*, October 7, 2016. https://www.marshallnewsmessenger.com/news/2016/oct/07/kelly-found-guilty-gets-life-no-parole-marshall-ba/. Accessed on November 12, 2017.

Index

A

AAFS, *see* American Academy of Forensic Sciences
Abusive head injury, 23
Acceleration, 55
Accident, 96
Acute abdomen, 189
"Adam Ruins Everything," 227–229
Adventist, 34
ALTE, *see* Apparent life-threatening event
Ambulance trip sheet, 69
American Academy of Forensic Sciences (AAFS), 61
American Board of Pathology, 61
Amigos de las Américas, 33
Andersen, H. C., 66
Andrew, T., 230
Anglophiles, 19
Apnea monitoring, 110
Apnea spell, 110
Apnoea, 84
Apparent life-threatening event (ALTE), 84
Autopsy standards, 67

B

Backward reasoning, 2
- deduction, 5
- effect on forensic pathology, 19
- example of, 3
- failures of, 2, 93
- and forward reasoning, 3–4
- problem with, 88
- syndrome, 37

Bandak, F., 56–57
Battered child syndrome, 23–24; *see also* Child abuse
- article, 43, 46
- offender evaluation techniques, 47
- signs, 46

Battered football player syndrome, 161
- chronic traumatic encephalopathy, 163
- Omalu, B., 161
- Webster, M., 161

Bayes' theorem, 89
Beliefs, 65
Bell, J., 9, 66
- skills, 10

Bennett, T., 205–207
Big thymus theory, 109–110
Bite-mark evidence, 185
Block, 86
Blood clotting, 83
Bloodstain evidence, 151
Body temperature, change in, 154–155
Bone disease, brittle, 73
Brainstem injury, 83, 84
Brand management, 163
"Brides in the Bath" murders, 12–15
Bridging veins, 83
British coroner system, 121
Broken bones in babies, 71; *see also* Child abuse
- chronic subdural hematomas and, 71
- diagnostic testing, 72
- metaphyseal lesions, 73
- mineralizing, 73–74
- osteogenesis imperfecta, 72
- temporary brittle bone disease, 73

Bryan Rein murder, 146–147
BSU, *see* Behavioral Science Unit

C

Caffey, J., 31, 35, 53, 60, 80, 167; *see also* Child abuse
- broken bones in babies, 71
- shaking and hemorrhages, 53
- whiplash shaken infant syndrome, 53, 60

Callery, R. T., 133; *see also* Chief medical examiner
Cardiopulmonary resuscitation (CPR), 8, 103
- injuries caused by aggressive, 192

Casey Anthony trial, 96–97
Categorical intuitive deduction, 20, 22, 23–24, 231; *see also* Deduction
Caylee Anthony's death, 96–97
Cerebral edema, 85
Chamberlain case, 41, 93
Charlotte Observer investigation, 120, 124
Chief complaint, 63
Chief medical examiner, 132; *see also* Medical examiner
  Callery, R. T., 133–134
  confessions of former, 239
  double dipping, 132
  ministering people with drug problems, 230–231
  public/private problem, 132–133
  speaking for dead, 220–221
  Sperry, K., 135–137
Child abuse, 43, 143; *see also* Caffey, J.; Broken bones in babies; Forensic pathologists
  acceleration and shakes, 54–55
  battered-child syndrome article, 43, 46
  medical diagnosis of, 44
  medicalizing, 43
  pediatrics, 62
  and shaking, 53
Child-abuse cases; *see also* Marshall baby death; Shaken baby syndrome
  common scenario, 55–56
  Darcey Iris death, 231–234
  deductive calculation and differential diagnosis, 44–45
  and emotions, 201
  encountering new information, 44
  evidence, 201
  evidence-based testimony, 74, 75
  evidence-based vs. belief-based, 65, 75
  numerical errors by Bandak, 56–57
  Reid Technique, 47
  and risk for forensic pathologists, 201
  risk with unreasonable conclusions, 67–68
  witnesses, 47–48, 143–145
Child maltreatment, *see* Child abuse
Christie, D. A., 153
Chronic, 163
Chronic subdural hematoma, 71
Chronic traumatic encephalopathy (CTE), 163; *see also* Omalu, B.
  constellation of symptoms, 167
  control cases, 165
  and whiplash-shaking, 167
Circular thinking, 166
Circumstantial evidence case, 96
Clarkson, L., 100
Clues, 6
Cognitive bias, 185–186
Concussion, 161, 168
Confessions, 65
Confirmation bias, 53–54
Conspiracy theory on Azaria's death, 94
Cory Maye case, 143
Co-sleeping deaths, 107
Court; *see also* Child-abuse cases
  authenticity of forensic testing, 183–184
  DNA as evidence, 182–183
  eyewitness misidentification case, 184–185
  vs. forensic science fiction, 226
  losing the focus, 181
  role of science in, 180, 181
CPR, *see* Cardiopulmonary resuscitation
Crib death, 108; *see also* Sudden infant death syndrome
  deciphering, 112–113
  doll re-enactment, 113
Crime investigation, real-life, 46
Crimes, 63
Crime Scene Investigation (CSI), 225–226
Criminal investigations; *see also* Death investigation; Scientific evidence
  cognitive bias, 185–186
  evidence detection, 179
CSI, *see* Crime Scene Investigation
CTE, *see* Chronic traumatic encephalopathy

D

Darcey Iris death, 231–234
Darwin, C., 33
Darwinian evolution, 33
Daubert hearing, 172
Daubert v. Merrell Dow Pharmaceuticals, 180, 181
  scientific testimony offered by expert, 181
  use of science in, 180
Davis, J., 42
Dean, D. E., 147
Death investigation; *see also* Trains of events
  Azaria's death, 93–95
  bloodstain evidence, 151

- British coroner system, 121
- Caylee Anthony's death, 96–97
- Cynthia Hubbard death, 28, 30
- Darcey Iris death, 231–234
- drug overdose deaths, 230
- inmate death, 68–70
- Jennifer Malkan death, 28, 30
- Kapsinow baby's death, 27–28, 30
- Kayaker's death, 213–216
- Kerry O'Clair Jefferson death, 145–146
- Margaret Purk death, 147–150
- Marshall baby death, 6–8, 15–17, 102–105, 176–176, 188–193
- medical examiners for, 122
- medicolegal death investigation officers, 67
- shaken-baby deaths, 203
- Sherlock Holmes in, 123
- South Main tree death, 229–230
- suspicious child death, 138–139
- techniques used to determine cause of death, 173
- training in, 122–123
- Vincent Viafore death, 213–216
- Violent deaths, 201
- Webster, M., 161, 162
- Wood's death, 95

Deceleration, 55
Deduction, 5, 22–23; *see also* Categorical intuitive deduction
Deductively valid, 184
Defense wounds, 146
Dementia pugilistica, 162
Deoxyribonucleic acid (DNA), 182–183
- evidence, 229

Deterryon Kelly's case, *see* Kelly, D. T.
Diagnosis, 24, 63
- differential, 45

Diaphragm, 86
DNA, *see* Deoxyribonucleic acid
Doctors as real-life Sherlocks, 11; *see also* Bell, J.; Sherlock Holmes-like experts
Doll re-enactment, 113
Double dipping, 132
- Callery, R. T., 133–134
- Sperry, K., 135–137

Doyle, A. C., 1
- inspiration for, 10

Drug overdose deaths, 230
Dural bleeding, cause of, 83

E

Edwards, R., 219
Emergency medical technicians (EMTs), 158
"Emperor's New Clothes, The," 66
EMTs, *see* Emergency medical technicians
Encephalopathy, 163
Evidence; *see also* Scientific evidence
- based science, 65
- in child-abuse cases, 201
- detection, 179

Eyewitness, 228
- misidentification case, 184–185

F

Facts, 65
Fairhurst, J., 143
- backward reasoning of, 144–145

Federal Rule of Evidence 702, 180, 181
Floating hypotheses, 153, 184
Forensic botanists, 61
Forensic doctor, 61
- experts, 131
- follies, 93
- forward reasoning, 64–65
- for Inferential Test, 64
- inventing trains of events, 81
- as vain emperors, 66

Forensic entomologists, 61
Forensic medicine, 11
- lack of challenge, 21–22
- lack of self-correction, 21

Forensic pathologists, 61, 67
- with alcoholic past, 76–80
- assessment of inmate death, 68–70
- categorical intuitive deduction in, 231
- considering child death as suspicious, 138–139
- fallen from grace, 202, 205
- flawed forensic thinking, 93
- Moritz, A. R., 19
- National Association of Medical Examiners, 62
- political influences, 67
- Pollanen, M., 203
- problem with, 88
- problems encountered by, 58–59
- risk in child-abuse cases, 201
- Spilsbury, B., 11, 12
- techniques used to determine cause of death, 173

Forensic pathology, 19
  mistakes in, 19–20
  North Carolina state budget, 121
Forensic science
  in Japan, 179
  scientific method, 89
  scientific tests, 228
  in United States, 179
Forensic science tragedy; *see also* Sudden infant death syndrome
  Bennett, T., 205–207
  death of Azaria, 93–95
  death of Caylee, 96–97
  JonBenet Ramsey Theory, 97–98
  shooting of Trayvon Martin, 99–100
  Smith, C., 202
  Spector murder trial, 100–101
  Wood's final events, 95–96
Forward reasoning, 3–4, 37
  forensic doctors, 64–65
  Marshall baby death, 6–8
Fowler, D., 124
Frye, J. A., 180
Frye v. United States, 180
  relevant issue in, 182
  use of science in, 180
Full evaluation, 46

G

Geddes, J., 82, 90
  brainstem injury, 83, 84
  cause of dural bleeding, 83
  unified hypothesis, 83–85
Gilliland, M., 150–152
Global hypoxia, 84
Good Cop, Bad Cop, 38, 139
  no-win situation, 39–41
  scenario building, 42
Gregory Parks murder case, 150–152
Griffin, D.
  interview techniques used by, 170
  testimony, 169–172

H

Hawley, D., 149
Hayne, S., 143
Hearst, P., 37
Heartland Forensic Pathology, LLC., 87
Hemorrhages, 83
Hurlburt, R., 24
  closing argument, 210–211
  meeting with Young, 101–105, 126
  questioning Sergeant Griffin, D., 169–172
  questioning Young, T. W., 172–176, 188–193
Hydrocodone, 146
Hypothesis, 5, 85, 184
Hypoxia, 104
Hypoxic encephalopathy, 86

I

Immunoperoxidase stains, 162
Infant bones, 73; *see also* Broken bones in babies
Infant deaths, 108; *see also* Sudden infant death syndrome
Inferential Test, 5, 186–187
  for forensic doctors, 64
Inmate death, 68–70
Innocence Project, 183
Intubation, 158
Intuitive, 23

J

Jack the Ripper, 218–220
  lack of witnesses, 219
  Russell's claim, 219–220
Jaspers case, *see* Jaspers, V.
Jaspers, V., 27, 39
  confessing foul play scenario, 30–31
  Cynthia Hubbard death, 28, 30
  evidence of foul play, 29
  as infant nurse, 27
  interrogation, 29–31
  Jennifer Malkan death, 28, 30
  Kapsinow baby's death, 27–28, 30
  no-win situation, 39–41
  proved pathogenic whiplash-shakings, 31, 32
Jimmie Duncan case, 143
JonBenét Ramsey mystery, 97–98
JP, *see* Justice of the peace
Justice of the peace (JP), 175

K

Kapsinow baby's death, 27–28, 30; *see also* Jaspers, V.
Kayaker's death, 213–216

Kelly, D. T., 6–8, 15–17, 24–25, 169; *see also* Marshall baby death
  arrest, 239
  sentence, 239–240
Kelly, K., 150–152
Kerry O'Clair Jefferson death, 145–146

L

Lack of witnesses
  Jack the Ripper, 218–220
  Kayaker's death, 213–216
  Spider bite, murder sparked by, 216–218
Lamb, S., 216–217; *see also* Spider bite, murder sparked by
Law of parsimony, 81
Limited liability company (LLC), 87
Lindy Chamberlain case, 93–95
Liver laceration, 175, 189
Lividity, 156
LLC, *see* Limited liability company
Logically valid, 184
Lyon, R. E., 16
  testimony, 138–141

M

Margaret Purk death, 147–150
Marshall baby death, 6–8, 15–17; *see also* Child-abuse cases
  autopsy on Ja'Keen Sanders, 138
  closing argument by District Attorney, 221–224
  closing argument by Hurlburt, R., 210–211
  closing argument by Kaye, K., 208–210
  closing argument by Young, T. W., 234–238
  Deterryon's recorded videos, 129–130
  Griffin, D. narration on, 127–129
  Griffin, D. testimony, 169–172
  Lyon, R. in witness stand, 138–141
  Morris, J. testimony, 153–159
  sentence, 239–240
  State of Texas v. Deterryon Tyrell Kelly, 113–117, 118
  surveillance videos, 126–127
  testimony of Young, T. W., 172–176, 188–199
  Young description on, 102–105
Massive brain swelling, 83
  hemorrhage in neck, 86
McKee, A., 164
Mechanical asphyxia, 174
Medical examiner, 67
  Charlotte Observer investigation, 120, 124
  chief medical examiner, 132
  death investigation, 122
  pay for North Carolina's, 119–120
  problems with, 125
Medicalizing child abuse, 43
Medicolegal death investigation officers, 67
Microscope, 179
Moritz, A. R., 19, 25
  intuitive deduction, 20, 22
Morris, J., 153–159
Murder on the Orient Express, 153

N

NAME, *see* National Association of Medical Examiners
NASA, *see* National Aeronautics and Space Administration
National Academy of Sciences, 183
National Aeronautics and Space Administration (NASA), 88
National Association of Medical Examiners (NAME), 62, 67, 122, 124; *see also* Medical examiner
National Institute of Standards and Technology (NIST), 183
NIST, *see* National Institute of Standards and Technology
Noguchi, T., 41
  on Wood's death, 95
Non-accidental injury, 144
North Carolina
  medical-examiner system, 124
  new state budget, 121
  pay for medical examiners, 119–120
No-win situation, 39–41, 54

O

Omalu, B., 161, 162, 163, 164, 166, 167, 168, 176, 177; *see also* Chronic traumatic encephalopathy
  alleged poisoning of Hillary Clinton, 169
  conspiracy theory, 169
  shaken-bottle scenario, 168

Omalu, B. (*Continued*)
  traumatic brain injury in infant, 168
  about Webster, M., 164
ONSH, *see* Optic nerve sheath hemorrhages
Optic nerve sheath hemorrhages (ONSH), 85
Organization of Scientific Area Committees (OSAC), 183
OSAC, *see* Organization of Scientific Area Committees
Osteogenesis imperfecta, 72

P

Parathormone, 72
Past events, 88–90
  deductively valid, 184
  and human body, 168
  testing for, 184
Past medical history, 63
Paterson, C., 73, 80; *see also* Child abuse
  evidence-based testimony, 74, 75
Pathogenic whiplash-shakings, 31, 32; *see also* Jaspers, V.
Pathologists, 11–12; *see also* Forensic pathologists
Pathology, 11
  department at Truman, 49–50
Patient-care setting, 62–63
Patient history, 9, 63
PBS, *see* Public Broadcasting System
PCAST, *see* President's Council of Advisors on Science and Technology
PEA, *see* Pulseless electrical activity
Peirce, C. S., 5, 32
Phrenic nerves, 86
Physical abuse, 46
Physical examination, 9–10, 63
Physician Diversion Program, 76
Poirot, H., 153
Poisoning of Hillary Clinton, 169
Pollanen, M., 203
Postulate, 89
President's Council of Advisors on Science and Technology (PCAST), 183
Public Broadcasting System (PBS), 161
Pulseless electrical activity (PEA), 103, 157, 194

R

Reasoning backward, *see* Backward reasoning
Reasoning forward, *see* Forward reasoning
Reid Technique, 47
Respirator, 82
Retinal hemorrhages (RH), 85, 86
Reversible error, 182
Review of systems, 63
RH, *see* Retinal hemorrhages
Rickets, 72
Rigor mortis, 156
Ross, J. M., 27, 35

S

Scenario building, 42
Science in courtroom, 180, 181
Scientific evidence; *see also* Criminal investigations
  bite-mark evidence, 185
  DNA as, 182–183
  general acceptance standard for admission of, 180
Scientific methodology, 184
Scurvy, 72
Self-correction in medical care, 21
Serious bodily injury, 189
Sevallius, J., 107
Seventh-day Adventist, 34, 41
Shaken baby syndrome, 23, 32, 83; *see also* Child-abuse cases; Jaspers, V.
  hemorrhage in neck, 86
  lack of oxygen, 83
  review of old shaken-baby deaths, 203
  triad of findings for, 86
Shaken-bottle scenario, 168
Shaking and hemorrhages, 53; *see also* Child abuse
Shaw, E., 74
Sherlock Holmes, 1
  backward reasoning, 2
  in death investigation, 123
  deductive calculation and differential diagnosis, 44–45
  doctors as real-life Sherlocks, 11
  encountering new things, 44
  Guinness World Records, 1, 8
  model for, 9
  popularity in China, 1, 8
  solving problem, 2
  in United States, 43
  Watson, Dr., 2
Sherlock Holmes-like behavior, 6

Sherlock Holmes-like experts, 164
  Dean, D. E., 147
  Fairhurst, J., 143–145
  Gilliland, M., 150–152
  Hawley, D., 149
  Kelly, K., 150–152
  Lyon, R., 138–141
  Thompson, J., 145–146
  Wigren, C., 146–147
SIDS, *see* Sudden infant death syndrome
Signs, 37
Smith, C., 202
Smith, G. J., 12–15
South Main tree death, 229–230
Spector murder trial, 100–101
Sperry, K., 135–137
Spider bite, murder sparked by, 216–217
  source of spider bite theory, 217–218
Spilsbury, B., 11, 12
  "Brides in the Bath" murders, 12–15
  Thorne's case, 12
Spitz, W., 97
Stockholm syndrome, 37
Subdural hematoma, 46
Subdural hemorrhage, 86
  bridging veins, 83
  in foetuses, 82
Sudden infant death syndrome (SIDS), 108; *see also* Crib death
  cause for, 109–110
  sleeping position and bedding environment, 110
  triple-risk model, 111
Sutton, W., 81
Swain, G., 107
Symptoms, 37
Syndrome, 37
Systolic blood pressure, 180

T

Tarte, J., 120
Tau protein, 165
Tautology, 187
TCDLA (Texas Criminal Defense Lawyers Association), 25
TCDLA LISTSERV, 25
Temporary brittle bone disease, 73
Testing present and past events, 63–64
Texas Criminal Defense Lawyers Association, *see* TCDLA
Texas Sharpshooter fallacy, 111, 112
Thompson, J., 145–146
Thorne, N., 12; *see also* Spilsbury, B.
Thorne's case, 12
Thymus, 109–110
Toxicology, 12
Trains of events, 2–3; *see also* Death investigation
  consistency with clues, 23
  example, 4
  vs. hypothesis, 5
  internal, 63
  inventing, 82
  unified hypothesis, 83
Traumatic, 163
Trayvon Martin shooting, 99–100
Triple-risk model, 111
Tyler Edmonds case, 143

U

Unanimity Race, The, 108–109
Unified hypothesis, 83–85

V

Victim of unsafe sleep environment, 107; *see also* Marshall baby death; Sudden infant death syndrome
Vincent Viafore death, 213–216
Violent deaths, 201
Vitamin D, 72

W

Wagner, R., 95
Watson, J. H., 2
Webster, M., 161; *see also* Chronic traumatic encephalopathy
  autopsy, 162
  Omalu, B. about, 164
Weekend at Bernie's, 125
Whiplash shaken infant syndrome, 53, 60, 71
Whiplash-shaking, 167
Wigren, C., 146
William of Ockham, 81
Witness, 90
Wood, N., 95
  final events, 95–96
  Noguchi's description on death, 95

Y

Young's Postulate, 89
Young, T. W., 32, 91
  assessment of inmate death, 68–70
  closing argument for *State of Texas v. Deterryon Tyrell Kelly*, 234–238
  cross-examination, 193–199
  in *Daubert* hearing, 187
  finding evidence, 42
  Forensic Scientific Method, 89
  in Georgia, 48
  Heartland Forensic Pathology, LLC., 87
  Inferential Test, 186–187
  influence of Seventh-day Adventist Church, 34–35
  interest in Darwin, 33
  interest in pathology, 34
  in Kansas City, 57
  letter to imprisoned victim of injustice, 240–245
  as *locum tenens* pathologist, 48
  in Loma Linda, 41
  on Marshall baby death, 102–105
  meeting with Attorney, 101, 126
  mistake of talking, 42
  pathology department at Truman, 49–50
  problems encountered by pathologist, 58–59
  reason for success as consultant forensic pathologist, 90
  testimony in Marshall baby death case, 176–176, 188–193
  trip to South America, 33–34
  Young's Postulate, 89

Z

Zimmerman, G., 99–100

For Product Safety Concerns and Information please contact our EU
representative GPSR@taylorandfrancis.com
Taylor & Francis Verlag GmbH, Kaufingerstraße 24, 80331 München, Germany

www.ingramcontent.com/pod-product-compliance
Lightning Source LLC
LaVergne TN
LVHW011122300926
849160LV00008B/474
* 9 7 8 1 0 3 2 4 0 1 9 0 4 *